# THE CHALLENGE OF
# MILITARY LEADERSHIP

## Other AUSA Books

Galvin THE MINUTE MEN—THE FIRST FIGHT: MYTHS & REALITIES OF THE AMERICAN REVOLUTION

Matthews & Brown THE PARAMETERS OF MILITARY ETHICS

Smith ASSIGNMENT: PENTAGON—THE INSIDER'S GUIDE TO THE POTOMAC PUZZLE PALACE

## Titles of Related Interest

Hunt & Blair LEADERSHIP ON THE FUTURE BATTLEFIELD

Laffin BRASSEY'S BATTLES: 3500 YEARS OF CONFLICT, CAMPAIGNS AND WARS FROM A-Z

Macksey GODWIN'S SAGA: A COMMANDO EPIC

Matthews & Brown ASSESSING THE VIETNAM WAR: A COLLECTION FROM THE JOURNAL OF THE US ARMY WAR COLLEGE

Matthews & Brown THE PARAMETERS OF WAR: MILITARY HISTORY FROM THE JOURNAL OF THE US ARMY WAR COLLEGE

Messenger HITLER'S GLADIATOR: THE LIFE AND TIMES OF SS-OBERSTGRUPPENFUEHRER AND GENERAL DER WAFFEN-SS SEPP DIETRICH

Moskos & Wood THE MILITARY: MORE THAN JUST A JOB?

Pakenham NAVAL COMMAND AND CONTROL

Perkins A FORTUNATE SOLDIER

Record BEYOND MILITARY REFORM: AMERICAN DEFENSE DILEMMAS

## Related Periodicals

Armed Forces Journal International

Defense Analysis

(Specimen copies available upon request)

# THE CHALLENGE OF MILITARY LEADERSHIP

Edited by

## Lloyd J. Matthews

and

## Dale E. Brown

Published under the auspices of the
U.S. Army War College Foundation, Inc.

Introduction by

## Lt. Gen. Walter F. Ulmer, Jr., U.S. Army (Ret.)

Selected by the Institute of Land Warfare
Association of the U.S. Army

## PERGAMON-BRASSEY'S
International Defense Publishers, Inc.

WASHINGTON · NEW YORK · LONDON · OXFORD · BEIJING
FRANKFURT · SÃO PAULO · SYDNEY · TOKYO · TORONTO

| | |
|---|---|
| U.S.A.<br>(Editorial) | Pergamon-Brassey's International Defense Publishers, Inc.,<br>8000 Westpark Drive, Fourth Floor, McLean,<br>Virginia 22102, U.S.A. |
| (Orders) | Pergamon Press, Inc., Maxwell House, Fairview Park,<br>Elmsford, New York 10523, U.S.A. |
| U.K.<br>(Editorial) | Brassey's Defence Publishers Ltd.,<br>24 Gray's Inn Road, London WC1X 8HR, England |
| (Orders) | Brassey's Defence Publishers Ltd.,<br>Headington Hill Hall, Oxford OX3 0BW, England |
| PEOPLE'S REPUBLIC<br>OF CHINA | Pergamon Press, Room 4037, Qianmen Hotel, Beijing,<br>People's Republic of China |
| FEDERAL REPUBLIC<br>OF GERMANY | Pergamon Press GmbH, Hammerweg 6,<br>D-6242 Kronberg, Federal Republic of Germany |
| BRAZIL | Pergamon Editora Ltda, Rua Eca de Queiros, 346,<br>CEP 04011, Paraiso, São Paulo, Brazil |
| AUSTRALIA | Pergamon-Brassey's Defence Publishers Pty Ltd., P.O. Box<br>544, Potts Point, N.S.W. 2011, Australia |
| JAPAN | Pergamon Press, 5th Floor, Matsuoka Central Building,<br>1-7-1 Nishishinjuku, Shinjuku-ku, Tokyo 160, Japan |
| CANADA | Pergamon Press Canada Ltd., Suite No. 271,<br>253 College Street, Toronto, Ontario, Canada M5T 1R5 |

Copyright © 1989 Pergamon-Brassey's International
Defense Publishers, Inc.

First edition 1989

**Library of Congress Cataloging-in-Publication Data**
The Challenge of military leadership/edited by Lloyd J.
Matthews and Dale E. Brown; introduction by Walter F.
Ulmer, Jr.—1st ed.
p. cm.—(An AUSA book)
"Published with the Institute of Land Warfare, Association
of the U.S. Army."
1. Leadership. 2. Command of troops. I. Matthews, Lloyd J.
II. Brown, Dale E. III. Institute of Land Warfare
(Association of the United States Army) IV. Series
UB210.C47 1989 355.3'3041—dc19    88-28967

**British Library Cataloguing in Publication Data**
The Challenge of military leadership.—(An AUSA book)
1. Military forces. Leadership
I. Matthews, Lloyd J. II. Brown, Dale E.
355.6

ISBN 0-08-035983-3 Hardcover
ISBN 0-08-035984-1 Flexicover

*Printed in Great Britain by A. Wheaton & Co. Ltd, Exeter*

# An AUSA Institute of Land Warfare Book

THE Association of the United States Army, or AUSA, was founded in 1950 as a not-for-profit organization dedicated to education concerning the role of the U.S. Army, to providing material for military professional development, and to the promotion of proper recognition and appreciation of the profession of arms. Its constituencies include those who serve in the Army today, including Army National Guard, Army Reserve, and Army civilians, and the retirees and veterans who have served in the past, and all their families. A large number of public-minded citizens and business leaders are also an important constituency. The Association seeks to educate the public, elected and appointed officials, and leaders of defense industry on crucial issues involving the adequacy of our national defense, particularly those issues affecting land warfare.

In 1988 AUSA established within its existing organization a new entity known as the Institute of Land Warfare. Its purpose is to extend the educational work of AUSA by sponsoring scholarly publications, to include books, monographs and essays on key defense issues, as well as workshops and symposia. Among the volumes chosen for designation as ''An AUSA Institute of Land Warfare Book'' are both new texts and reprints of titles of enduring value which are no longer in print. Topics include history, policy issues, strategy, and tactics. Publication as an AUSA Book does not indicate that the Association of the United States Army and the publisher agree with everything in the book, but does suggest that the AUSA and the publisher believe this book will stimulate the thinking of AUSA members and other concerned about important issues.

# Contents

## III. Case Studies in Combat Command

## IV. The Ethical Dimension of Leadership

## V. Military Leadership—The Larger Vision

# Acknowledgments

Perhaps even more difficult than assembling an anthology is the task of acknowledging properly and within sufficiently brief compass the numerous deserving individuals who rendered indispensable assistance at some point along the way.

We begin with the 17 authors themselves. Their willingness at a busy stage of their careers to pause, reflect, and record their thoughts on the subject of military leadership has resulted in an enduringly valuable legacy to national security.

In the larger context, we owe a deep debt of gratitude to the Commandant of the U.S. Army War College, Major General Howard D. Graves, who has so successfully engendered an intellectual climate at the war college within which this and similar projects could grow. Thanks go also to Colonel Donald E. Lunday, Director of Academic Affairs at the college, who in ways large and small has consistently advanced the cause of unfettered intellectual inquiry within the national defense dialogue. Our sponsor for this project has been the Army War College Foundation, Inc; its Executive Director, Colonel LeRoy Strong, U.S. Army Ret., has stood ever ready at hand with invaluable advice and assistance.

Past *Parameters* editors under whose tutelage the present articles made their original appearance—the late Colonel Paul Goodman, Colonel Alfred J. Mock, Colonel Paul R. Hilty, and Colonel William R. Calhoun, Jr.—deserve a warm and grateful remembrance. Finally, we express our appreciation to the present *Parameters* editorial staff—Mr. Gregory N. Todd, Mrs. Lisa A. Ney, and, however brief her tenure, Miss Jennifer L. Cunningham—who with their various gifts worked a transmutative magic on the manuscripts now seen here on the printed page.

The Editors

# Introduction

What phenomenal technological and sociological change in the past 50 years! From the old reliable DC-3 transport to exotic stealth aircraft. From the crystal radio set to the satellite relays into the TV sets. The nearly incomprehensible impact of technology may have been outpaced by revolutionary modifications in lifestyles and human expectations. Family patterns, job mobility, traditional sexual and social taboos, access to information, sensitization to issues of race and gender, the search for satisfaction in the workplace—dynamic developments in all these and more have transformed the environment in which we live.

Despite the extraordinary technological and sociological revolutions of the past 50 years, however, the key player in warfare remains the soldier. The basic makeup of that soldier seems not to have changed much over the last millennium or longer. We have, then, the profound challenge of tailoring leadership styles to acknowledge the enormous but deceptively incremental changes wrought by societal and technical forces while attending to perennial human imperatives. S.L.A. Marshall, for example, once said in *The Armed Forces Officer* (the best book ever written on leadership in American units and one that should remain required reading): "The art of leadership, the art of command . . . is the art of dealing with humanity." As described by John Shortal in "MacArthur's Fireman: Robert L. Eichelberger," chapter 10 of this volume, General Eichelberger's actions as division and corps commander at Buna and Biak in the Pacific in 1942–43 are surely as relevant to leadership studies today as they were 45 years ago.

There are many justifications for revisiting the military leadership scene through a collection of readings such as *The Challenge of Military Leadership*. Because military leadership remains basically an exercise in human motivation, we will always prize intelligent analysis of the traditional leader's attributes. Thus, for example, in any predictable circumstance, courage and commitment will remain essential—for leaders at all levels. The fundamentals that motivate the platoon cannot be discarded as one moves upward in seniority; however, the challenges stemming from societal and technological factors converge most forcefully at senior leadership levels. Leaders at those levels must gain the appropriate frame of reference. They must adjust their leadership styles to the demands of a high-tech battlefield and the legitimate expectations of today's generation of soldiers. We do not have a comprehensive strategy in place today for coping with these challenges.

Each of the pieces in the present book—a collection of outstanding articles on military leadership previously appearing in the pages of *Parameters*—focuses on one facet or another of the key issues of winning the battle and sustaining the force. The selections include the following themes of particular relevance:

- Identifying and developing the strengths of character essential to successful leaders of American soldiers;
- The crucial role of intellect;
- The need to build and coach a staff;
- The difficulty of evaluating, selecting, and developing leaders; and
- A key contemporary challenge—the need for conceptual integration of operations and leadership doctrines.

Before discussing how the articles touch upon these issues, a few assumptions, definitions, and semantic distinctions should be understood. First, "leadership," however it is defined, is not the only contributor to organizational outcomes. There are resource constraints, third-party initiatives, and even natural phenomena that also affect mission accomplishment.

Second, there is for our purposes a distinction between "leaders" and "leadership." Leaders can be described as people who have been placed in charge of something. They may or may not be able to motivate or influence others toward an organizational goal, which is the essence of the process of leadership. History has seen kings, presidents, CEO's, and generals who could not gain the confidence of their subjects, constituents, associates, or potential followers. As we normally define it, *leadership* is a process depending ultimately on the willingness of followers to move toward the goal set by the *leaders*. In motivating followers, the leader may use the power of his office or his physical presence, but if the prevailing method relies essentially on bribery, coercion, or fear, the leader is not "leading." As General Bradley put it, "The test of a leader lies in the reaction and response of his followers."

Third, effective leadership is more than personality; wondrous charisma alone will not guarantee success. Success requires mutual trust in all cases and respect in most cases. Trust derives primarily from a perception of leader competence in essential tasks plus a perception that the leader will treat others fairly and will share the risks to which the group is exposed. The competence ingredient is in all situations a cornerstone—dramatically more important than such nice-to-haves as being approachable or even moral—and is obviously akin to the world of management.

Finally, good intentions do not count for much even though they are essential! Leaders long before the days of the disastrous 1915 Gallipoli expedition to the abortive Iranian hostage rescue mission of 1980 have seen good intentions lead to misfires. Most internally induced failures to execute properly in large and complex organizations, military or civilian, are not the work of fools or knaves. They are instead the unanticipated by-products of uncoordinated or poorly conceived policies or insensitivity to systemic mismatches, which can create an intractable morass at the operating level.

Also by way of preliminaries, we can properly establish an important assumption regarding how leadership challenges of the 1990s might be different from those of 60 or even 30 years ago: we can assume that the transition-to-war period will be very short. So short, in fact, that we will not have time to unlearn bad peacetime habits such as beginning rifle range instruction with the admonition, ''Now the most important thing on this range is safety!''; or to relieve large numbers of unfit colonels and generals as we did on stateside maneuvers in the early 1940s and later on in the Southwest Pacific and North Africa campaigns; or to convert our training incrementally from unit/team to combined arms task force to joint force and so on. Perhaps never before in our history has war doctrine, as articulated by Donn Starry (''Running Things'') in this collection and explained by Charles Sutten (''Command and Control at the Operational Level'')—dispersed, multiple-threat, fast-moving, continuous, and acting on commander's intent—been so dependent on a particular style of leadership: attend to coaching, develop initiative, build a sense of responsibility, and promote vertical and horizontal cohesion.

## The Criticality of Character

It would be impossible to rank order those words most precious and powerful in the leadership vocabulary of the American military, but *character* would be near the top, along with *integrity* (with which it is closely associated). Lewis Sorley in ''Doing What's Right: Shaping the Army's Professional Environment'' declares that character is the essence of professionalism, while General Omar Bradley's ''On Leadership'' also posits character as an essential quality for effective leadership. Although definitions of character differ, Bradley's view that a person with character is one ''who has high ideals, who stands by them, and who can be trusted absolutely'' is certainly suitable.

Other important components of character are boldness (or courage), steadfastness, tenacity, and a strong sense of individual responsibility. We find each of these qualities epitomized, incidentally, in the actions of Union Colonel Joshua Chamberlain, whose famed order to his unit on Little Round Top—''Bayonets to the right!''—led to repulse of the attacking Confederates and prevented a major Union disaster during the Battle of Gettysburg. In the present volume, Jay Luvaas in ''Napoleon on the Art of Command'' invokes Napoleon's sentiment that boldness is ''the common denominator among the Great Captains.'' Current U.S. Army doctrine embraces a leadership philosophy aimed at developing initiative on the part of subordinates. In

*"Auftragstaktik*: A Case for Decentralized Combat Leadership,"John Nelsen II demonstrates how behavioral and cultural factors can either constrain or enhance a leader's ability to implement a truly decentralized modus operandi.

Recent surveys of the army officer corps reveal significant doubt about the typical boldness of our senior officers. Assuming that boldness needs attention, the challenge to our institution is how to develop or nourish it, or can it be developed at all? Napoleon seemed to believe that "everything depends on the character that nature has given to the general. All that I am," he said, "I owe to the work habits I have acquired from my boyhood." General Bradley noted, "Once having been maturely formed, I don't think a man's character ever changes." The born vs. made argument has not been put to rest and should not be.

Our assumption is that behaviors *can* be taught and nourished. Whether those basic attitudes underlying leaders' behavior can be greatly modified remains of major import to our leader identification and selection systems. I agree with Sorley that organizational climates can be developed that support the practice of good leadership and stimulate such practices as risk-taking and fairness. We should arm our colonels and generals with a clear understanding of the role of climate in creating high-performing units. But there are limits to what even field experience under good coaching (the optimum scenario for leader development) can do to produce bold and sensitive leaders. Quoting from Colonel Red Reeder's *Born at Reveille*, Bradley cites Colonel Bryant Moore's comment concerning Guadalcanal: "The good leaders seem to get killed; the poor leaders get the men killed. The big problem is leadership and getting the shoulder straps on the right people."

Of course, it is possible that we study too much the giants of military history (who may be born rather than made) and too little the performance of the sergeants, captains, and colonels on whose collective shoulders so much rests. After all, over 80 percent of the leadership positions in our army are within the company level. The mystique of the Napoleons and the MacArthurs can easily obscure the fact that leadership training continues to play a major role in molding the thousands of commissioned and noncommissioned officers who in unheralded moments across the world are motivating others to do their best every day.

Perhaps, but only perhaps, the more pragmatic ethics of the marketplace have intruded, thus eroding character within military leaders. Clay Buckingham in "Ethics and the Senior Officer" identifies the temptations toward character lapses that sneak into the milieu of higher bureaucracies today. Contrast, for example, General Ulysses Grant's calm and confident reply when awakened by a panicked staff officer during the battle near Richmond— as recounted by Bradley—with the typically hyperactive response of the contemporary senior Pentagon leadership to untoward accidents or incidents half a world away. But if, in fact, we have been imperfect in identifying or building the requisite character in all of our leaders, it is also clear that by luck or design we continue to produce in large numbers leaders at all levels whose commitment and sacrifice are more akin to the traditional military mold than to the least attractive managerial models of a materialistic society. Today's followers have less toleration for poor leadership than did their grandfathers, yet they seem to blossom at least as well under good leadership. In any case, few initiatives have greater potential for long-term positive impact than those set forth by Philip Lewis, Karl Kuhnert and Robert Maginnis in "Defining Character in Military Leaders" regarding how officer character can best be understood and enhanced.

## The Role of Intellect

Through its understandable emphasis upon warfighting and the martial virtues, the U.S. Army may inadvertently have sustained a mild case of anti-intellectualism. Still, we return to the power of the intellect as an essential component of leadership, especially senior leadership. Correlations between measurable intelligence and promotion to general officer appear quite high. Because intellect—just as some facets of body build, susceptibility to disease, and tendencies toward certain personality characteristics—is dependent on heredity (and modified mostly in the very early years), our success in developing outstanding leaders is limited by our success in attracting a pool of manpower within which lies the essential intellectual equipment. As Starry tells us, empires, corporations, and civilizations decay because their leadership cannot assimilate or react to change. Sensing trends, creating adaptive mechanisms, and modifying organizational climates are intellectual sports.

In "The Pillars of Generalship," John Vermillion notes Field Marshal Bernard Montgomery's great strengths as getting the right man for the job and being able to think abstractly. Mitchell Zais's "Strategic Vision and Strength of Will Imperative for Theater Command" reminds us that Clausewitz saw the need for intellectual power. Donald Bletz in "The 'Modern Major General,'" as well as Vermillion and Zais, insists on the need for change of perspective, enlargement of vision, and conceptual differentiation as leaders move up the ladder of responsibility. Zais maintains that "strategic vision and strength of will seem to be the only attributes which consistently characterize the best theater commanders." Research on corporate executives indicates that those who are able to envisage the differing challenges as they move upward are more likely to succeed. Recent official efforts to describe the unique tasks of leadership at the operational and strategic levels—as seen in Field Manual 22-103, *Leadership and Command at Senior Levels*, and DA Pamphlet 600-80, *Executive Leadership*—should stimulate discussion of the role of conceptual as well as experiential challenges to leader development.

## The Need to Build and Coach a Staff

As Luvaas, Vermillion, Bradley, and Thomas Stone ("General William Hood Simpson: Combat Commander") mention in their articles, leaders such as Napoleon, Montgomery, Patton, and Simpson among others saw staff selection and operation as crucial. The ability to recruit and mold a staff receives inadequate attention as an aspect of senior commandership. Montgomery's first requirement for a good general was to "have a good chief of staff." Portrayals of Patton and Simpson show them not only as commanders with great tactical instincts but also with the ability to coach and use their staffs. Open dialogue, trust, and latitude to disagree were hallmarks.

Vermillion writes that "superior generals surround themselves with staff officers who complement them by covering their blind spots." Another task, then, is to assist senior officers in recognizing and admitting to blind spots and encouraging them to think as seriously about the leadership of their staffs as about the leadership of their subordinate echelons. Systematic opportunities for self-assessment (the absolute prerequisite for continued growth) and for gleaning insight from perceptions of subordinates are not available to today's officers—senior or junior.

## Evaluating, Selecting, and Developing Leaders

"We have forgotten the heart of our leadership training and how to grow sergeants," says Larry Ingraham in "Fear and Loathing in the Barracks—And the Heart of Leadership." We may not have forgotten exactly, but we often appear unable to handle leadership development within the hectic world of a marginally resourced Army.

The U.S. Army spends more time on leader education and training than does any other large contemporary institution. A lot of that effort, combined with the native talents of our people, is paying off reasonably well. Indicators of combat readiness are up and those showing lack of discipline are down. Few would argue, however, that the leader screening or developmental processes are as good as they could be. Perceptions of mediocre leadership at battalion and higher levels are too widespread to be ignored—alongside equally strong perceptions of outstanding leadership in similar circumstances. Evidently the possibility exists of attaining higher levels of leadership proficiency even within the current imbalance of missions and resources. It would be tragic were we unable to exploit this possibility universally.

Difficulties in our leader selection-and-development methodology derive in large part from the difficulty of measuring leadership or commandership (encompassing all of the commander's responsibilities). Even winning or losing the battle might not indicate the best leader, but in any case after the battle is too late to determine who is the best. The National Training Center at Fort Irwin, California, is a great developmental laboratory. Its lessons at the battalion task-force level could be interpreted to provide some leader-selection as well as developmental insights. Fortunately, as Lieutenant General Arthur Collins concluded in "Tactical Command," most good leaders in peacetime seem to translate into good combat leaders. But assessing combat readiness and its contributing components remains more of an art than a science.

General Bradley wrote, "I had to relieve a senior commander because I learned that his men had lost confidence in him." How did he learn that? Was it appropriate for him to find out? Could he have found out before the battle? In the late 1960s when, as Ingraham describes, officers in some units were afraid to go above the first floor of the barracks, at least a few generals were ignorant of that situation. (Some were also astonished that AWOL statistics were being doctored.) General Collins tells how outstanding leaders get out to take the pulse of the troops. He also recognized that too few above the muddy-boots level "will ever suspect or appreciate the great talents" of many of their tactical commanders. In the collective literature on leadership, a powerful argument supports bringing the perceptions of the led systematically into the process of evaluating leadership! As a final but not inconsequential note on the need for both openness to feedback from subordinates and a system for providing it, Buckingham reminds us that ethical misbehavior is most obvious to peers and subordinates.

Technical competence remains a cornerstone of effective leadership, of course, but the mix of required competencies changes as one advances in responsibilities, and complexity taunts us at every turn. Thus, career preparation for senior positions presents a tremendous challenge. Further, we may no longer be able to provide traditional opportunities for command at general-officer levels before moving senior officers to key three- and four-star positions. (A few years ago, three of the seven four-star army generals in the United States had been division commanders; none had commanded a corps.) If this trend of relatively limited opportunity to serve with troops as general officers prevails, then we can logically anticipate the possible emergence of leaders who are in some aspects less knowledgeable, less comfortable, less secure in their roles as senior commanders.

Zais notes that Eisenhower had the insight and self-discipline "not to interpose himself in tactical decisions." But, as General Collins remarks, the importance of decentralization is sometimes "neglected or deliberately avoided by commanders whose lack of confidence results in their failure to delegate authority." In a similar vein, Nelsen sees overcontrol as "the reflex of the commander's own insecurity." (It is noteworthy that in the midst of World War II, General Marshall had the confidence and sense of independence to often leave the Pentagon at 1500 hours.)

## Integrating Operational and Leadership Doctrines

Peacetime habits become wartime habits. The predominant elements of non-materiel combat power—such as discipline, boldness, technical competence, physical fitness and trust—obviously have long gestation periods.

Sutten discusses the links between leadership doctrine and operational doctrine. We know, for example, that neither "management by exception" (establishment of an information flow to management confined to identification of problems demanding management's attention) nor the zero-defects model is compatible with current operational doctrine. We know that "management by objective" (management by systematic goal-setting, with some collaboration between manager and subordinate in specifying measurable goals) is also suspect in a sophisticated setting. A compelling argument remains for a range of leadership styles adapted to the circumstance at hand, with a particularly formidable argument for frequent use of a transformational style that nourishes a strong sense of responsibility and initiative among subordinates. Transformational leadership, by the enlightened use of inspiration, communication, and understanding of human behavior, can motivate subordinates to achieve more than could ordinarily be expected.

In his discussion of the evolution of *Auftragstaktik* (maximum tactical autonomy and decentralization, with heavy emphasis upon lower-echelon initiative), Nelsen describes how that concept faded in World War I as German army reserve officers were unable to handle it. We may have multiple issues to ponder from that bit of history.

A leadership doctrine that supports AirLand Battle doctrine—or any other warfighting approach dependent on individual initiative and decentralized decisionmaking—may be more difficult to put in place than the operational doctrine itself. Nelsen and many others including myself see routine decentralization efforts today as being quietly undermined. Efforts to empower downward and encourage prudent risk-taking on the part of subordinates require almost Herculean energies if they are to prevail against the tide of hierarchical conservatism. If getting our leadership ducks in order—creating climates, expectations, and routines that will optimize our warfighting capabilities—is not the absolute first order of the day, I do not know what is.

The contributors to these pages—ranging from young majors to perceptive historians to proven senior combat leaders—have given us more than food for thought. Together they have mandated a prescription for greater awareness and provided a tonic for renewed action on the military leadership front.

Lieutenant General Walter F. Ulmer, Jr.
U.S. Army, Retired

# I.  THE FOUNDATIONS OF LEADERSHIP

# 1

# On Leadership

## By OMAR N. BRADLEY

Military men are expected above all else to be leaders. What they do may well dignify the past, explain today, and secure—for all of us—tomorrow.

I would like to touch upon a few factors that will underscore the value of good leadership. Leadership is an intangible. No weapon, no impersonal piece of machinery ever designed can take its place.

This is the age of the computer, and if you know how to program the machine you can get quick and accurate answers. But how can you include leadership—and morale, which is affected by leadership—into your programing? Let us never forget the great importance of leadership; and while we use computers to obtain certain kinds of answers, let us not try to fight a whole war or even a single battle without giving proper consideration to the element of leadership.

Another element to be considered is the Man to be led, with whose morale we are concerned. I am constantly reminded of this point by a cartoon which hangs over my desk at home depicting an infantryman with his rifle across his knees as he sits behind a parapet. Above him is the list of the newest weapons science has devised, and the soldier behind the parapet is saying: "But still they haven't found a substitute for ME."

In selecting a company in which to invest our savings, we often give primary consideration to the company with good leadership. In similar manner, a military unit is often judged by its leadership. Good leadership is essential to organized action where any group is involved. The one who commands—be he a military officer or captain of industry—must project power, an energizing power which marshals and integrates the best efforts of his followers by supplying that certain something for which they look to him, whether guidance, support, encouragement, example, or even new ideas and imagination.

The test of a leader lies in the reaction and response of his followers. He should not have to impose authority. Bossiness in itself never made a leader. He must make his influence felt by example and the instillment of confidence in his followers. Remember, a good leader is one who causes or inspires others, staff or subordinate commanders, to do the job. His worth as a leader is measured by the achievements of the led. This is the ultimate test of his effectiveness.

While it takes a good staff officer to initiate an effective plan, it requires a leader to ensure that the plan is properly executed. That is why the work of collecting information, studying it, drawing a plan, and making a decision is only a small part of the total endeavor; seeing that plan through is the major part. During World War I, while inspecting a certain area, General John J. Pershing found a project that was not going well, even though the second lieutenant in charge seemed to have a pretty good plan. General Pershing asked the lieutenant how much pay he received. On hearing the lieutenant's reply of "$141.67 per month, Sir," General Pershing said: "Just remember that you get $1.67 per month for making your plan and issuing the order, and $140.00 for seeing that it is carried out."

Similarly, I can recall a former vice-president of an industrial company with which I am familiar. He would formulate some good plans but never followed up to see that his plans got the expected results. I knew he had served in World War II; out of curiosity, I looked into the nature of his service and found that his entire period of service was as a staff officer. He had never had the advantage of a command job; thus his training was incomplete. Maybe if he had remained in the service longer, we could have developed his leadership qualities as well—and this man would still be with the company.

Certainly in these days, however, problems are complex and good staff work plays a large part in resolving them. I have known commanders who were not too smart, but who were very knowledgeable about personnel and knew enough to select the very best for their staffs. No leader knows it all (though you sometimes find one who seems to think he does). A leader should encourage the members of his staff to speak up if they think the commander is wrong. He should invite constructive criticism. It is a grave error for the leader to surround himself with "Yes" men.

General George C. Marshall was a strong exponent of the principle of having his subordinates speak up. When he first became Chief of Staff of the Army, the secretariat of that office consisted of three officers, including myself, who presented orally to General Marshall the staff papers coming from the divisions of the General Staff. We presented the contents of the staff studies in abbreviated form, citing the highlights of the problem involved, the possible courses of action considered, and the action recommended.

At the end of his first week as Chief of Staff, General Marshall called us into his office and opened the discussion by saying: "I am disappointed in all of you." When we inquired if we might ask why, he said: "You haven't disagreed with a single staff recommendation all week." We told him it so happened that we were in full agreement with every paper that had been presented, and that we would add our frank comments to any proposal we considered dubious. The very next day, we briefed a paper as written and then pointed out some factors which, in our opinion, made the recommended action questionable.

General Marshall responded: "Now that is what I want. Unless I hear all the arguments concerning an action, I am not sure whether I have made the right decision or not."

Thus, if an officer happens to be detailed to a staff, he should try to avoid being a "Yes" man. I would recommend to all commanders that they inform the members of their staffs that anyone who does not disagree once in a while with what is about to be done is of limited value and should probably be shifted to some other place where he might occasionally have an idea.

Of course, I am thinking about the decisionmaking process. After a decision is made, everyone must be behind it 100 percent. I thought the British were admirable in this respect during World War II. No matter how much discussion there had been on a subject, as soon as a decision was made you never heard any doubts expressed. You would have the impression that no one involved in making the decision had ever entertained a contrary point of view.

I don't want to overemphasize leadership of senior officers; my interest extends to leaders of all ranks. An essential qualification of a good leader is the ability to recognize, select, and train junior leaders. During World War II in the Pacific, Colonel Red Reeder was on a trip for General Marshall. One of his assignments was to inquire into junior leadership. In a book entitled *Born at Reveille*, Colonel Reeder records an account of his conversation with Colonel Bryant Moore on Guadalcanal:

> "Colonel Moore," I said, "tell me something about leadership." I had hit a sensitive spot. He forged ahead. "Leadership! The greatest problem here *is* the leaders, and you have to find some way to weed out the weak ones. It's tough to do this when you're in combat. The platoon leaders who cannot command, who cannot foresee things, and who cannot act on the spur of the moment in an emergency are a distinct detriment.
>
> "It is hot here, as you can see. Men struggle; they get heat exhaustion. They come out vomiting and throwing away equipment. The leaders must be leaders and they must be alert to establish straggler lines and stop this thing.
>
> "The men have been taught to take salt tablets, but the leaders don't see to this. Result, heat exhaustion.
>
> "The good leaders seem to get killed; the poor leaders get the men killed. The big problem is leadership and getting the shoulderstraps on the right people."
>
> Sixty-millimeter Japanese mortar shells fell about thirty yards away and attacked a number of coconut trees. I lost interest in taking dictation and the colonel stopped talking. When the salvo was over and things were quiet again, Bryant Moore said, "Where was I? You saw that patrol. I tell you this, not one man in fifty can lead a patrol in this jungle. If you can find out who the good patrol leaders are before you hit the combat zone, you have found out something.
>
> "I have had to get rid of about twenty-five officers because they just weren't leaders. I had to *make* the battalion commander weed out the poor junior leaders! This process is continuous."

What, then, are the distinguishing qualities of a leader? There are many essential characteristics, but I will mention a few that come to mind as perhaps the most important. First, he must know his job, without necessarily being a specialist in every phase of it. A few years ago it was suggested that all engineering subjects be eliminated from the required studies at West Point. I objected. For example, bridge building is a speciality for engineers; yet, I think every senior officer should have some idea of what is involved. When we reached the Rhine in World War II, it was not necessary that I know how to build a bridge, but it was very helpful that I knew what was involved so that I could see that the bridge engineers received sufficient time and proper logistical backup.

Specialization figures in almost every problem faced today by the military leader or the business manager. This person must get deeply enough into his problem to be able to understand it and manage it intelligently, without going so far as to become a specialist himself in every phase of the problem. One doesn't have to be a tank expert in order to use a tank unit effectively.

Thomas J. Watson of IBM once said that genius in an executive is the ability to deal successfully with matters he does not understand. This leads to another principle of leadership which I have often found neglected, both in the military and in business. While one need not be a specialist in all phases of his job, he should have a proportionate degree of interest in every aspect of it—and those concerned, the subordinates, should be aware of the leader's interest.

Thus, leaders must get around and show interest in what their subordinates are doing, even if they don't know much about the techniques of their subordinates' work. And, when they are making these visits, they should try to pass out praise when due, as well as corrections or criticism.

We all get enough criticism and we learn to take it. Even Sir Winston Churchill, despite his matchless accomplishments, found occasion to say: ''I have benefited enormously from criticism and at no point did I suffer from any perceptible lack thereof.'' But let us remember that praise also has a role to play. Napoleon was probably the most successful exponent of this principle through his use of a quarter inch of ribbon to improve morale and get results.

We tend to speak up about our subordinates' performance only when things go wrong. This is such a well recognized fact that a ''Complaint Department'' is an essential part of many business firms. To my knowledge, no comparable department exists anywhere to handle praise for a job well done. Praise, incidentally, need not be extravagant.

Both mental and physical energy are essential to successful leadership. How many really good leaders have there been who were lazy or weak, or who couldn't stand the strain? Sherman was a good example of a leader with outstanding mental and physical energy. During the advance from Chattanooga to Atlanta, he often went for days with only two or three hours of sleep per night and was constantly in the saddle reconnoitering. He often knew the dispositions and terrain so well that he could maneuver the enemy out of position without a serious fight and with minimum losses.

Conversely, a sick commander is of limited value. It is not fair to the troops under him to have a leader who is not functioning at 100 percent. I had to relieve several senior commanders during World War II because of illness. It is often pointed out that Napoleon didn't lose a major battle until Waterloo, where he was a sick man.

A leader should possess human understanding and consideration for others. Men are not robots and should not be treated as such. I do not by any means suggest coddling. But men are intelligent, complicated beings who will respond favorably to human understanding and consideration. By these means their leader will get maximum effort from each of them. He will also get loyalty—and, in this connection, it is well to remember that loyalty goes down as well as up. The sincere leader will go to bat for his subordinates when such action is needed.

A good leader must sometimes be stubborn. Here, I am reminded of the West Point cadet prayer. A leader must be able to "choose the harder right instead of the easier wrong." Armed with the courage of his convictions, he must often fight to defend them. When he has come to a decision after thorough analysis—and when he is sure he is right—he must stick to it even to the point of stubbornness. Grant furnishes a good illustration of this trait. He never knew when he was supposed to be licked. A less stubborn man might have lost at Shiloh.

During the Richmond campaign, after being up all night making his reconnaissance and formulating and issuing orders, Grant lay down under a tree and fell asleep. Sometime later, a courier rode up and informed the general that disaster had hit his right flank and that his troops at that end of the line were in full retreat. General Grant sat up, shook his head to clear the cobwebs, and said: "It can't be so," and went back to sleep—and it wasn't so.

Of course, in commending stout adherence to one's chosen course of action I do not mean to imply that there is always just one solution to a problem. Usually there is one best solution, but any good plan, boldly executed, is better than indecision. There is usually more than one way to obtain results.

Actually, what I have referred to as Grant's stubbornness might better be called confidence. Leaders must have confidence in themselves, their units, their subordinate commanders—and in their plans. Just before the invasion of Normandy in 1944, a story went around in some of the amphibious assault units that they would suffer 100 percent casualties—that none of them would come back. I found it necessary to visit these units and talk to all ranks. I told them that we would, naturally, suffer casualties, but that our losses would for certain be manageable and that with our air and naval support we would succeed. After our landing, a correspondent told me that on his way across the Channel in one of the leading LSTs he had noticed a sergeant reading a novel. Struck by the seeming lack of concern of the sergeant, he asked: "Aren't you worried? How can you be reading at a time like this?" The sergeant replied: "No, I am not worried. General Bradley said everything would go all right, so why should I worry?"

I might relate another incident involving confidence. I had to relieve a senior commander because I learned that his men had lost confidence in him. This meant, of course, that we could not expect maximum performance by that division. After being relieved, the officer came back through my headquarters and showed me a file of statements given him—at his request, I am sure—by the burgermeisters of all the towns his division had passed through. After seeing the letters, I told the officer that if I had ever had any doubts as to whether to relieve him, those doubts were now removed. His letters proved beyond question that he had lost confidence in himself, so it was no wonder the men had lost confidence in him.

A leader must also possess imagination. Whether with regard to an administrative decision or one made in combat, the leader must be able to look ahead: what will be the next step—and the one after that? Imagination is the quality that enables him to anticipate the train of consequences that would follow from his contemplated courses of action. He can thus minimize error and be prepared for likely contingencies.

While there are other qualities which contribute to effective leadership, I will mention just one more—but it is a vital one—character. This word has many meanings. I am applying it in a broad sense to describe a person who has high ideals, who stands by them, and who can be trusted absolutely. Such a person will be respected by all those with whom he is associated. Such a person will readily be recognized by his associates for what he is.

It has been said that a man's character is the reality of himself. Once having been maturely formed, I don't think a man's character ever changes. I remember a long time ago when someone told me that if a mountain was reported to have moved, I could believe or disbelieve it as I wished, but if anyone told me that a man had changed his character, I should not believe it.

All leaders must possess those positive qualities which I have been discussing, and the great leaders are those who possess one or more of them to an outstanding degree. Some leaders just miss being great because they are weak in one or more of these areas. There is still another ingredient in this formula for a great leader that I have left out, and that is *luck*. He must have the right opportunity. Then, of course, when opportunity knocks, he must be able to rise and open the door.

Some may ask: "Why do you talk about the desirable traits of leadership?" They maintain that you either have leadership or you don't—that leaders are born, not made. I suppose some are born with a certain amount of leadership. Frequently, we see children who seem inclined to take charge and direct their playmates. The other youngsters follow these directions without protest. But I am convinced nevertheless that leadership can be developed and improved by study and training.

There is no better way to develop a person's leadership than to give him a job involving responsibility and let him work it out. We should try to avoid telling him how to do it. That principle, for example, is the basis of our whole system of combat orders. We tell the subordinate unit commander what we want him to do and leave the details to him. I think this system is largely responsible for the many fine leaders in our services today. We are constantly training and developing younger officers and teaching them to accept responsibility.

However, don't discount experience. Someone may remind you that Napoleon led armies before he was 30, and that Alexander the Great died at the age of 33. Napoleon, as he grew older, commanded even larger armies. Alexander might have been even greater had he lived longer and gained more experience. In this respect, I especially like General Bolivar Buckner's theory that "Judgment comes from experience and experience come from bad judgment." Thus, all other factors being equal, the leader with experience will have a considerable advantage over the leader who lacks it.

This article appeared in the autumn 1981 issue of *Parameters*.

# 2

# Running Things

By DONN A. STARRY
© *1987 Donn A. Starry*

Despite the differences between the military and industry, the practice of leadership and management in the two arenas is not so dissimilar as one might think. Cut to the bone, it's a matter of running things. That is what leaders and managers do, whether in uniform or mufti. They run things, do things, get things done. They take finite resources, organize them, and direct their application toward finite goals, tasks, aims, and objectives, always cognizant of what those goals are, always mindful of the resources at hand and what must be achieved.

It is not my purpose here to tell you how to run things; each of you will decide that on your own. That you are reading this book testifies to your interest in the subject of leadership, which has doubtless helped you to form your own ideas about how to run things. So I will try not to bother you with things you already know. My purpose is to distill for you some observations from 44 years of running things and watching other people run things, in the hope that the product will be of some value.

One of the most elemental complications in running things is *change*. Change is constant, unceasing, and ever-accelerating. True, this has always been the case, but today the pace of change is much more rapid and we have to swallow it in much greater doses than ever before. Change is inherently confusing, upsetting; change is dysfunctional. It is imperative that leaders or managers accommodate to change while pursuing goals which don't change very much. That brings us to an important second point: despite the pace and magnitude of change, some things don't change very much at all. In fact, if we are to be successful, our core objectives likely should not change at all; what changes is the variety of ways in which we seek to achieve those relatively static goals. With change swirling all about us, affecting much of what we do, consistency and stability are essential qualities of sound leadership and management.

Running things involves four fundamental factors that determine what is done and how it gets done:

- *Vision*. At the beginning there must be some vision of what is being attempted. What are we trying to accomplish? Vision varies with perspective. Your vision if you are taking command of a brigade won't be the same as it will if you're about to take over as chief operating officer of a division or a company in industry, but presumably you will set goals in either case. What do you want to get done on your watch? Your answer to that question is what I call *vision*. Vision is expressed largely in terms of what the leader senses, what his intuition tells him, as opposed to some more rational process. Please understand, though, that what is required in this sense is informed intuition, not just some seat-of-the-pants guesswork. To be useful, vision must be believable; it must be something that those charged with achieving it can understand and believe to be a good, achievable idea, one they can eventually embrace as their own. In fact, one of the keys to getting anything done is to convince a lot of people that what is being attempted is a good idea; to really move things it is necessary also to convince them it was their idea in the first place. If you can do that, you can accomplish almost anything!
- *Strategy*. Next, you need a description of how the *vision* is to be achieved. How do we get from where we are to where we want to be? The answer is our game-plan—our *strategy*.
- *Operations*. Specific tasks must be accomplished to achieve the strategy. The strategy becomes a series of mission statements with accompanying tasks. These tasks describe the *operations* to be undertaken in order to get things done. In the business world, this includes how the company is to be organized. What market segments are to be embraced by what organizational divisions and in what segments of the market will each business entity operate, grow, and yield profit? In the military, campaign plans and their ensuing operational-level implementation determine how things get done at the operational level of warfare.
- *Tactics*. Finally, there is the set of business practices one employs to get things done. In the military these are called *tactics*, and so they might be called in industry. They involve the lower-level schemes which win the bid, the program; which take the hill, the objective; which mark success for the lowest levels of the organization as that success has been spelled out in operations plans and orders, in budget plans and instructions.

Long years ago, a new commander took charge of a unit in which I commanded a subordinate element. One of his first acts was to summon me to issue instructions. What he said went something like this: "I want you to understand why I am here. I am here because it is necessary for me to command this unit for a year—no more, no less—in order to get to be a general. I am going to be a general. Now, your outfit has a tendency to do things differently, to attract attention. I don't like that. For the year I am in command, I don't want anything to happen. I don't just mean anything bad—I mean anything that will call the attention of higher headquarters to us as being different from anyone else. We are just going to go along. That's my vision [his word] for the next year. Don't rock my boat. Do you understand?''

Of course, I affirmed that yes, I understood. Then I went back to my unit to report on our instructions. First, I relayed what the new commander had said to me. Then, after some discussion, we decided what we would do: We *would* rock the boat, and hard, but in such a way that our boss couldn't accuse us of screwing up his vision. We went right along as he had said, but with the firm determination to be the best, to win everything in sight. The boat was constantly rocking, but our commander really couldn't say much to stop us—*his* boss was forever congratulating him on how well we were all doing under his enlightened leadership! My commander never spoke with me again about this, but I'm sure that by his standards he had a very miserable year.

In another setting, at another time, a new chief executive officer took over a fairly large company with a diversified portfolio of businesses. In setting out his vision for his business units, the CEO issued the pronouncement that his vision for one unit was that it become, in five years, number three in the market segment in which it was involved. When asked how he arrived at the number three, he replied that ''intuitively it seemed about right.'' At the time, the business unit in question was number 29 in an industry which had an annual growth rate of about eight percent. In order to achieve the number three position, that business unit would have to grow at a rate six times the market growth rate and invest a sum four times the total corporate allocation for that function. The CEO's vision was clearly out of sync with reality. As a consequence, the business unit manager and his staff ignored the vision. The unit did grow, and at a rate somewhat better than the market rate, but against a totally different set of criteria from those laid down by the CEO. His vision was simply not relevant; it may have been intuitive, but it was certainly not informed.

The management texts will tell you that the chief executive officer must be involved in strategy formulation. Several studies of military leadership cite the same notion. But it is very difficult to get the boss involved in the vision or strategy part of the operation. It is perhaps more difficult in the business world, where the all-pervasive concentration on profit and the chief executive's inability to unharness himself from budget details distract his attention visibly, sometimes completely, and perhaps even fortuitously, from what in reality should be his fundamental role.

Military estimates call for a commander's guidance; military orders call for a commander's concept of the operation. Yet how many times have you ever seen a commander sit down to think and write about those things himself? He's too busy to think—the staff keeps him that way. Besides, he is almost always more comfortable with the nits and details than with vision and strategy. The latter require that a commander think creatively; the former, only that he have an accountant's grasp of what's going on, and usually he's far more comfortable in that role.

In the automobile industry, Ford lost its market share lead to General

Motors in the 1920s largely because of Henry Ford's unwillingness to give up the Model T and build the cars that technology was making possible and that customer demands were making necessary. Ford's dominant position in the auto industry was lost. While his vision of providing the car for the common folk may have been a correct one, Henry Ford was unable to tolerate the changing demands of the common folk. Chevrolet and GM overtook him, and it was not until 1986, 62 years later, that his successors were able to push his company's performance past that of General Motors.

The Ford Motor Company had a problem with its vision—its strategy—even into the recent past. One way to decide on a strategy is to watch carefully what the competition does and, if they're successful, then jump in and carve out your own market share before the competition's share grows too large. This was essentially the strategy followed by Ford in the 1970s. With the first oil crisis came the need to produce smaller, more fuel-efficient cars for the US market. GM moved off in this direction. The GM strategy was to seize the dominant share of that market. Ford's strategy was to see how well GM did, then jump in. The belated jump, ill-timed according to some, did not capture a sufficient market share, and only after huge capital investment and complete redesign has Ford begun to recoup the losses suffered by the wait-and-see strategy.

But let's face it: not many people in charge, in the military or in industry, are intuitively or consistently good at running things. It would be difficult to say whether there is more or less ineptitude on one side than on the other. Military people certainly have had far more formal education and schooling to equip them for running things than the chief executives in industry. By and large, they seem to do better than the average industry exec, but given the differences in background, education, and training specifically directed at the art of running things, one would expect a much better than average performance from the average military leader. Why doesn't it happen?

In large measure, it seems to me, the problem devolves to the need for an individual to take the time to figure out who he is and what his role is to be at each new command. If a CEO is managing programs, and many of them can't resist the temptation, then what in the world are the division general managers and operations directors doing? If a corps commander is running battalions, then what, indeed, are the division and brigade commanders doing?

Several years ago, I succeeded to command of V Corps, my predecessor having been relieved for cause. Assumption of command was by signature in the airport lounge on a Sunday. The following Wednesday, the G3 marched into my office to announce it was time to check the readiness of the corps. We went to a special room in the headquarters, a place called the "Cutting Edge Room." There, a major and several captains and sergeants were posting readiness data off the DA Form 2715 reports onto side-lighted plexiglass boards arranged around the room. Each company in the corps had a line; columns displayed the data from the readiness reports. There were reds, yellows, and greens to show at a glance how things were going. Deadlined vehicles were indicated in red by bumper number. The corps operational readiness rate for tracked vehicles was at about fifty percent, so there were lots of red entries. When I asked, the G3 reported that I was supposed to come here, look at the red numbers, then call the company commanders to see what they were doing about the deadlined vehicles, by bumper number. What, I asked, were the division, brigade, and battalion commanders doing? They were, I was told, waiting for the company commanders to call in reports of their conversation with the corps commander. Now, you'll recall that the corps commander is not in that reporting chain. Having listened and observed, I left instructions to get rid of the whole thing. I went to my office, called the division commanders, and explained that henceforth materiel readiness and its reporting system were in their hands, that I expected an operational readiness rate of 95 percent or better, and that if they had problems attaining and sustaining that rate they were to call me. The OR rate began a slow but perceptible climb. It reached 95 percent in a few months, and stayed at that level or better. Now and then I'd check to see that the numbers were real, that they were not just cobbled-up to meet my standards. Satisfied that the reporting was honest and fairly accurate, I concluded that the problem had been solved.

Another important thing to remember—after answering the question of the boss's role at each level of responsibility—is that at every level—strategic, operational, or tactical—everything that is done depends on people. So, success at running things is a function of getting people to do what is necessary to accomplish the vision and implement the strategy. Concurrently, we must realize that there are a whole lot of average people out there trying to get things done, and that the challenge of command, or of being the chief executive, is to get great things done using those average people to execute the operational- and tactical-level schemes that implement the strategy, the vision.

An example. In V Corps, when I was its commander, there were 72 battalion-sized units. Twenty-six were maneuver battalions or squadrons; nearly 30 more were fire support units; the remainder were support battalions of various types. We spent the whole of our 16 months together doing two things. First, we went to the General Defense Positions, where the division and brigade commanders and I listened to each battalion-level commander tell how he intended to fight the battle, or provide the support, from his positions, with the resources he had been assigned. Then, we went to each battalion in turn and heard the battalion commander and his command sergeant major explain how they intended to train their battalion to fight the battle, or provide the support, we had just previewed on the ground. On a little score sheet, I noted that of the 72 battalions, about eight or nine of the commanders were so good at what they were doing that it probably was not necessary for us to go through the routine I just described. Another 15 were so poor at what they were doing that the commanders clearly should never have been posted to command. The rest were in the middle. In other words, 12 percent or so were OK, about 21 percent were unsatisfactory, and two-thirds were in the middle. The real challenge of command or management is this: to somehow bring the level of performance of the middle two-thirds up to something like the top 12 percent. The United States Army simply does not have enough battalions to afford having 85 percent of them less than exemplary. Nor in industry can you expect to run a company at above-market growth rates unless something is done to improve the proposals, performance on contracts, technology development, planning, and budgeting to some level well above the industry average. That is the challenge of management. There must be a willingness to replace the less-than-average performers, regardless of the system by which they were chosen. That also is the job of the management, the job of leaders; indeed, it is probably their toughest job of all.

What is it, more often than not, that's wrong with the folks who don't know how to run things? Why are the good leaders or managers and the not-so-good the way they are? The simplest explanation I know comes from our attempts to figure out how to fight outnumbered below the nuclear threshold and win. What became clear was the idea that regardless of the force ratios extant at the beginning, and regardless of who attacked whom, the winning side was the side which seized the initiative and held it to the end. The lesson for leaders is clear and unequivocal: to win it is necessary to seize the initiative; and the person running things is responsible for taking the initiative.

Taking the initiative is not easy. First, it requires some thought, and we've already noted the problems of thinking about things at the managerial level. Second, it requires the ability to describe one's vision in terms that cause the people who must realize that vision to say, "That's a damned good idea." Third, it requires the ability to lay down strategies for achieving the vision in terms that those people embrace, even to the extent that they come to believe they invented the strategies themselves. This takes time, a certain craft, and a well-developed skill in communicating with people. But it is essential. Finally, taking the initiative means doing something. Doing something means taking risk. He who would get out in front and lead things—take the initiative—does so at some risk to himself. It is always much easier to let the other guy go first and test the market, test the water, then jump in if it seems OK. It is always safer from the standpoint of making general to command an organization that just "goes along."

As an illustration of initiative in the vision-strategy-operations-tactics context consider for a moment the military concept called AirLand Battle. Its basic vision is the notion that it is necessary for us to be able to fight outnumbered and win, below the nuclear threshold at the operational level of war. The basic strategy is to so control and moderate the force ratios at the FLOT (forward line of own troops) that it is possible to seize the initiative by maneuvering forces to defeat the enemy. To do that, it is necessary to attack enemy follow-on forces at the same time the FLOT battle begins, and to do so in such a way that the FLOT battle is manageable and opportunities are created for forces to maneuver.

That fairly straightforward set of ideas forms the basis for the constellation of doctrine, organization, equipment, and training which the Army and the Air Force have been developing for several years.

Broadening this concept to embrace the national level, there seems to me to be an urgent need for some fundamental initiatives and a baseline statement of vision-strategy-operations-tactics as the nation moves ahead to the turn of the century. The central aim of our nation is to preserve our democratic institutions, to foster their well-being, growth, and development. How that is to be done is a matter for debate. But the central point is that inherent in that goal is the issue of survival: for in order to preserve, foster, and grow, one must first survive. Survival is at the root of every corporate strategy in the industrial world. Other things will be laid on as goals, aims, and objectives, but the fundamental imperative is to stay in business. In the ever-changing global environment, our ultimate nonchanging goal as a nation is survival.

Now, the problem we face in insuring achievement of that goal is that we are quite likely engaged in what will turn out to be a century or more of global conflict, for there is no objective evidence that the Soviet Union will cease to be a Leninist state, run by a collective tsardom, in which the secret police enforce the will of the central authority. In my opinion, anybody who holds that Gorbachev is a political moderate and modernizer is just not thinking clearly. Gorbachev's Russia is a slightly modern version of the Russia of Nicholas the First. A Sovietologist friend once said to me that the frightening thing about studying the Soviet Union is just that—nothing changes. The basic system has remained in place, perhaps a little more grotesque under Stalin, a little less grotesque under someone else, but it is still the same system. If that is true, we must find the initiatives to contain the Soviet empire in order to preserve peace. If we are to do that, our national goals must not simply cope with the Soviets, they must accelerate our rate of change as a society so that we pull away from the Soviet system, leaving it, in effect, a modern-day Ottoman Empire. Remember the Ottoman Empire: in 1600, it was yet a great threat to Europe; by 1800, it was irrelevant; and by 1900, it was routinely described as the sick man of Europe. It could not adapt, could not make the cultural and economic changes necessary to cope with the changing world. Its leadership could not accommodate change.

Peace is a noble goal, one to be sought after, but it is not the ultimate goal. The ultimate goal is survival in order that preserving, growing, fostering, and developing can take place uninhibited. Those who would have peace would be well advised to gird for conflict—political, economic, social, and perhaps even military—over the long term.

Cast in that framework, then, our national challenge is not at all unlike the challenge facing every company in the corporate world. The difference is, of course, that the nation must engage in a global competition over the next two or three generations to decide if the inhabitants of this planet are to be free or slave. If we lose that competition, the corporate world will have nothing to worry about, for it will not survive either. So the challenges inherent to running things extend to all levels of endeavor, from government to small business, from civilian to military.

In industry, success is built very much on common ingredients—the dedication and motivation of the workers, the quality of the leadership, and the excellence of the training provided to the working team. If the standards are high, the dedication to excellence ever present, the team working in concert, then better-than-average companies led by managers seeking always to take the initiative can go to battle in the bidding environment, fully confident of winning, growing, and prospering.

The military is not so different, after all. Wars are won by the courage of soldiers, the quality of leadership they are provided, and the excellence of the training the soldiers, leaders, and units have been through before the battle. If the training has been tough, demanding, unrelenting, then better-than-average units, led by officers seeking ever to take the initiative, are prepared to go to battle; and that's what it takes to win.

This article appeared in the September 1987 issue of *Parameters*.

# 3

# Napoleon on the Art of Command

By JAY LUVAAS

"My son should read and meditate often about history," Napoleon asserted to one of the generals sharing his last days on St. Helena: "This is the only true philosophy. He should read and meditate about the wars of the Great Captains; that is the only way to study war."[1]

Although much has been written about Napoleon as a general, analyzing in elaborate detail his tactical and strategical maneuvers from the Italian campaign of 1796 to the repulse of the Imperial Guard at Waterloo, surprisingly little attention has been paid to what Napoleon thought and *wrote* about leadership. His 78 maxims, which were extracted from his dictations on St. Helena several years after his death, contain practical advice on what a general should do in planning marches, fighting battles, and conducting sieges, but only three or four maxims have to do with leadership per se, ending with the startling revelation that "generals in chief are guided by their own experience or genius."[2]

When Napoleon advised his son to study the campaigns of the Great Captains, it was not so much to discover the principles of war as it was to see how these had been applied. Only by imitating these great models, that is, by understanding the basis for their decisions and studying the reasons for their success, could the modern officer hope to approach them.

Had Napoleon wished to instruct his son on the fine points of military leadership, however, he could have found no better way than to make available a selection of his own letters and papers, which contain a wealth of information and insights on the art of command. His letters to his brother Joseph and his stepson Eugene are especially revealing, for here Napoleon clearly was trying to educate members of his family to become good military leaders. To his marshals and other subordinates he said in effect, "do it," and sometimes when he was impatient of delay, Napoleon would invoke a convenient "principle" to lend infallible authority to his wishes. (This may be one reason why Napoleon often was ambivalent about the so-called "principles of war," asserting that genius acts by inspiration, that what is good in one case is bad in

18

another, and that when a soldier becomes accustomed to affairs he tends to scorn all theories.)[3] To his brother and stepson, however, Napoleon went to great lengths to explain *why* and *how* they should execute his wishes, in the process revealing many of his secrets of leadership.

Although he did not express himself in the analytical terms of the famed Prussian theorist on war, Karl von Clausewitz, Napoleon would have agreed that good leadership was a combination of two kinds of qualities—qualities of the intellect, which are trained and cultivated; and those of temperament, which can be improved by determination and self-discipline. Good military leadership therefore is a blend of the two, the product of superior insight and will, and rarely, according to Napoleon, do all of the qualities that produce a great general combine in a single individual. When this happy combination does occur, the result is a military genius, "a gift from heaven."[4]

Of those intellectual qualities essential for high command, Napoleon would probably have placed calculation at the head of his list. "I am used to thinking three or four months in advance about what I must do, and I calculate on the worst," he explained to Joseph. "In war nothing is achieved except by calculation. Everything that is not soundly planned in its details yields no result."[5] "If I take so many precautions it is because it is my custom to leave nothing to chance."[6] A plan of campaign was faulty in Napoleon's eyes unless it anticipated everything that the enemy might do and provided the means for outmaneuvering him.[7] Napoleon recognized, of course, that in all affairs one must leave something to circumstances: the best of plans can fail as a result of what Clausewitz called friction, that is, "the factors that distinguish real war from war on paper," those "countless minor incidents" a general never could foresee.[8] Conversely, sometimes even poor plans succeeded through a freak of fortune.[9]

To be a good general, Napoleon once commented to one of his military entourage on St. Helena, "you need to know mathematics. That is useful in a thousand circumstances to correct ideas. Perhaps I owe my success to my mathematical ideas; a general must never make a picture for himself. That is the worst thing of all."[10] Toward the end of his career Napoleon sometimes was guilty of "making pictures," but in his early days he had the ability to penetrate to the heart of a question and to see the entire situation clearly.

If there were two intellectual qualities that set Napoleon apart from most men, it was his prodigious memory and his infinite capacity for mastering detail. "A very curious thing about me is my memory," he told Gourgaud. "As a young man I knew the logarithms of more than thirty to forty numbers. I knew, in France, not only the names of the officers of all the regiments, but the places where the regiments were recruited and had gained distinction."[11]

Napoleon constantly fretted in letters to his generals about the need for them to pay strict attention to their muster rolls.

> The good condition of my armies comes from the fact that I devote an hour or two every day to them, and when I am sent the returns of my troops and my ships each month, which fills

twenty large volumes, I set every other occupation aside to read them in detail in order to discern the difference that exists from one month to another. I take greater pleasure in this reading than a young lady would get from reading a novel.[12]

Napoleon kept a critical eye on every detail of military intelligence, the movement and supply of troops, and army organization and administration. Woe to the subordinate general who failed to provide the date, place, and even the hour where a dispatch had been penned, or who did not provide information in sufficient detail. "The direction of military affairs is only half the work of a general,"[13] Napoleon insisted. Obviously, the other half involved a detailed knowledge of all parts of the military machine. In large measure, Napoleon's own mastery over men was possible because of his mastery of information, for as he explained to one of the generals sharing his captivity: "All that I am, everything that I have been I owe to the work habits that I have acquired from my boyhood."[14] There can be no doubt that Napoleon, had he been spared to supervise the military education of his own son, would have driven this point home time and again, and with all the forces at his command.

In Napoleon's case, a trained memory was reinforced by an absorbing interest in the minutiae of military activity. One cannot read his dictations on St. Helena without being impressed by the facts at his fingertips—how much dirt a soldier could dig in a specified time; minute details of tactics, and organization, and logistics; the smallest facts from his own campaigns and those of the other Great Captains. When asked one day how, after so many years, he could recollect the names and numbers of the units engaged in one of his early combats, Napoleon responded: "Madam, this is a lover's recollection of his former mistresses."[15]

Brilliance was not essential for a general, at least not so far as Napoleon was concerned. "Too much intellect is not necessary in war," he once reminded his brother Jerome. What was essential was precision, a strong personality, and the ability to keep things in a clear perspective.[16] Probably the most desirable attribute of all, or so he told Las Cases, "is that a man's judgment should be . . . above the common level."[17] Success in war depends on prudence, good conduct, and experience.[18]

By prudence Napoleon did not mean that a good general should be cautious in the conduct of operations. *Au contraire*: a good general "must be slow in deliberation and quick in execution."[19] Whenever Napoleon used the term prudence, what he intended to convey was careful management and presence of mind.

We have now slipped over into what Clausewitz called "moral qualities," and what Napoleon undoubtedly had in mind at the time he urged that his son should read and re-read the campaigns of the Great Captains. "But all that . . . he will learn will be of little use to him," Napoleon warned, "if he does not have the sacred fire in the depths of his heart, this driving ambition which alone can enable one to perform great deeds."[20]

The moral quality that Napoleon most admired was boldness; here again, he would have agreed with Clausewitz, who asserted that "a distinguished commander without boldness is unthinkable."[21] Napoleon saw boldness as *the* common denominator among the Great Captains. Alexander succeeded because "everything was profoundly calculated, boldly executed, and wisely managed."[22] Hannibal was bolder still,[23] and Caesar was "a man of great genius and great boldness."[24] Napoleon did not consider Gustavus Adolphus in a league with the others, if only because his early death meant that he must be judged on the basis of only a few campaigns, but he was impressed by the "boldness and swift movements" of the Swedish king's last campaigns.[25]

Clausewitz in one of his more discerning passages observed that "boldness grows less common in the higher ranks. . . . Nearly every general known to us from history as mediocre, even vacillating, was noted for dash and determination as a junior officer."[26]

Napoleon probably would have concurred, for he once described Turenne as "the only general whose boldness had increased with the years and experience." Napoleon, it should be added, preferred Turenne for another, more personal reason. "I like him all the more because he acts exactly as I would have done in his position. . . . He is a man who, had he come near me at Wagram, would have understood everything at once." From St. Helena he mused: "If I had had a man like Turenne to assist me in my campaigns, I would have been master of the world."[27]

In Napoleon's comments about Prince Eugene, we again read of a "very bold march crowned by the most brilliant successes,"[28] and while he often criticized the tactics and strategy of the Great Frederick, he had only praise for the "bold resolutions" that had enabled Frederick to survive the Seven Years' War and emerge with his state—and his army—intact.[29]

> Frederick possessed great moral boldness. . . . What distinguishes him most is not the skill of his maneuvers, but his boldness. He carried off what I never dared attempt. He abandoned his line of operation and often acted as if he had no knowledge of the military art. Always superior to his enemies in numbers at the beginning of a campaign, he is regularly inferior to them on the field of battle.

"I may be daring," Napoleon concluded, "but Frederick was much more so."[30] He was especially great "at the most critical moments," which was the highest praise that Napoleon could bestow.[31]

A general was expected to be brave, but Napoleon insisted that bravery be tempered by good judgment. If courage was the predominating quality of a general, he would be apt to "rashly embark in enterprises above his conception." On the other hand, if a general lacked character or courage he probably would not venture to carry out his ideas.[32]

Marshal Ney, "the bravest of the brave," was a case in point. "He was good when it came to leading 10,000 men," Napoleon acknowledged, "but beyond that he was a real fool." Always the first under fire, Ney was inclined to forget those troops who were not under his immediate supervision.[33] Murat was another who was brave in action but in other respects had "neither vigor nor character."[34] Napoleon distinguished between the bravery that a commander must display and that required of a division commander, and neither, he wrote, should be the same as the bravery of a captain of grenadiers.[35]

When he mentioned courage, Napoleon had also in mind moral courage—what he liked to call "two o'clock in the morning courage." When bad news comes to a person at that hour, it is dark, he is alone, and his spirits are at low ebb; it requires a special brand of courage at such a time to make the necessary decision. Such courage is spontaneous rather than conscious, but it enables a general to exercise his judgment and make decisions despite the unexpected or the unfortunate surprises.[36]

Firmness—what Clausewitz would call perseverance—was another requisite for good generalship. "The most essential quality of a general is firmness of character and the resolution to conquer at any price."[37]

> The foremost quality of a commander is to have a cool head, receiving accurate impressions of what is happening without ever getting excited, or dazzled, or intoxicated by good or bad news. The successive or simultaneous sensations that the commander received during the course of a day are classified in the mind and occupy only as much attention as they deserve, for good sense and judgment flow from the comparison of several sensations taken into equal consideration. There are men who, by the moral and physical composition, distort a picture of everything. No matter how much knowledge, intellect, courage and other good qualities they might have, nature has not called them to command armies or to direct the great operations of war.[38]

The worst error a general can make is to distort what he sees or hears. Merely because some partisan has captured an enemy picket is no reason for the general to believe that the entire army is on hand. "My great talent," he told Gourgaud, "the one that distinguishes me the most, is to see the entire picture distinctly."[39]

Because of the variety of intellectual and moral factors, Napoleon recognized that "in the profession of war, like that of letters, each man has his style." Messena might excel in sharp, prolonged attacks, but for defensive purposes Jourdan would be preferable.[40] Reynier, a topographical engineer, was known as a man of sound advice, but he was a loner, cold and silent by nature and not very communicative. Obviously, he was no man to electrify or dominate soldiers. Lannes was "wise, prudent and bold," a man of little formal education but great natural ability and a man of imperturbable *sang froid*. Moreau was personally brave but knew nothing of grand tactics. Desaix, on the other hand, understood *la grand guerre* almost as well as Napoleon—or so Napoleon claimed after he had been sent into exile.[41]

It follows, therefore, that generals were not to be treated as interchangeable parts. Each was particularly well suited for some kinds of tasks, but as Napoleon wrote on more than one occasion, a great general—by which he may well have meant a complete general—"is no common thing."[42]

Because Napoleon never bothered to write a book of practical advice to his son, of the kind written by several contemporaries in France and England,[43] we can only surmise some of the things he might have said. Nevertheless, many of his strong convictions snap to attention and salute as one reads his published correspondence. The following excerpts probably should be considered for promotion to the level of maxims, to serve as pithy aphorisms on the art of command.

There are no precise or determined rules; everything depends on the character that nature has given to the general, on his qualities, his shortcomings, on the nature of the troops, on the range of firearms, on the season and on a thousand other circumstances which are never the same.[44]

War is a serious sport, in which one can endanger his reputation and his country: a rational man must feel and know whether or not he is cut out for this profession.[45]

The honor of a general consists in obeying, in keeping subalterns under his orders on the honest path, in maintaining good discipline, devoting oneself solely to the interests of the State and the sovereign, and in scorning completely his private interests.[46]

In war one sees his own troubles and not those of the enemy.[47]

In war the commander alone understands the importance of certain things. He alone, by his will and superior insight, can conquer and overcome all difficulties.[48]

Hold no council of war, but accept the views of each, one by one. . . .The secret is to make each alike . . . believe that he has your confidence.[49]

Take nobody into your confidence, not even your chief of staff.[50]

Soldiers must never be witnesses to the discussions of the commanders.[51]

Generals always make requests—it is in the nature of things. There is not one who cannot be counted upon for that. It is quite natural that the man who is entrusted with only one task thinks only about it, and the more men he has the better guarantee he has for success.[52]

One always has enough troops when he knows how to use them.[53]

Once you have made up your mind, stick to it; there is no longer any *if* or *but* . . . .[54]

War is waged only with vigor, decision and unshaken will; one must not grope or hesitate.[55]

It is at night when a commander must work: if he tires himself to no purpose during the day, fatigue overcomes him at night. . . . A commander is not expected to sleep.[56]

Give your orders so that they cannot be disobeyed.[57]

It is not enough to give orders, they must be obeyed.[58]

In military operations, hours determine success and campaigns.[59]

The loss of time is irretrievable in war: the excuses that are advanced are always bad ones, for operations go wrong only through delays.[60]

You must be slow in deliberation and quick in execution.[61]

Intelligent and fearless generals assure the success of affairs.[62]

I may be accused of rashness, but not of sluggishness.[63]

It is by vigor and energy that one spares his troops, earns their esteem, and forces some of it on the reprobates.[64]

You must not needlessly fatigue troops.[65]

You must avoid countermanding orders: unless the soldier can see a good reason for benefit, he becomes discouraged and loses confidence.[66]

Pay no attention to those who would keep you far from fire: you want to prove yourself a man of courage. If there are opportunities, expose yourself conspicuously. As for real danger, it is everywhere in war.[67]

In war the foremost principle of the commander is to disguise what he does, to see if he has the means of overcoming the obstacles, and to do everything to surmount them when he is resolved.[68]

True wisdom for a general is in vigorous determination.[69]

In war everything is perception—perception about the enemy, perception about one's own soldiers. After a battle is lost, the difference between victor and vanquished is very little; it is, however, incommensurable with perception, for two or three cavalry squadrons are enough to produce a great effect.[70]

If one constantly feels humanity he cannot wage war. I do not understand war with perfume.[71]

An army of lions commanded by a deer will never be an army of lions.[72]

Whether these or other maxims still apply today is for others to determine. The point is, they applied in Napoleon's day. At least they reflected his experience, and for that reason alone they reveal much about Napoleon and his philosophy of command.

## NOTES

1. "Extraits des récits de la captivité," *Correspondance de Napoléon 1er* (32 vols.; Paris, 1858-70), XXXII, 379.
2. There are many editions of Napoleon's maxims: this quotation is from the translation by L. E. Henry, *Napoleon's War Maxims* (London, 1899), p. 39. In *The Mind of Napoleon*, J. Christopher Herold includes a conversation recorded by Las Cases and a letter from Napoleon to one of his generals on the subject of command, and additional insights can be inferred from extracts of Napoleon's views of the Great Captains. (See Ibid., pp. 220-21, 224-30.) The comprehensive collection of Napoleon's thoughts on military topics assembled by Lieutenant Colonel Ernest Picard devotes only three out of 575 pages to the heading "Qualities of Command." *Préceptes et jugements de Napoléon* (Paris, 1913), pp. 214-17.
3. Napoleon to Joseph, 4 May 1807, *Corres.*, No. 12530, XV, 188; General Gourgaud, *Sainte-Hélène, Journal inédit* (2 vols.; Paris, 1899), II, 20.
4. Comte de Montholon, *Récits de la captivité de l'empereur; Napoléon a Sainte-Hélène* (2 vols.; Paris, 1847), II, 240-41; Carl von Clausewitz, *On War*, in Michael Howard and Peter Paret, eds. and trans. (Princeton, N.J.: Princeton Univ. Press, 1976), pp. 190-92.
5. Napoleon to Joseph, 18 September 1806, *Corres.*, No. 10809, XIII, 210; XII, 442.
6. Napoleon to Marshal Murat, 14 March 1808, *Corres.*, No. 13652, XVI, 418.
7. "Ulm-Moreau," *Corres.*, XXX, 409.
8. Clausewitz, *On War*, p. 119.
9. To Vice Admiral Decres, 16 June 1805, *Corres.*, No. 8897, X, 529; "Notes sur l'art de la guerre," XXXI, 417.
10. Gourgaud, *Journal*, II, 460.
11. Ibid., p. 109.
12. Napoleon to Joseph, 20 August 1806, *Corres.*, No. 10672, XIII, 87.
13. Napoleon to Eugene, 20 June 1809, *Corres.*, No. 15388, XIX, 140; to Berthier, 28 June 1805, No. 8957, X, 571; to Murat, 12 October 1805, No. 9372, XI, 316.
14. Montholon, *Récits*, I, 321.
15. Count de Las Cases, *Memoirs of the Life, Exile and Conversations of the Emperor Napoleon* (4 vols.; London, 1836), II, 349.
16. Napoleon to Jerome, 2 May 1804, *Corres.*, No. 8832, X, 474; to Jerome, No. 12511, XV, 178.
17. Las Cases, *Memoirs*, I, 251.
18. "Note sur la situation actuelle de l'Espange," 5 August 1808, *Corres.*, No. 14245, XVII,429.
19. Napoleon to Eugene, 21 August 1806, *Corres.*, No. 10681, XIII, 9.
20. *Corres.*, XXXII, 379.
21. Clausewitz, *On War*, p. 21.
22. Las Cases, *Memoirs*, IV, 140-41.
23. "Notes sur l'art de la guerre," *Corres.*, XXXI, 349.
24. Gourgaud, *Journal*, II, 162.
25. "Notes sur l'art de la guerre," *Corres.*, XXXI, 354.
26. Clausewitz, *On War*, p. 191.
27. Gourgaud, *Journal*, II, 135-37.
28. "Notes sur l'art de la guerre," *Corres.*, XXXI. 355.
29. "Précis des guerres de Frédéric II," *Corres.*, XXXII, 238-39.
30. Gourgaud, *Journal*, II, 17, 20, 33,34.
31. "Précis des guerres de Frédéric II," *Corres.*, XXXII, 238.
32. Las Cases, *Memoirs*, I, 250-51.
33. "Campagne de 1815," *Corres.*, XXXI, 206-07; Gourgaud, *Journal*, I, 585.
34. Napoleon to Murat, 26 January 1813, Léonce de Brofonne, *Lettres inédities de Napoléon 1er* (Paris, 1898), No. 1033, p. 423.

35. "Campagne de 1815," *Corres.*, XXXI, 207.
36. Las Cases, *Memoirs*, I, 251.
37. Montholon, *Récits*, II, 240–41; Gourgaud, *Journal*, II, 426.
38. "Précis des guerres de Frédéric II," *Corres*, XXXII, 182–83.
39. Gourgaud, *Journal*, II, 460.
40. Napoleon to Joseph, 6 June 1806, *Corres.*, No. 10325, XII, 440.
41. "Notes-Moreau," *Corres.*, XXX, 496; "Notes sur l'art de la guerre," *Corres.*, XXXI, 380; Montholon, *Récits*, I, 176.
42. Gourgaud, *Journal*, II, 423–24.
43. See *A Series of Letters recently written by a General Officer* to his son . . . (2 vols.; Salem: 1804). This American edition was from the second English edition, which bears a striking resemblance to M. le Baron D'A . . . , *Conseils d'un Militaire a son Fils* (Paris, 1874).
44. "Notes sur l'art de la guerre," *Corres.*, XXXI, 365.
45. Napoleon to Eugene, 30 April 1809, *Corres.*, No. 15144, XVIII, 525.
46. Napoleon to Marshal Berthier, 8 June 1811, *Corres.*, No. 17782, XXII, 215.
47. Napoleon to Eugene, 30 April 1809, *Corres.*, No. 15144, XVIII, 525.
48. "Observations sur les campagnes de 1796 et 1797," *Corres.*, XXIX, 341.
49. Napoleon to Joseph, 12 January 1806, *Corres.*, No. 9665, XI, 535.
50. Napoleon to Jerome, 26 May 1812, *Corres.*, No. 18727, XXIII, 436.
51. Napoleon to Marshal De Moncey, 31 March 1805, *Corres.*, No. 8507, X, 279.
52. Napoleon to Joseph, 4 March 1809, *Corres.*, No. 14846, XVIII, 308.
53. Napoleon to Joseph, 26 June 1806, *Corres.*, No. 10416, XII, 489.
54. Napoleon to Marshal Marmont, 18 February 1812, *Corres.*, No. 18503, XXIII, 229.
55. Napoleon to General Bertrand, 6 June 1813, *Corres.*, No. 20090, XXV, 363.
56. Napoleon conversation with Gourgaud, *Journal*, II, 159.
57. Napoleon to Marshal Berthier, 29 March 1811, *Corres.*, No. 17529, XXI, 521.
58. Napoleon to Eugene, 11 June 1806, *Corres.*, No. 10350, XII, 270.
59. Napoleon to Admiral Mazarredo, 20 March 1800, *Corres.*, No. 4689, VI, 199.
60. Napoleon to Joseph, 20 March 1806, *Corres.*, No. 9997, XII, 204.
61. Napoleon to Eugene, 21 August 1806, *Corres.*, No. 10681, XIII,96.
62. Napoleon to Marshal Mortier, 29 November 1806, *Corres.*, No. 113255, XIII, 588.
63. Napoleon to the Executive Director, 6 May 1796, *Corres.*, No. 337, I, 237.
64. Napoleon to Joseph, 28 July 1806, *Corres.*, No. 10558, XIII, 9.
65. Napoleon to Eugene, 29 July 1806, *Corres.*, No. 10563, XIII, 13.
66. Napoleon to Eugene, 5 August 1806, *Corres.*, No. 10699, XIII, 38.
67. Napoleon to Joseph, 2 February 1806, *Corres.*, No. 9738, XI, 573.
68. Napoleon to Marshal Berthier, 9 April 1810, *Corres.*, No. 16372, XX, 284.
69. Précis des guerres de Frédéric II," *Corres.*, XXXII, 209.
70. Napoleon to Joseph, 22 September 1808, *Corres.*, No. 14343, XVII, 526.
71. Napoleon conversation with Gourgaud, *Journal, II*, 449.
72. "Campagnes d'Egypte et de Syrie," *Corres.*, XXX, 176.

This article appeared in the summer 1982 issue of *Parameters*.

# 4

# *Auftragstaktik:* A Case for Decentralized Combat Leadership

By JOHN T. NELSEN II

The main question this article attempts to answer is whether the U.S. Army should formally adopt a concept akin to what is called *"Auftragstaktik."*[1] That this question needs answering may be surprising to many readers, since the much ballyhooed emphasis upon mission orders in the 1982 and 1986 editions of Field Manual 100-5, *Operations*, has been linked to *Auftragstaktik.*[2] But the German concept means far more than mission orders. Indeed, it means more even than "task-oriented or mission-oriented tactics," which though certainly a more sophisticated definition is still a rough and imperfect approximation.

There are significant problems in attempting to identify the nature of *Auftragstaktik.* Chief among them is that not until after World War II did the term come into general use. At that time, former German generals coined the term to label certain aspects of the German Army's approach to war in the past. Adding to the confusion, West Germany's *Bundeswehr* adopted the term but applied it narrowly to their own system of command and control, translating it as "mission-oriented orders." In short, the term *Auftragstaktik* is an artificial, after-the-fact construct whose meaning has never been defined with any precision. How then should one use the term? It is particularly useful as a rubric for denominating those aspects of German Army methodology prior to 1945 that led to the exercise of such impressive initiative in battle by its leaders at all levels. To study these aspects, however, one must examine the German Army's regulations and military literature of the period, as well as the writings of former German officers. One must be wary of focusing on any single aspect in isolation; what is now termed *Auftragstaktik* formed part of a seamless fabric in the German Army's warfighting philosophy. Virtually all notions were interrelated in some fashion. They were not grafted piecemeal onto this philosophy, but evolved organically over a period of at least eighty years. Thus, the concept of *Auftragstaktik* is a useful analytical tool—the more so as one bears in mind its limitations and views it in its proper historical setting.

## The Historical Backdrop

*Auftragstaktik*, as demonstrated in World War II, was the product of an evolutionary process dating from the 19th century. The driving force for it was the necessity of developing greater initiative in leaders at all levels. At the tactical level, the Prussian Army discovered both during the Austro-Prussian War (1866) and the Franco-Prussian War (1870–71) that the increased lethality of weapons forced greater dispersion across the battlefield. Commanders of armies, corps, divisions, brigades, regiments, and often battalions could neither fully observe nor control their forces in the detail previously allowed. Frequently, captains and lieutenants were forced to employ their units in fast-moving situations without detailed instructions from superiors. In short, they had to make decisions on their own which in the past had been reserved for higher-level commanders. The results were frequently disastrous. Prussian junior leaders were untrained for this and often proved inadequate to the task.[3]

Of necessity, the new Prussian army studied the problem, seeking a way to better prepare leaders at lower levels for independent decisionmaking. Without allowance for this, decisions on the dispersed battlefield threatened to be too time-consuming. Speed of decisive action would be lost. The result of the study was a new provision in the Drill Regulations of the Infantry (1888). It stipulated that commanders should give subordinates general directions of *what* was to be done, allowing them freedom to determine *how* to do it. This approach, it was felt, would stimulate development of the "thinking leader" who was used to making tactical judgments in his own right. Such leaders would less likely freeze up when faced with new situations in the absence of detailed instructions from above. By 1914, the spirit of this provision had taken root.[4]

World War I saw pendulum-like swings in the application of this provision. In the initial campaigns, it was fully applied with good results. However, the high attrition rates and the great influx of reserve officers who had not received adequate training caused the application to wane. In the West, the more centralized nature of trench warfare also had an influence. Commanders issued increasingly detailed orders that gave subordinates few opportunities to exercise much initiative. Then, the German development of elastic defense-in-depth tactics (1916–18) and assault tactics (1918) changed the situation. Both demanded great initiative and creativity from leaders down to the noncommissioned-officer level, often in fluid situations and in the absence of orders. The Germans trained hard for such leadership behind the lines and enjoyed impressive success at the tactical level. As a consequence, the German army of the post-World War I era evinced a strong institutional commitment to developing leaders who were willing and able to take prudent, independent action to handle the unexpected.[5]

This desire for increased leader initiative was in full consonance with the German Army's perception of the nature of war. First, speed was considered imperative for victory at both strategic and tactical levels. German field service regulations emphasized that "the first demand in war is decisive action." As a country with a central position in Europe, Prussia/Germany always faced the specter of a two-front war. Rapid defeat of an enemy through offensive action was essential. This discouraged opportunistic countries from joining the conflict to gang up on Germany. It also reflected the view that in a two-front war, victory was possible only by defeating one foe quickly before the second one was ready to fight. This allowed the fullest concentration of German forces at chosen decisive points, in a way which favored a series of decisive victories. At the tactical level, the idea was to react after enemy contact with a series of rapid maneuvers to force the adversary into a largely reactive posture. He would than be vulnerable to defeat in detail through a series of subsequent engagements forced on him at great disadvantage.

Second, the Germans believed that the appropriate maneuvers to take in the face of the enemy could not be pre-planned in meticulous detail. They subscribed to the elder Moltke's dictum that "no operation plan extends with any certainty beyond the first encounter with the main body of the enemy." Since war was viewed fundamentally as a "clash of wills," enemy action would seldom conform to expectations. Added to this was a keen appreciation for the disruptive effects of friction on military activities.[6]

Third, the Germans considered every situation in war unique. This required competent leaders to make rapid estimates and decisions, and then to act on them swiftly. Furthermore, such decisions would always be made with incomplete, inaccurate, or conflicting information. Uncertainty and the fog of war stalked the battlefield. Thus the leader had to be a thinking soldier. He needed both intuitive powers to interpolate correctly and creative powers to devise a successful course of action. Each situation required a unique application of tactical principles which could not be prescribed by universal recipes or by detailed planning. This view of war was subsumed by the first article in the Field Service Regulations of 1933: "Leadership in war is an art, a free creative activity based on a foundation of knowledge. The greatest demands are made on the personality."

Thus the German view of war fully supported granting junior leaders great scope for initiative—if that was what it took to generate the speed necessary for victory. At the same time, this situational and artistic perspective on war shaped the framework for the exercise of leader initiative. This framework provided for three essentials: proper leader character, sound methodology for issuing and carrying out orders, and enlightened senior-subordinate relations.

So far as leader character was concerned, initiative in a leader flowed from his willingness to step forward, take charge of a situation, and act promptly—completely on his own authority, if necessary. Not surprisingly, the German field service regulations stressed that the noblest quality of a leader was his willingness to assume responsibility. To do so under stressful conditions required considerable moral courage, self-reliance, and self-confidence—attributes the German Army prized highly.

Closely related were the attributes which stressed risk-taking and decisive action. Since all decisions were made under conditions of uncertainty and since every situation was unique, there could never be a demonstrably perfect solution. Therefore, one should not demand one. There were theoretically several workable solutions for every tactical problem. "Many roads lead to Rome" was a common refrain heard in this regard. The object was to pick any reasonable plan swiftly and then to execute it with energy and dispatch. Leaders were cautioned against waiting to gather more information so as to reach a perfect decision, or even the best decision possible. Good leaders made a rapid estimate, adopted as sound a course of action as feasible, and executed it decisively. In this view, speed was more essential than precision; a decent plan carried out immediately was superior to a superb plan carried out much later.[7]

To operate in this way, a leader had to assume great risk willingly. To encourage this, the German Army framed two rules. First, in situations clearly requiring independent decisions, a leader had not only the latitude to make them, but the solemn *duty* to do so. A good leader cultivated a will to action. Second, inaction and omission in such situations were considered much worse than judgmental error based on a sincere effort to act decisively. The former was the shameful antithesis of leadership. The latter was an honorable effort to practice the art of warfighting, in which no single action was guaranteed success. While errors in judgment might cause unsuccessful local engagements, the broad exercise of initiative by all leaders, it was felt, would carry the battle. Thus no opprobrium was associated with failure resulting from prudent risk-taking by the thinking leader. Such setbacks were simply the breaks of war.

The second part of the framework for exercising initiative consisted in the methodology of issuing and carrying out orders. In present-day terminology, this falls chiefly under the heading of command and control. As mentioned earlier, the Germans adopted a system of orders in 1888 giving subordinates as much latitude as possible in implementing assigned tasks. They refined the methodology over time. Insofar as he could, the commander told subordinates *what* tasks to accomplish, but not *how* to accomplish them. He also gave them sufficient resources to accomplish those tasks, stated any restraints, and provided required coordinating information. The goal was to allow subordinates as much freedom of action as the situation permitted. Orders were brief and usually verbal.

Leaders so trained, it was thought, would better handle the unexpected in battle, where split-second decisions were often decisive. Such leaders would also feel more ownership for their actions, thereby stimulating greater determination in carrying them out. Self-reliant leaders would derive more personal pride and satisfaction from their duties, causing them to identify more closely with their units. This, in turn, would strengthen unit cohesion.

In issuing orders, the most important part was the statement of the commander's intent. This related the various assigned tasks and provided a vision of the desired result of an operation. In carrying out their tasks, subordinates were always to focus on the intent. It was virtually sacrosanct. Subordinates using initiative in response to the unexpected had to conform, insofar as possible, with this intent. Thus the commander's intent promoted unity of effort in fluid situations which failed to conform nicely to plans and expectations. The intent, therefore, both circumscribed and focused the exercise of initiative in subordinates.

Under exceptional circumstances, a subordinate could even modify or abandon tasks if he could still satisfy the commander's intent. This, however, was a serious matter. Prior approval was required if possible. If that proved impossible, the subordinate assumed full responsibility for the decision. He would have to justify his action later to his superior.

This system of operating did not lessen the need for commanders to control their subordinates. Commanders habitually positioned themselves well forward. They kept themselves informed of the situation as well as the actions of their subordinates, whom they visited frequently. In no way did commanders relinquish any command authority or responsibility. They would intervene when subordinates were doing something clearly unsound. They would add or delete assigned tasks, or change their intent, as they saw fit. In short, they supervised and controlled, but in a manner encouraging initiative and thinking in subordinates. Subordinates, on the other hand, made every effort to maintain contact with their commander and to keep him fully informed of the situation. They were expected to solve problems which could be surmounted at their level, and to recommend changes to orders based on a continual evaluation of the situation.[8]

A third element of the framework for exercising initiative was that of senior-subordinate relationships. This falls under today's rubrics of leadership, command and control, and tactics. Commanders were responsible for developing in their subordinates the desired character and leadership attributes discussed earlier. Equally important, they spent much time teaching subordinates how to think on their feet in making estimates of the situation and in applying tactical principles. The object was not only to train subordinates but to educate them. Leaders were taught not so much what to think about, but, more important, how to think. Superiors and subordinates spent time together in map exercises, terrain walks, sand-table exercises, and field exercises discussing tactical problems. A central focus of every field exercise was the development of subordinate leaders. This involved a close teacher-student, coaching-like relationship.[9]

The result was that the leader and his subordinate got to know how each other thought. This was important to the subordinate in helping him to read between the lines of his commander's intent. This was also important to the commander; it allowed him to anticipate intuitively how his subordinate would exercise freedom of action in various situations. From this close relationship flowed mutual trust, which in turn nourished initiative. The subordinate would feel confident that his exercise of initiative in battle generally conformed to his commander's intent. The commander would trust his subordinate with greater rein in accomplishing tasks.[10]

The training and education process, both in units and military schools, facilitated the exercise of initiative in another way. It promoted among leaders a common outlook on the nature of war, on desirable character and personality traits, on the importance of initiative, on proper senior-subordinate relationships, and on how to issue orders. It also taught a common approach in understanding and applying tactical principles to the different types of operations, emphasizing the peculiar features and characteristics of each. Military terminology was precise, standard, and widely understood. The result was a remarkably uniform perspective in tactical operations which facilitated concise orders, accurate but brief communication of intent, and a sensing of how the unit as a whole might respond in given situations. This common outlook and language reassured both leaders and subordinates, reinforcing that sense of mutual trust and dependability so conducive to initiative and freedom of action.

The standard approach for conducting critiques of tactical exercises promoted initiative as well. Since every situation was unique and since no training situation could encompass even a fraction of the peculiarities of a real tactical situation, there could be no approved solutions. One acceptable solution was as good as another. Critiques of leader actions focused on identifying the student's rationale for doing what he did. What factors did he consider, or not consider, in making his estimate of the situation? Were the actions taken consistent with this estimate? How well were orders communicated? Were the actions taken tactically sound? Did they have a reasonable chance of being successful? These questions served as the basis for critiques. The idea was to broaden the leader's analytical powers, experience level, and base of knowledge, thereby enhancing his creative ability to devise sound, innovative solutions to difficult problems. Critiques were lenient and understanding, rather than biting and harsh. Mistakes were considered essential to the learning process and thus cast in a positive light. The focus was not on whether the leader did well or poorly, but on what progress he was making overall to develop as a leader. Damaging the leader's self-esteem, especially publicly, was strictly avoided. A leader's self-confidence, it was felt, was the wellspring from which flowed his willingness to assume responsibility and exercise initiative.

It becomes clear that *Auftragstaktik* was an extraordinarily broad concept, holistically embracing aspects of what today would be called a theory of the nature of war, character and leadership traits, tactics, command and control, senior-subordinate relationships, and training and education. In addition, these aspects were organically consistent, mutually reinforcing, and inseparably interwoven. *Auftragstaktik*, then, was much more than a mere technique of issuing orders. It was nothing less than a comprehensive approach to warfighting. Its first imperative was speed, to be achieved by the intelligent and aggressive exercise of initiative at all levels.

## The Demands of the Modern Battlefield

To what extent are the main features of *Auftragstaktik* applicable to the needs of the modern battlefield—today and tomorrow? Certainly speed of decisive action—the fundamental rationale for *Auftragstaktik*—is essential for success in contemporary war. Fluid situations, fleeting opportunities, and chaotic conditions will require rapid decisionmaking under conditions of great uncertainty. Furthermore, speed will often demand a conscious sacrifice of precision and will be critical for a smaller force to defeat a larger force. In the words of FM 100-5:

> Agility—the ability of friendly forces to act faster than the enemy—is the first prerequisite for seizing and holding the initiative. Such greater quickness permits the rapid concentration of friendly strength against enemy vulnerabilities. This must be done repeatedly so that by the time the enemy reacts to one action, another has already taken its place, disrupting his plans and leading to late, uncoordinated, and piecemeal enemy responses. It is this process of successive concentration against locally weaker or unprepared enemy forces which enables smaller forces to disorient, fragment, and eventually defeat much larger opposing formations.[11]

There is a broad consensus that speed can result only from decentralized decisionmaking in conformity with *Auftragstaktik*. The exercise of initiative by subordinates at all levels is considered essential.[12] First, the general tempo of war has increased significantly since World War II. In many cases, junior- and mid-level leaders will have no time to request instructions from superiors before having to act. There is less time for decisionmaking and communicating than ever before. Second, battlefield conditions will cause units at all levels to lose radio contact frequently with their headquarters or to become isolated physically from parent units. This will result from intense electronic warfare and from the fluid shape of the battlefield. To await reestablishment of contact with superiors before acting would court disaster by yielding the initiative to the enemy. Third, unit dispersal will be much greater than in past wars. Experiences at the National Training Center indicate that battalion commanders who attempt detailed control over even a portion of their force are usually overwhelmed by the tempo of the enemy's attack. Distances between subordinate units preclude this kind of control. As Major General E. S. Leland, former NTC commander, wrote: "A unit that does well only those things the boss checks will have great difficulty." Initiative at all levels is a must.[13]

There is widespread agreement on the needed framework for decentralized decisionmaking. It is the system of mission-oriented orders. Commanders should tell subordinates *what* to do, but allow them as much leeway as possible to determine *how* to do it. The commander also communicates his intent—as well as that of his next senior commander—along with any pertinent restraints or coordinating information. The intent is the subordinate's guidepost as he strives to deal with unexpected threats or opportunities, friction, and the fog of war.[14] As FM 100-5 emphasizes, the leader must avoid dependence on constant direction. Rather, he should

> conduct his operation confidently, anticipate events, and act fully and boldly to accomplish his mission without further orders. If an unanticipated situation arises, committed unit commanders should understand the purpose of the operation well enough to act decisively, confident that they are doing what their superior commander would order were he present.[15]

Not surprisingly, the leadership and character attributes commonly associated with stimulating battlefield initiative bear a strong resemblance to those associated with *Auftragstaktik*. Most important, the leader must be an aggressive thinker—always anticipating and analyzing. He must be able to make good assessments and solid tactical judgments. These must be based on a thorough grounding in doctrine, and on the creative ability to apply it to specific situations. He must take pride in his ability to solve problems at his own level, improvising as necessary to accomplish assigned missions without detailed, blow-by-blow instructions or continual supervision. He must be tough-minded, acting decisively and independently when contact with superiors is impractical or impossible. This behavior requires moral courage, self-reliance, and self-confidence. It also involves a willingness to assume responsibility and take risks in order to do the right thing at the right time. Finally, the leader must be both trustworthy and trusting. As a subordinate, he must faithfully adhere to his commander's intent in exercising whatever freedom of action he is given. As a superior, he must trust his subordinates with as much freedom of action as possible and encourage them to exercise initiative.[16]

This composite view of war thus echoes an old German army belief. It is the ability of small units—acting with coherence and synergism in behalf of a central plan in chaotic and potentially panicky moments—to shape decisively the whole course of battles. This comment by S. L. A. Marshall is more pertinent today than in the late 1940s when he made it:

> The great lesson of minor tactics in our time . . . is the overpowering effect of small amounts of fire when delivered from the right ground at the right hour. . . . The salient characteristic of most of our great victories (and a few of our defeats) was that they pivoted on the fire action of a few men.

The increased firepower, lethality, and ranges of modern weapons dramatically increase the effect that small units can have at pivotal times and places.[17] What emerges from this overall mosaic of future war is the strong suggestion for the need of an approach roughly approximating *Auftragstaktik*.

*John T. Nelsen II*

# Where Do We Stand Now?

The Army, it can be argued, has two opposing traditions of exercising command—centralized and decentralized. They have developed side by side over time, although they have seldom been formally recognized. The personal inclinations of the commanding officer have been the greatest influence in determining which tradition would predominate in a unit.

The centralized philosophy of command visualizes war more as a science than an art. At its extreme, the centralized approach sees a higher-level commander attempting to make precise decisions in a virtual zero-defects fashion. He then devises detailed plans to carry them out, and supervises the execution by micromanagement. All key decisions are referred to this commander. Decisions are based on massive amounts of information designed to cut through uncertainty. Slow responses are compensated for by massing overwhelming men and materiel against the enemy. In this view, far-reaching initiative from subordinates is not critical to success. Massive relative combat power is. In fact, there is an inherent skepticism that subordinates can make judgments which are precise enough. The centralized plan is sacred. Decentralized decisionmaking is seen as likely to undermine this well-oiled plan. To make the wrong decision is worse than making no decision at all. This approach tends to produce junior leaders who are reactors rather than initiators and who are risk-aversive. S. L. A. Marshall lamented that the Army in World War II, Korea, and Vietnam leaned too heavily toward this style of command.[18] One of the most vivid pictures of it in action is seen in the following passage from Lieutenant General Dave Palmer's *Summons of the Trumpet*:

> In the final analysis, the helicopter's most pernicious contribution to the fighting in Vietnam may have been its undermining of the influence and initiative of small unit commanders. By providing a fast, efficient airborne command post, the helicopter all too often turned supervisors into over-supervisors. Since rarely was there more than one clash in any given area at any given time, the company commander on the ground attempting to fight his battle could usually observe orbiting in tiers above him his battalion commander, brigade commander, assistant division commander, division commander, and even his field force commander. With all that advice from the sky, it was easy to imagine how much individual initiative and control the company commander himself could exert on the ground—until nightfall sent the choppers to roost.[19]

This tradition continues. Experiences at the NTC show that in many units subordinates lack a sense of responsibility as thinking actors. They are used to their commanders doing their tactical thinking for them. Since their role has been one of executing detailed plans, they do not feel they have the latitude to make on-the-spot adjustments demanded by the situation. Nor do they tend to make recommendations or suggest changes to established plans. Junior leaders often do things at the NTC they know are inappropriate because they were ordered to do them.[20] In 1984, the Army surveyed 23,000 officers from second lieutenant through colonel on a number of issues. Of those who responded, 49 percent said that "the bold, original, creative officer cannot survive in today's Army."[21]

The decentralized style of command, on the other hand, views war more as an art than a science. It values the initiative of subordinates, striving especially to harness their creative energies toward simultaneous problem-solving at all levels. The desired effect is speed based on sound judgmental ability developed by trial and error. Adequate, not perfect, solutions are sought. In this view, commanders issue general instructions, relying on subordinates to get the job done within a broad charter for action. Plans are viewed as provisional, with the understanding that no plan is ever implemented exactly as envisioned. The leader must continue to think on his feet, aggressively analyzing, recommending, anticipating, and adjusting.

This style has deep roots. Grant's instructions to Sherman during the Civil War bear its imprint: "I do not propose to lay down for you a plan of campaign . . . but simply to lay down the work it is desirable to have done and leave you free to execute it in your own way."[22] Lee operated similarly. In fact, as that war progressed, both sides relied increasingly on decentralized decisionmaking to tap the enormous resources of initiative in subordinates down to regimental and sometimes even company level.[23]

As Assistant Commandant of the Infantry School in the late 1920s, George Marshall did all he could to develop young officer-students into thinking leaders who could operate in a decentralized manner. He often issued students foreign or outdated maps, provided only sketchy intelligence, and compelled them to make their own decisions by cutting off communications with higher headquarters. He routinely made them face the unexpected in order to stimulate their imagination and ingenuity. One of his first orders was that "any student's solution of a problem that ran counter to the approved school solution and yet showed independent, creative thinking would be published to the class."[24]

Another supporter of the decentralized style of command was General George S. Patton. He allowed his subordinates great freedom of action, being tolerant and patient with their errors. He demanded speed and risk-taking. "Never tell people *how* to do things," he said. "Tell them *what* to do and they will surprise you with their ingenuity."[25]

This tradition, too, continues. Generally among subordinates today, the idea of a favorable command climate implies one in which their commanders allow them enough freedom of action, based on trust, to make their own decisions and perform their duties without over-detailed guidance or supervision. It is also a climate that readily forgives honest errors as part of the learning process. Furthermore, the growing number of journal articles advocating adoption of some sort of *Auftragstaktik* suggests that the decentralized tradition is alive and well. In one such article, the results of a poll of a number of former battalion commanders in Europe were reported: "All of them demanded that their company commanders be prepared to take appropriate action on the battlefield in the absence of specific orders." All of them wanted active, thinking leaders with the well-developed capacity to exercise initiative at every opportunity.[26]

There is thus plenty of fertile ground for an *Auftragstaktik*-like approach to grow in the U.S. Army. But as long as the centralized command tradition remains alive and respectable, such growth will be uneven, confusing, and occasionally contentious.

## What Is to Be Done?

The strongest psychological impediment to *Auftragstaktik* in the U.S. Army is fear on the part of the commander that his subordinates' mistakes resulting from their loosened rein would make the command look bad and thus jeopardize the commander's own success. Overcontrol, to be honest, is the reflex of the commander's own career insecurity. The antidote to such insecurity is a *top-down* command climate which deliberately tolerates the possibility of greater tactical error in confident expectation that the resulting explosion of initiative at all tactical echelons will provide a massive multiplication of combat effectiveness at the operational level.

To secure the manifest benefits of the decentralized approach, the Army should formally and systematically adopt an *Auftragstaktik*-like doctrine. Only thus, it might be added, will the centralized tradition ever be effectively confronted. Any process of formal adoption would require a codified doctrinal articulation of exactly what was meant. Without such an articulation, it would be virtually impossible for service schools and units around the globe to implement the approach in a uniform way. It should as a minimum articulate an integrated theory of the nature of war, desirable character and leadership attributes, command and control, senior-subordinate relationships, application of tactics, and leader education and training. The ideas linking all these aspects together are complex, reinforcing, and interwoven. By explaining fully the rationale for this approach and by thus tying it directly to warfighting and war readiness, formal adoption would facilitate acceptance, especially among many steeped in the centralized tradition of command.

Broad acceptance is particularly important since any *Auftragstaktik*-like approach must be implemented from the top downward in the chain of command. Implementation can be blocked by any commander who wishes to operate in a centralized fashion. Having the imprimatur of doctrine would increase the perceived legitimacy of *Auftragstaktik*, making efforts to circumvent general implementation clearly improper.

A concept like *Auftragstaktik*, if formally articulated as doctrine, offers advantages that range beyond the battlefield. For example, the concept could serve as a valuable prism through which one could better envision the development and integration of technology. The German army between 1933 and 1945 integrated the tank, the airplane, and other emerging technologies without changing or altering in any way their system of *Auftragstaktik*. The Germans recognized that man, not machine, was the first factor in achieving victory. To the extent that technology could support the notions associated with *Auftragstaktik*, it was integrated. If it worked against those notions, it was set aside or adapted. The German Army credited their success against France in 1940 to the manner in which they integrated technology in their system rather than to the presence of the technology itself. One should not forget that the French and British had more tanks than the Germans did in this campaign. Besides that, the overall quality of most French and British equipment was better. The German view emphasized not what one had, but how one used it.

This has important ramifications for the Army today. For example, the Army is developing two pieces of communications equipment which could provide senior commanders with the capability of readily micromanaging subordinate units. One is Mobile Subscriber Equipment, a system of highly mobile radiotelephones which greatly increases battlefield communications but which would enable corps and division commanders to dial battalion commanders directly. Another item being developed is the Position Location and Reporting System/Joint Tactical Information Distribution System Hybrid. Among other capabilities, this system would locate for a maneuver brigade commander by automatic, periodic electronic signal every platoon leader's vehicle in the brigade. Positions would be indicated on a computer screen that even a battalion commander would not have in his command post. One can only imagine the temptation a brigade commander would have to try to maneuver platoons, especially if he were an advocate of the centralized tradition of command. Such speculations are not to say the Army should refuse to develop these items, but rather that it must carefully consider how best to integrate them doctrinally.

The situation hearkens back to the old German Army's special concern about any communications equipment which allowed a commander to bypass intermediate command levels. Over time, this would cause a withering away of initiative, of a sense of responsibility, and of imagination at those levels. The German army used *Auftragstaktik* as a framework to circumscribe the use of such equipment for the larger good of a healthier command climate.[27] Perhaps such notions in doctrinal form could serve as an equally valuable framework for command in the U.S. Army.

The time for the formal adoption of *Auftragstaktik* by the U.S. Army has arrived. The success of AirLand Battle demands it. FM 100-5 tells us so. But adoption entails more than occasional lip service. It entails a recognition by the Army's leadership of the all-encompassing application of an *Auftragstaktik*-like concept, and then the systematic, top-down implementation of the concept through command leverage, doctrinal and regulatory changes, and service school indoctrination. To generate the necessary change in command climate will be the work not of weeks or months, but of years.

In this monumental redirection of leadership philosophy, we would seek to develop thinking, tough-minded, self-reliant, confident, and courageous leaders who can respond to friction, the fog of war, and unexpected enemy actions with initiative and grim determination—but with no guarantee of success. Such leaders, to paraphrase Teddy Roosevelt, will at best know the triumph of high achievement, but even in failure they will at least fail while daring greatly.[28]

## NOTES

1. This chapter is an abridged version of a monograph titled, "Where to Go from Here?: Considerations for the Formal Adoption of *Auftragstaktik* by the U.S. Army," School of Advanced Military Studies (Ft. Leavenworth, Kans., USACGSC, 5 December 1986). The monograph contains more comprehensive documentation of sources as well as a complete bibliography. It is on file in the Ft. Leavenworth Combined Arms Reference Library and in the Defense Technical Information Center (DTIC) system.

2. John L. Romjue, *From Active Defense to AirLand Battle: The Development of Army Doctrine 1973-1982* (Ft. Monroe, Va.: USATRADOC, 1984), pp. 58–59, 67.

3. Except where otherwise noted, the elaboration of the German concept of *Auftragstaktik* is based generally on the following sources: German army, *Exerzir-Reglement fuer die Infanterie* (Berlin: E. S. Mittler und Sohn, 1889), pp. 108–09; *Exerzir-Reglement fuer die Infanterie* (Berlin: E. S. Mittler und Sohn, 1906), pp. 78, 90–91; *Truppen fuehrung, Teil I* Heeresdienst vorschriften 300/1 (Berlin: E. S. Mittler und Sohn, 1936), pp. 1–5, 10, 15–16; *Fuehrung und Gefecht der verbundenen Waffen, Teil I* (Berlin: Verlag Offene Worte, 1921), pp. 6–9, 21–22, 30; Friedrich E. E. A. von Cochenhausen, *Die Truppenfuehrung, Teil I: Mittlere und untere Fuehrung*, 6th ed. (Berlin: E. S. Mittler und Sohn, 1931), pp. 25–26, 105; and *Die kriegswissenschaftliche Fortbildung des Truppenoffiziers* (Berlin: E. S. Mittler und Sohn, 1926), pp. 1–30, 50, 91–97, 153–56; Burkhart Mueller-Hillebrand, *Deutsche und soujetrussische militaerische Fuehrung im Zweiten Weltkrieg* report prepared for the Historical Division, U.S. Army, Europe, no date (c. 1954), pp. 24–25, 28, 31, 52–53; Friedrich von Bernhardi, *How Germany Makes War* (New York: George Doran, 1914), pp. 213–21.

4. Fritz Hoenig, *Inquiries into the Tactics of the Future*, 4th ed., trans. Carl Reichmann (Kansas City, Mo.: Hudson-Kimberly Publishing Co., 1898), pp. 25–27, 43, 45, 220, 232–34, 267, and 311; Tim Lupfer, *The Dynamics of Doctrine: The Changes in German Tactical Doctrine During the First World War*, Leavenworth Papers, no. 4 (Ft. Leavenworth, Kans.: Combat Studies Institute, USACGSC, July 1981), pp. 15–21, 41–46.

5. Herbert Rosinski, *The German Army*, ed. Gordon Craig (London: Pall Mall, 1966), p. 310.

6. Baron von Freytag-Loringhoven, *The Power of Personality in War*, trans. US Army War College (Harrisburg, Pa.: The Military Service Publishing Co., 1955), p. 91.

7. Guenther Blumentritt, *The Dangers of Operational and Tactical "Systems,"* ed. A. Hall, trans. H. J. Baerwaldt, report prepared for the Historical Divison, European Command, 1948, p. 6.

8. Lothar Rendulic, *Combat Orders*, trans. U.S. Army (Historical Division, U.S. Army Europe, 1947), pp. 5, 11.

9. Lothar Rendulic, *The Command Decision*, trans. M. Bauer (Historical Division, U.S. Army Europe, 1947), p. 9. Reassuringly, the U.S. Army's present emphasis upon "mentorship" in the superior's dealings with his subordinate leaders has many of the earmarks of *Auftragstaktik.*

10. Richard E. Simpkin, *Race to the Swift* (London and New York: Brassey's, 1985), pp. 230–31, 239. Martin van Creveld, *Fighting Power: German and U.S. Army Performance, 1939-1945* (Westport, Conn.: Greenwood Press, 1982), p. 36.

11. U.S. Department of the Army, *Operations*, Field Manual 100-5 (Washington: G.P.O., May 1986), pp. 15–16, 24, 97. The quotation is from p. 16.

12. Van Creveld, p. 35.

13. U.S. Department of the Army, "National Training Center: Lessons Learned," Commander's memorandum signed by Brigadier General E. S. Leland (Ft. Irwin, Calif.: National Training Center, 20 November 1985), p. 1.

14. FM 100—5, *Operations* (1986), pp. 17-18, 21; John M. Vermillion, "Tactical Implications of the Adoption of Auftragstaktik for Command and Control on the AirLand Battlefield," monograph, School for Advanced Military Studies (Ft. Leavenworth, Kans.: USACGSC, 2 December 1985), p. 36.
15. FM 100-5, *Operations* (1986), p. 22.
16. Ibid., pp. 15-16, 26.
17. S.L.A. Marshall, *Men Against Fire: The Problem of Battle Command in Future War* (Washington: Infantry Journal, 1947; reprinted, Gloucester, Mass.: Peter Smith, 1978), p. 68.
18. Ibid., pp. 114-15.
19. Dave Richard Palmer, *Summons of the Trumpet: U.S.-Vietnam in Perspective* (San Rafael, Calif.: Presidio Press, 1978), p. 142.
20. Vernon W. Humphrey, "NTC: Command and Control," *Infantry* 74 (September–October 1984): 36.
21. Benjamin Schemmer, "Internal Army Surveys Suggest Serious Concerns about Army's Senior Leaders," *Armed Forces Journal International* 122 (May 1985): 18-19.
22. Quoted in Marshall, p. 189.
23. F. W. von Mellenthin, *Armored Warfare in World War II*, Conference Report (Columbus, Ohio: Battelle, 10 May 1979),p. 5. Von Mellenthin likens Lee to the elder Moltke in the common approach of aligning their forces in the right direction for the decisive battle and then letting subordinates actually conduct the fight.
24. Forrest C. Pogue, *George C. Marshall: Education of a General, 1880-1939* (New York: Viking Press, 1963), pp. 248-57.
25. Porter B. Williamson, *Patton's Principles* (Tucson, Ariz.: Management and Systems Consultants, 1979), pp. 36-38, 45-47, 104-08.
26. John W. Mountcastle, "On the Move: Command and Control of Armor Units in Combat," *Military Review* 65 (November 1985): 37-38.
27. General Frido von Senger und Etterlin, *Neither Fear Nor Hope*, trans. George Malcolm (New York: E. P. Dutton, 1964), p. 220.
28. The full quotation appears in Vince Lombardi, *Vince Lombardi on Football*, ed. George L. Flynn (New York: Graphic Society Ltd. and Wallynn Inc., 1973), I, 16.

This article appeared in the September 1987 issue of *Parameters* under the title *"Auftragstaktik*: A Case for Decentralized Battle."

# 5

# Fear and Loathing in the Barracks—And the Heart of Leadership

By LARRY H. INGRAHAM

The smart guys have taken the U.S. Army about as far as we can go with respect to weapon systems that bust up things and hurt people. The next advance in creating a more effective army will be done with people. People require leadership. That's what worries me, and lots of others.

The Army is now in the throes of a blizzard of memos, manuals, and pamphlets on leadership. But they miss the point. What gets left out is the heart of leadership, which cannot be taught from the platform. To make you understand what I'm talking about, I have to tell you a story told to me by some wise old NCOs who understood the heart of leadership, and how we lost it.[1]

Once upon a time, long ago, there was an army. It was a pretty good army, too, by world standards. One day it got committed to the jungles of Southeast Asia. It was committed with an unclear mission by a commander-in-chief who hoped to wage a major war without pain to his people. He therefore refused to call up the reserves. To further reduce pain he agreed to a 12-month rotation and increasingly heavy draft calls. Within five years the Army was bloated on rapid promotions. Repeated tours wore down the NCO corps, adding the burned-out to the killed and the wounded. But the war continued. Draft standards were lowered to spare the sons of the middle class. Project 100,000 scraped the bottom of the nation's poor and disadvantaged to man that once-magnificent army.

Many dedicated NCOs and officers tried to carry on, but the task became increasingly difficult. War protests eroded essential civilian support for the war, and soldiers became "pigs" to their fellow citizens. Racial violence flared throughout the country and spilled over into the Army. Drug use permeated both civilian and military sectors. And, on top of all this, the legal system of the country took a sharp turn in support of individual rights over collective obligations. Charlie Company refused to move out when ordered. Discipline broke. The Army and the nation trembled in disgust and frustration at revelations of atrocities symbolized by My Lai. Senior officers looked the other way. The war continued.

The 12-month rotation cycle worked reasonably well, except for one small problem—the Army quickly ran out of junior NCOs. Developing sergeants takes time. More time than 12 months. The Army tried to solve the problem by school-training junior NCOs, who were derisively called "shake and bakes." The scorn was not altogether deserved. They were well-trained at school, and got a few months jump on learning to be a sergeant in the jungle. Unfortunately, while they knew how to lay a Claymore, they often had trouble getting others to follow their example. Telling somebody else where to go and what to do (and having them respect you for it)—that's something you don't learn in any school. You have to learn by watching somebody with the knack and then trying to copy. Well you can imagine the time those NCOs had when all hell broke loose in the Army, when discipline collapsed, and when nobody could tell anybody anything.

Those were times when many NCOs and officers were more afraid of their own troops than the enemy. Those were days of fraggings, and of racial protests on the commanding general's front lawn. Those were days when in some units in Germany no officer or NCO dared to go above the first floor of the barracks. Those were days of hassling over haircuts, of confiscating drugs only to be told the seizure was illegal, and of being verbally assaulted as a "lifer" for giving a legitimate order.

When the war finally ended, the Army was in a damn sorry shape. It was combat ineffective throughout the world. It was morally rotten. The jungle massacres were bad enough, but on top of that the Sergeant Major of the Army and the Provost Marshal General so much as admitted to being crooks. Oh, it looked like an army on the outside, but inside it was hollow. All the depots had been picked clean, operations and maintenance funds diverted, and serious unit training eliminated. What was left of the Army sat in ratty facilities maintaining worn-out equipment, with no funds to practice being an army with.

Many experienced senior NCOs quit in disgust at what had become of the Army they had grown up in. The Army they loved lay in shambles around them, a paper model of its former self. They quit for many reasons. The end of the draft reduced the pay differentials between privates and sergeants. The "New Volunteer Army" marched to the tune, "The Army Wants to Join You." It seemed like the privates got every benefit, everything but standards and discipline.

Others quit because their work had been contracted out to civilians during the war. Others found the MOS reclassifications difficult to swallow, while still others found it more profitable to retire than to continue to serve. They left with heavy hearts. The spirit of their army was gone. And with them went not man-years, but man-centuries of experience.

These centuries of experience included an understanding of the difference between recruit billets and the barracks of real soldiers; how to inspect a mess hall; drill ceremonies for fun; full field layouts; little pocket books with personal data on each soldier; how to housebreak lieutenants so you could show them off in company as captains; how to teach and how to train; when to joke and when to growl; and, most important, how to love soldiers and the Army.

The NCOs who stayed to put the Army back together again had a hell of a job on their hands. Remember, too, that they were comparatively inexperienced. They had gone to the jungle, done well, been promoted fast, and returned home. But they didn't know all the tricks of the old sergeants. Why, some of them couldn't march a squad to the motor pool when the formation was directly outside the gate! Sure, they could lay down indirect fires in the jungle, but nobody had shown them how to keep floor buffers operational in garrison ("You gotta teach 'em not to snap that long cord or it'll rip the socket right outta the wall and ruin the plug, too").

To make matters worse, the officer corps lost confidence in the NCO corps, and blamed it directly for all the trouble. It didn't seem like things could possibly get any more confusing and discouraging. But they did. The Army in its wisdom put male and female soldiers in the same barracks. Sometimes with only a week's notice and no guidance other than "do it," the NCOs had to sort out latrine and shower facilities, kitchens and sewing machines, visitation and inspection policies. It was bad enough getting the men to make their beds and keep the place looking like an army barracks, but allowing teddy bears and bedspreads was going too far!

So the Army up and did something smart. If NCOs could be school-trained for the jungle, then they ought to be school-trained for garrison, too. From that little insight grew a whole new concept in developing noncommissioned officers, the Noncommissioned Officers Education System. Slowly, painfully over the years, with the help of the remaining senior NCOs who remembered how a good army was put together, the young pups learned the technical skills required. Schools are good for teaching technical how-to's and the young sergeants took the opportunity and ran with it.

There was one important thing, however, that the schools either didn't or couldn't teach. That was the heart of leadership. Caring for soldiers was an aspect of leadership the schools weren't very good at teaching. They taught sergeants to record birthdays, but they didn't teach them why. The old sergeants knew the value of greeting a private, "So, Smitty, how does it feel to be 19 today?" And they knew how to arrange for a steak at the mess hall. They knew this because these things happened to them when they were 19. The schools taught how to inspect a wall locker, but not how to sit on a footlocker and get a soldier to pour out his heartache. The schools taught about caring for soldiers, but nobody said that meant caring for their wives and kids, too. And the schools never mentioned a sergeant getting his goof-offs out of jail in the middle of the night, for no other reason than that he was responsible for them. Good or bad, for better or for worse, they were their sergeant's responsibility.

These things are not learned from the platform; they must be learned from example in the school of hard knocks, with demonstration, imitation, practice, and critique being the key ingredients. The old sergeants knew there was no limit to what they could ask of soldiers when there were no limits to NCO concern for their troops. But too many old sergeants were gone.

There was all that rah-rah stuff about teamwork, morale, and esprit that was taught in school. The words were right, but the rhythm was wrong. Again, these things had to be experienced coming up before they could be practiced going down. Oh sure, some of the old timers remembered how competition could make even the most disagreeable work seem tolerable. Those old first shirts could set one platoon against another until it looked like they'd destroy each other, but just in the nick of time they'd set them all against the company next door. The old-timers also knew they were players on the team, not just coaches on the sidelines. They could manage a drink with the guys, or even a poker game, without compromising their authority. They too could have fun at unit socials, because both work and play were just different aspects of family life. The youngsters who grew up in the jungle, especially after 1969, seemed to forget, or not to have understood to begin with. The only lesson they seemed to bring home was to be an adversary of their own soldiers. They weren't dumb. They were inexperienced. And the times were against them.

Remember the difference between laying the Claymore yourself and insuring somebody else did it right? The same thing happened in garrison. The senior sergeants didn't have much time to teach their juniors a patient, caring coaching leadership style. They had to act fast. They taught the shortcut, the "Poor Protoplasm Theory of Leadership." The troops were just no damn good; the only solution was to kick ass and take names, yell and holler, be strict and arbitrary, even capricious, if necessary—whatever it took to maintain authority and discipline.

Back in the early 1970s, when the Army was flat on its back, sergeants had a real enemy, all right: their own soldiers. The difference between an army and a mob is discipline. The first order of business amid the racial incidents, drug use, and thuggery was to reestablish good order and discipline. They succeeded, too, with the tried and true ways that scared leaders always use: social distance and the whip. NCOs despised privates as dirtballs and scumbags because they feared them. They whipped them with chickenshit inspections, extra duties, expeditious discharges, and both judicial and nonjudicial punishments. They sought additional administrative ways to get rid of the riffraff. And, by golly, they got their soldiers' attention. They surely did, and the Army knew discipline once more.

Those who brought the Army back from chaos have a lot to be proud of, and their country owes them a debt that will never be acknowledged. But the Army paid dearly for the restoration of discipline. In the process, something happened to the noncommissioned officer corps and the officer corps, something that grew more worrisome the more healthy the Army appeared.

Previously the NCOs had always prided themselves in making the Army work, despite their officers. Now they started picking up all the bad habits of the officer corps. They weren't sure enough of their own authority to talk to either their soldiers or their officers. They talked only to each other, mostly about their insecurities (but of course they didn't use that term). They said they were "professionals" (which nobody who knew the Army ever doubted for a minute), but they confused professionalism with status symbols like office furniture and having a tactical vehicle. They equated school learning with professional competence, but sometimes a little learning *is* a dangerous thing. They became obsessed with whistle-clean efficiency reports required by centralized promotion boards.

Saddest of all, when they stopped talking to their soldiers, unwritten rules got set. Rules like, "professionals" don't drink a beer with the unit after work. And "professionals" don't have the unit over to the house for a cookout, because that's fraternization. "Professionals" attend to the barracks, because that's where the rater looks, but pay no mind to where married soldiers live. "Professionals" leave work at a reasonable hour, but the junior NCOs and privates stay until the work is finished. Scheming to give soldiers time off just isn't "professional." Since a "professional" tells other people what to do, he has to maintain a sharp image; "professionals" don't have to get their hands dirty any more. A "professional" is loyal and never laughs at the turkeys at headquarters (especially if he hopes to be a turkey himself, someday). A "professional" doesn't laugh much at all; soldiering is serious business. If "professionals" laugh at all, it's at the expense of the troops, not the officers or the crazy Army bureaucracy.

It's not the fault of the NCOs, really. It's not the fault of the officer corps. It's not the system's fault, either. It's nobody's fault, at least nobody who's identifiable and still around. Things just turned out that way. Not all NCOs turned "professional." The Sergeant Morales Club represents NCOs who were nurtured in the old ways.[2] Many of the other sergeants we see now weren't so fortunate, for whatever reasons, to have had superb role models. They are good products considering their times and circumstances. But they may not be good enough for war.

They grew up fearing their troops; in war they must trust them. They grew up despising their soldiers; in war they must love them. They grew up whipping the unit into shape; in war they must lead it. They grew up commanding respect; in war they must command devotion. They grew up keeping their distance and maintaining their proper place; in war they must hold the hands of the uncertain, cradle the anguished, and change the underwear of the scared, all without a second thought, because they're all family.

In the long march back from the days of the mutinous mob, the Army got confused about intimacy and authority, maybe for good reasons at the time. Leaders saw intimacy and authority as opposites and incompatible. They confused camaraderie with fraternization, equal opportunity with coed living, training-by-example with instruction from the podium, and soldierly irreverence with insubordination. They assumed social relations with their soldiers should be different in garrison than in combat. Maybe they're right. Maybe everything will be different in combat. Maybe the troops will come together when the fighting starts, just like they were supposed to in the jungle, before Charlie Company said, "We won't go." Maybe it's all bull that as an army practices in peace so will it perform in war. Maybe. I hope so for the sake of the Army and the Republic. But, maybe it's not all bull.

I wish this story had a happy ending, but it has no ending at all. The story is still being written, unfortunately by NCOs and officers who grew up in an army that lacked heart. If you doubt me look at the way we act in our leader training schools, not at what we say. We fail to teach the heart of leadership as the old-timers understood it, in terms of the four Cs: Competence, Candor, Compassion, and Commitment. That is the heart of leadership. I send my young NCOs to school. They learn to buff floors, but not to build cohesion. They learn to file counseling statements but not to console a troop in the face of a "Dear John" or a dead buddy. They learn to instill fear, but not to inspire affection.

The head learns from the platform, but the heart learns from practice. We have forgotten the heart in our leadership training. The Army once knew how to teach that kind of leadership, and how to grow sergeants and officers who could practice it. Maybe the Army could teach that kind of leadership again, while there's still time, before it's too late.

## NOTES

1. This article is based on the "NCO Career Histories Project," funded entirely by the U.S. Army Medical Research and Development Command. The project included some 500 hours of interviewing 20 senior noncommissioned officers.
2. The Sergeant Morales Club, open only to NCOs who demonstrate exemplary professionalism, originated in Europe several years ago. Each club nominee goes before a board of five to seven command sergeants major who examine the nominee's record, appearance, and conformity to the Morales ideal, epitomized by an NCO's dedicated attention to the needs of his soldiers throughout the 24-hour day. See "Focus on People," *Soldiers* 41 (October 1986): 26.

This article appeared in the December 1988 issue of *Parameters*.

# II. LEADERSHIP AND THE LEVELS OF WAR

# 6

# Tactical Command

## By ARTHUR S. COLLINS, JR.

My approach in this article will be to comment briefly on the level at which tactical command is most pertinent and then to make some observations on the impressions good tactical commanders have conveyed to me. These thoughts on tactical command stem from personal experience as a subordinate commander looking up the chain of command and as a senior commander looking down; from observation of hundreds of tactical commanders, especially at the battalion and brigade level; and from study and reading.

## Levels of Command

At the outset, at what levels of command is tactical command of primary importance? Is tactical command pertinent above the battalion and combat command levels?

Before answering these questions, there is need for some clarification. *Joint Chiefs of Staff Publication 1* defines tactical command as "authority delegated to a commander to assign tasks to forces under his command for the accomplishment of the missions assigned by higher authority." This is clear enough, but it is so broad that it could apply at any level of command and for all types of units. To bring this subject into focus, I will put rather severe limits on the levels at which I consider tactical command to be truly pertinent. Although I realize that some manifestations of tactical command can occur at almost any level of command, there are levels at which the *active exercise* of command responsibility is most constant, obvious, personal, and effective in operations and training, and that is what tactical command is all about. Then I will describe the *manner* in which the best combat arms tactical commanders exercise their authority and responsibility.

My experience, observations, and study persuade me that battalion command is the essence of tactical command. The battalion is the highest level at which a commander consistently lives and deals with people and facts that can be seen firsthand. The battalion commander normally sees his subordinate commanders and troops daily, and even if he has communications problems,

49

he can still get around to talk to commanders, check conditions, and see the terrain.

At the next level of command—brigade, combat command, and regiment—the level of command of a full colonel, there is still considerable tactical command. The commander, however, is more dependent on staff reports and the observations of others; in a combat zone the area to be covered precludes easy movement from one unit to another. If communications break down, it is not always possible to visit all the major subordinate commanders or to assemble them for a face-to-face discussion.

Above that, at division and corps, there is limited tactical command in the context of which I address it. Division and higher commanders are more constrained by time and space and their overall responsibilities in support of their own subordinate tactical commanders. However, the outstanding generals under whom I served in combat invariably got out with the troops and saw some elements of their command every day. It may have been more for "tactical inspiration" than exercise of command, but it worked.

In time of war, the division, corps, and army commanders—who should be the outstanding field commanders of the Army as a result of their training, background, and ability—will be at the critical point in operations to sense the situation or to encourage or direct a subordinate. Battalion and brigade commanders, however, will be the principal executors of any plan of action adopted.

One of the things that I have observed time and again throughout my service is that division commanders think in terms of the combat power of the battalions in the division. When a division gets in a tight spot in combat, it is often difficult to disengage a brigade and move it on short notice. So sometimes division, or even corps, directs the movement of a battalion-sized combined arms task force to plug a hole, to cover a flank, or to carry out a special mission. The brigades then spread out to cover the gaps left by the units that have been moved.

For the reasons noted, I believe that the primary exercise of tactical command takes place at battalion level and below. At levels below battalion—company, battery, troop, platoon, and on down the chain of command—tactical command is constant and, in time of war, is exercised under the most demanding conditions of the combat environment. The guiding spirit for the company-sized units, however, will continue to be the battalion commander, since the battalion has more autonomy in planning and executing missions than the units below battalion.

## The Tactical Commander's Three Roles

Over a period of many years, I have observed that the best tactical commanders did certain things well. The learning and maturing process was an important part of their development, and this was most evident in the ranks of lieutenant colonel and colonel. I know I will strike a sympathetic chord with those who have commanded when I say that the *good* tactical commanders were successful in most of the capabilities and characteristics that will be discussed below—the *best* had totally mastered all of them.

## Trainer

First and foremost, the effective tactical commander is a first-class trainer, and this is nowhere more evident than in a battalion. A well-trained battalion uses weapons efficiently, effectively, and in concert; it maintains its equipment as it operates; and it communicates well both up and down the chain of command. The service and support elements are geared to support the fighting elements of the battalion, and the commander trains them to function as a team. The smooth integration and interaction of each unit's capabilities is apparent as the battalion operates. The subordinate units work so well together that you don't think of them as separate elements; there is a complete melding of all the units. But this doesn't happen automatically or overnight. Practice, it is said, makes perfect; it does, but only realistic practice of correct tactics, techniques, or skills. This is what makes the well-trained battalion I have described possible; this is what I mean by the training ability of the battalion commander.

## Teacher

During the training process, the tactical commander also emerges as a demanding teacher. He teaches constantly, and that is chiefly what makes him a good trainer. When he observes some activity that warrants corrective attention, he asks the senior officer or noncommissioned officer present for a diagnosis and a cure, but is prepared to give his own if needed. He sees a weapon in position, and just maybe he will get behind it to see if there is a good field of fire; he knows the fundamentals of his unit's equipment and how it should be employed; he has high standards and insists that these standards be met in the day-to-day training and operations of his subordinate units. When he recognizes voids in the military education of his officers and NCOs—and there is so much to learn that there are always voids—he conducts schools for his subordinate leaders.

The teaching and stress on high standards in daily training activities are major factors in creating disciplined, well-trained combat units, without which no tactical commander could be effective. The best commanders continue to conduct the training and the teaching even when in combat, adjusting to new conditions as they develop.

Delegation of authority is important in the development of subordinate leaders and is an important part of the teacher-trainer role of the tactical commander. I make special note of this because in peacetime it is sometimes neglected or deliberately avoided by commanders whose lack of confidence results in their failure to delegate authority.

Delegation is essential so that competent subordinate commanders will be ready to step forward when those above them are killed or wounded. At other times units may be out of communications with higher headquarters, or sudden and unanticipated events may demand that the commander act swiftly on his own initiative. This is a talent that can be developed only by giving subordinate commanders an opportunity to act on their own without fear of relief. Commanders who are overly concerned about their own image are slow to delegate. They fail to give subordinates a chance to learn from their mistakes, which in most cases teach valuable lessons with no great loss except for a little personal embarrassment. The good tactical commander learns early the importance of subordinates taking action on their own, and he delegates responsibility routinely.

## Student

To train, teach, and develop subordinates to conduct military operations and to plan and direct the execution of military missions, a tactical commander must himself be thoroughly familiar with all aspects of the systems that contribute to the operational capabilities of the units under his command: effective range of weapons; movement times for different types of units; logistic, communication, and maintenance requirements, and which units provide them.

This is manageable for competent commanders at battalion level and below. At higher levels of command, a wider array of different weapon and support systems is often available for a commander to use. Few commanders have the time and capacity to acquire expertise in the details of all these systems; that can be left to the battalion commanders and their subordinates. Regardless of the level of command, however, the tactical commander must know what the other arms and services can contribute to the accomplishment of his missions, so that he can accomplish them expeditiously and with a minimum of casualties. The best tactical commander grasps quickly the significance of this wider range of capabilities and knows how and when to ask for them.

In this connection, the importance of the contributions of different arms and services to success in combat has always been recognized, but they have often been neglected because of parochial branch interests or the emphasis of enthusiasts. Advances in technology and the mechanization of forces in recent years have forced the operation of combined arms task forces lower and lower in the chain of command. Infantry and armored units learn quickly in combat that there is a limit to what either of them can do alone. They also realize that to keep casualties down, the support of other arms and services is essential.

As late as World War II there was a tendency for infantry or armor to operate independently, until they got into trouble. Then, cross-attaching and supporting infantry with armor—or vice versa—was common until the trouble was cleared up. Modern weapons are so lethal and expensive that recent conflicts—notably the brief but violent battles in the Arab-Israeli wars—make clear that pronouncements about the importance of combined arms teams must be translated into reality in early phases of training, and this down to the company level.

An understanding of human nature is a most complex subject, and it confronts the tactical commander every day. He must be aware of the mental and physical condition of his men and the effects of fatigue on his soldiers who may be worn and weary from the demands of combat. He must also know when and how to demand the last reserves of strength and energy, as in a pursuit, and when to husband the troops' strength under adverse conditions.

Thorough grounding in basic Army matters; a keen sense of the American soldier; and a willingness to accept responsibility for all that goes on in his unit—these are what is required of a tactical commander. The ideal tactical commander knows how all these subjects and conditions interrelate because he is a student: of people and what motivates them; of weapons systems; of the enemy; of tactics; and of military history. The knowledge acquired by his study and his experience breeds a confidence that enables the tactical commander to interact in a positive fashion with his subordinates and his superiors. Study, hard work in the field with troops, and constant attention to detail in the execution of all missions, administrative as well as tactical—these are the best ways to learn.

As an aside, I believe that in recent years many battalion and brigade commanders did not have the knowledge of the fundamentals of their respective branches of the service—and some of them who were promoted to general officer carried this deficiency into higher grades. Lacking this knowledge, they did not know what to look for; they did not recognize what they should be teaching their subordinates; and they had few standards to go by. Officers with these shortcomings may command units, but they are not tactical commanders. They most often commanded at the expense of their subordinates.

## Further Qualities

In addition to a high degree of skill in fulfilling the roles we have just discussed, there are many other qualities, skills, characteristics, or traits—call them what you will—which the better tactical commanders I have known all uniformly possessed. Taken together, these qualities are such that they have set off the great commanders from those who just do well. Let me mention several of those I consider to be most significant.

### Integrity

Integrity is an absolutely vital quality in a tactical commander. To be brief, integrity as I use it here means that the commander of Company A knows that if his unit gets in trouble, his battalion commander is going to come to the aid of his outfit if there is any way to do so. Keeping the soldier fully informed, caring for his basic needs, and standing up for his legitimate interests help build this sense of trust. Once the troops have confidence in a commander, believe he can be trusted with their lives, and want to be with *him* when the chips are down, there is a special spirit that flows through the unit; and there is nothing that will give a tactical commander more satisfaction. Knowledge of human nature and concern for the troops creates this atmosphere over time. An important feature of this is for a commander to be himself and not try to emulate someone else. That seldom works because the troops spot a false front very quickly. Learn from others, but don't try to copy their ways.

## Terrain Appreciation

The best tactical commanders have a keen appreciation of terrain. In some, it is inherent; in some, it is acquired; in most, it is probably a combination of the two. Such a commander's unit experiences one tactical success after another. There is no doubt in my mind that a commander's ability to see the advantages and disadvantages in terrain for attack or defense is a major contributing factor to his unit's success. Associated with terrain appreciation is an understanding of the effects of the weather and the elements on operations: the difficulties of movement in rain, snow, or under icy conditions; the influence of fog, darkness, and clouds on visibility; the time span of darkness or light available to complete a mission.

I do not believe we give terrain appreciation the attention it warrants. In the training of other armies—the British, Israeli, and German armies in particular—they stress terrain. They study it, walk over it, and examine its advantages and disadvantages in different situations; there is constant and exhaustive simulation using the sand table. We would be wise to pay more attention to terrain and weather in our unit training and in our schools.

## Presence I

Presence is difficult to describe because it reflects the individuality of each person's makeup. Varied though it is, presence is real and important in tactical command, so the effort must be made to describe it. I will discuss presence in two modes. The first is a physical presence on the ground that for convenience I will refer to as "Presence I." This presence is easy to see, but the ability to be at the right place at the right time—which is an important part of the true meaning of presence—is an art. It is not blind luck.

I have often heard officers talking about some fortunate fellow officer who happened to be at the right place at the right time. This happens, but in the field of tactical command that lucky fellow just didn't happen to be there. He had no doubt been there about 95 percent of the time, because the effective tactical commander is out where the action is. I don't mean that he is leading the attack in the first tank or the first squad, but he is not in the command post, and he is not in the operations center. Some people get confused about this and think the outcome of the fight will be decided at one of those vital focal locations with all the maps and blaring radios. Not so; it is decided out where the troops are. Someone taught me that in a dozen different ways when I was a young officer, and perhaps it was the most valuable lesson I ever learned as a soldier.

The true tactical commander is with one of the lead units, or at a forward observation post where he can see the ground being fought over, or at a critical crossroad or stream crossing, or at the forward collecting point talking to men who have just been wounded in battle. In the course of a day, he will have been at several such points. All the time he is weaving a web of knowledge of the terrain, the effectiveness of his unit's firepower, and of that of the enemy. He is aware of the hardships and pressures his troops are being subjected to and how they are reacting in a given situation. He is consistently sensitive to his unit, his troops, and the conditions under which his unit is fighting. The same applies in peacetime training and operations.

Familiarity with the area; knowing the mental and physical condition of the troops; being up-to-date through having talked to or observed a variety of commanders and their troops; all this contributes to—and results from—presence with a capital "P." This intangible quality—which is endowed by the creator to a fortunate few, but which comes to most of us by hard work—permits a commander to react vigorously and rapidly to changing conditions. There is no substitute for this physical presence on the ground. It is the launching point for boldness, imagination, and ingenuity, all marks of the great tactical commanders in time of war.

This is a good place to reiterate that it is the battlefield that provides the payoff for the Army's emphasis on physical fitness. If a commander is to be bold and aggressive he had better give thought to staying in top physical condition. The demands of combat on an individual cannot be appreciated until they are experienced. The lack of sleep; the ever-present minor infections from the flies, waste, and decay in the front-line areas; the ever-present danger; and the constant concern for the lives of subordinates all make heavy demands on the system. Soldiers are always tired in combat, and the heaviest fatigue hovers over those with the greatest responsibility. Weariness will soon wear down a tactical commander unless he maintains good physical condition. Once a commander succumbs to fatigue, fear and foreboding creep into the decisionmaking process, and the boldness, drive, and confidence required in tactical operations are lost. Stalemate and unsuccessful operations then become the norm.

## Presence II

A second form of presence—I term it here "Presence II"—is the manner or impression the commander conveys; often he conveys one impression to his troops and another to outsiders. This is more a matter of the personal makeup of the commander and his reactions to events that impinge on his unit.

Many people find it hard to maintain a calm air in time of stress and danger, but this the successful commander must do. When the going gets tough, the good tactical commander does not get rattled, does not rush about, and does not do a lot of shouting. The greater the pressure, the cooler that commander gets—or at least he appears to—and the unit will reflect his actions. It is easy for a battalion commander to create a businesslike atmosphere in his unit, and the time to do it is in training; the brigade commander can do it with a little more effort. In training, some battalion and brigade commanders create a lot of unnecessary pressure because they are chiefly concerned with their own successful image. Personal ambition leads to excessive display of a "can do" attitude which is not in the best interest of the troops. If the commander finds himself trying to put on a show or look better than a fellow commander, he had better reconsider why he is commanding a unit.

The battlefield is characterized by abnormal stress, uncertainty, confusion, and apprehension. This in turn demands that the tactical commander require tight discipline, act confident, and remain calm. In a unit's early enemy contacts there can be considerable scurrying about because most of us are scared and worried when the shooting starts, but nonetheless people try to do their jobs. Sometimes people think that noise and rushing about is a good way to show they are involved, but it is a poor substitute for moving and acting with purpose. Whenever troops are new to combat, a good tactical commander makes it a point to get around to visit his subordinates' areas and look over the units with the commanders. If things are a bit hectic, he can suggest that they just dampen the excessive activity. This only has to be done a few times because most commanders are perceptive, and they get the message. From then on, their operations are purposeful and steady. One of the hallmarks of a good unit is a businesslike attitude when the pressure is on. A good tactical commander can create the proper atmosphere, and his demeanor—which is the second form of presence—is reflected in the unit presence.

This second form of presence is not a surface appearance, although it starts with the personal appearance of the commander. Presence II is affected to a degree by personal appearance, but appearance alone is not the key to establishing a commanding, confident presence. That comes from the commander's inner self; it emerges and takes shape over a period of time. It is difficult to predict what it will be, so don't be fooled by surface impressions.

One thing has struck me at all levels of command: commanders who cared for their troops, who had clean barracks, good messes, good maintenance, and good training in preparation for combat, invariably performed well in battle. These results can be achieved only when a commander establishes and maintains high standards in operations and training, and this requires pressure in the development of capable and competent units. There is a dividing line between the unnecessary pressure of the commander driven by personal ambition and the necessary pressure of the commander determined to create an effective unit, but it is not always clear.

There are times when commanders do well in a peacetime environment and fail in combat, but generally the commanders who do their jobs well every day go right on doing the same when the shooting starts. This means there is a bit of the tactical commander in all of us. How well we do depends on how much effort we put into learning about the military profession and improving our units.

A point worth stressing is that good tactical commanders do not necessarily come in heroic models. The military image would be great if all commanders could pose for the fashion magazine ads. I think of General Creighton W. Abrams, Jr., on this point. He was visiting U.S. Army, Europe, sometime in 1972-73 and was making some observations to its Commander-in-Chief, General Mike Davison, at the end of his trip. He told about a lieutenant he had seen in one of the units. "He was just a little fellow, his raincoat was too long, he wore glasses, and he sure didn't look like much. Then I started talking to him about his platoon, and his eyes lit up. He could tell you about every man in his platoon and where each one came from, and he could tell you about their families. Then I looked at some of the weapons, watched the training, and talked to some of the men." Then suddenly the room rattled as General Abrams banged his fist on the table and exclaimed, "By God, what a commander he is! The men in his platoon know it, and you can feel it when you are with them."

I have seen many outstanding commanders that no one would ever have picked from a crowd; some tall and scrawny, others small and lean or short and stocky—even pudgy—and those built to be a guard or a tackle. Most of them were just ordinary-appearing individuals with nothing to distinguish them until they were doing a commander's job. Then on some raw, cold night when I, as their next higher commander, was there face-to-face with them during some crisis, and they stood there in all the noise and confusion, tired, unshaven, rain dripping from their helmets, splattered with mud, and told me what was going on and what their units were doing, I fully understood the extraordinary character and quality of these seemingly ordinary people. Unfortunately, too few outside that immediate circle will ever suspect or truly appreciate the great talents they had as tactical commanders. *That* is what I mean by Presence II.

## In Conclusion

I have tried to depict here some of the images that emerge as a competent tactical commander goes about a soldier's business—teacher, trainer, student, physically present in time of crisis, and present day-to-day as he exercises responsible leadership. The end result of all of his efforts is that when missions are assigned, his unit is ready to execute them, whatever they may be. Units trained by good tactical commanders accomplish their missions because the units are disciplined and they are trained through the full range of the capabilities of the men, weapons, and equipment available to them. At each level of command, the trained unit is a team and is ready to combine with other well-trained units to carry out the vast variety of tasks that are assigned to Army units in peace and in war.

History does not dwell on the low-level tactical commanders who fight the wars and win or lose the battles. Quite understandably, only the most famous senior commanders are singled out for study. Only the tip of the iceberg is visible, but what a tip it is, because these great field commanders are largely the latter-day reflection of the superb tactical commanders they were in earlier years as company and battalion commanders.

Witness Guderian on 12-13 May 1941 at the crossing of the Meuse. At this critical point of the attack in the west, he is there talking to the battalion and regimental commanders making the attack. Follow his footsteps during the period 9-24 May 1941, as he describes these actions in his book, *Panzer Leader.* You will see that he understood and practiced these things we have been discussing.

Rommel, the peerless tactical commander, is an even better example. Just after World War I he had written a book, *Infantry Attack,* based on his experiences as a company and battalion commander. It was little noticed outside the German Army until Rommel became famous as the "Desert Fox" in World War II. Speidel, in writing about Rommel as a company and battalion commander in World War I, said Rommel was always at the critical point of the action. It seems only natural, then, that in World War II they used to say, "The front is where Rommel is."

General Abrams—Colonel Abrams then—was famous for the same thing as a battalion and combat command commander in World War II. The great and famous field commanders at corps and army levels were almost always in their early years superb tactical commanders. They were intensely interested in their profession and the technical developments that might change tactics and methods of operation.

It seems to me, the goal of every combat arms officer should be competence as a tactical commander. Those who are the most competent, and whose intellectual and leadership qualities enable them to handle more complex organizations and greater responsibilities, should be the division, corps, and army commanders of the future. These same qualities—combined with the troop experience that provides the foundation for tactical competence—should make superb staff officers too, so no one loses in his endeavor to be proficient in tactical command.

This article, slightly revised, appeared in the September 1978 issue of *Parameters.*

# 7

# The Pillars of Generalship

By JOHN M. VERMILLION

A review of the spate of literature on the operational level of war published within the past two or three years suggests that the Army (at least those officers writing on the subject) is finally agreeing on how the term should be defined. Working definitions of the concept generally argue that the operational level of war encompasses the movement, support, and sequential employment of large military forces in the conduct of military campaigns to accomplish goals directed by theater strategy.[1]

Just as the Army has been able to perceive more clearly what warfare at the operational level entails, so also has it observed that the requirements of leadership at that level differ in some important respects from leadership at the tactical level. Indeed, the term operational art implies that the commander at this echelon requires special talents. To identify these special requirements should be a matter of high concern not only to those who aspire to command at the operational level, but also to all field-grade officers who might be staff officers at operational-level headquarters.

If it is advisable, then, to learn about the unique demands of leadership at the operational level, where does one look for instruction? The ideal circumstance is to serve with a latter-day Clausewitzian genius personally and directly. Commanders with transcendent intellectual and creative powers are rare, however, so to have a chance to observe a genius personally is nearly impossible. A second way, open to all, is through study of the sequence and tendencies of past events and the key personalities who drove them. The present essay rests mainly on this method. As a matter of plain fact, though, most U.S. Army officers do not read military history with a critical eye. The majority of officers look for a third way.

The Army has tried to provide just such a third way. In Field Manual 22-103, *Leadership and Command at Senior Levels*, Army leaders have provided guidance for leadership and command at the large-unit level in the context of AirLand Battle as described in Field Manual 100-5, *Operations*. Even the most biting critics must applaud the hard work and serious study which obviously underpin the new manual. Nonetheless, the work suffers badly precisely because of its sheer

59

exhaustiveness. Every significant utterance on leadership seems to have found its way into the manual. It is full of lists, generally in threes. For example, the reader learns that senior leaders teach, train, and coach; that they must possess certain attributes, perspectives, and imperatives; and that they ought to possess three groups of skills—conceptual, competency, and communications. Subdivisions of major headings also commonly occur in threes, as in three types of attributes—standard bearer (read "example"), developer, and integrator.

By the time one finishes wading through endless alliterative lists of traits desirable in the operational-level commander, he has had drawn for him a commander with the piety of St. Paul, the intellect of Einstein, and the courage of Joan d'Arc. In short, FM 22-103 lacks focus and a selective sense of what is fundamentally important. To say everything is to say nothing. The purpose of this essay is to draw sharper distinctions between the junior and senior levels of leadership, and to offer a considered opinion about what characteristics seem to be most essential to those commanders whom, in AirLand Battle, we associate with the operational level of war.

## On the Corporate Nature of Leadership

A false idea, namely that discussions about leadership need take into account the leader only, has spread throughout the Army and slowly influenced at least a generation of soldiers. The word leadership implies that a relationship exists between the leader and something else. The "something else," of course, is followers. By followers, however, I am not speaking of the subordinate commanders or the men in ranks. Entire books have been written on how various generals have inspired their troops to success in war. Rather, in the present context, I am speaking of those followers who comprise the general's staff—that immediate circle of assistants who act to translate the commander's operational will into battlefield reality. Little first-class work has been done to appraise the dynamics of leader-staff interaction. It is time to examine the evidence regarding leadership in this sense and then to hold the findings up to the bright light of common sense.

The exercise of generalship today carries with it tremendous difficulties. A division today is expected to cover a frontage comparable to that assigned to a corps in World War II. As the numbers and varieties of machines and weapons have multiplied, so also have logistical requirements. The higher the echelon of command, the more the general has to be responsible for, yet the less direct control he has over subordinate forces. With the advent of night vision equipment and vehicles with longer ranges of operations, combat operations can proceed unremittingly. Command functions combine into a process that is progressive and continuous. While a commander is exercising military command, he is responsible without respite for the effective and vigorous prosecution of the operations which will achieve his objectives and contribute to the execution of the overall mission. Obviously, no single man, unaided, can do this properly. He must have, as we have seen, a close circle of functional assistants.

But such a requirement is by no means new. From the middle of the last century, the tasks of the general in command have been too numerous and too complex for any one man to manage effectively, and the general staff system thus gradually emerged. Helmuth von Moltke saw that the Industrial Revolution had let loose the powers to mobilize, equip, and direct enormous armies, and that this development demanded the creation of a complex and highly professional staff. In fact, "the General Staff was essentially intended to form a collective substitute for genius, which no army can count on producing at need."[2] The Army need not aim so high as to produce geniuses, but generals solidly grounded in the fundamentals of the profession. With a wise selection of subordinates, the "average" general can have a successful command. On the other hand, history demonstrates conclusively that some of its most acclaimed generals have failed when stripped of their right-hand men.

Superior generals surround themselves with staff officers who complement them by covering their blind spots. Consider the case of Napoleon Bonaparte, widely acknowledged to be the most esteemed soldier who ever led troops into battle. Some histories depict Marshal Berthier, the Emperor's chief of staff, as nothing more than an exalted clerk. Napoleon from time to time spoke publicly about Berthier in such pejorative language, but this probably was a consequence of the Emperor's personal insecurity. Napoleon needed a chief of staff who would endure the waspish sting of his burning intellect, and, yes, even occasional humiliation. The fact is, though, that Berthier's responsibilities were heavy, to such a degree that he often worked 20-hour days. He personally controlled the division of labor on Napoleon's staff, all finances, and all appointments. Most important, he supervised the issue of all of Napoleon's orders regarding troop movements, operations, and artillery and engineer employment.[3]

Napoleon was an operational-level planner nonpareil. Nonetheless, he needed someone with Berthier's energy, dedication, and retentive capacity to translate broad instructions into polished orders fit to be delivered to the corps commanders. Berthier had an exceptional talent for drafting clear, concise orders. As David Chandler notes, "Bonaparte owed much of his early success to the administrative talents of Berthier."[4]

Only at the end, in 1815, did Berthier's worth to his Emperor become clear. On 1 June 1815, during the Waterloo campaign, Berthier reportedly committed suicide, possibly because of his inability to tolerate any longer the rebukes of his commander. Napoleon thereupon was forced to substitute Soult, an able corps commander. Almost immediately, "Soult was to be responsible for perpetuating several mistakes and misunderstandings in the written orders he issued, and these, taken together, account for a great deal of Napoleon's ultimate difficulties."[5] At Waterloo, Napoleon is said to have cried out, "If only Berthier was here, then my orders would have been carried out."[6]

In analyzing the dynamics of the Napoleon-Berthier relationship, it seems fair to suggest that Berthier was not flashingly quick. He was a man of deeply intelligent judgment rather than of brilliance. He was capable of making Napoleon's desire, if not vision, his own, of knowing how the Emperor wanted things to appear, then of being tough and stubborn enough to make them turn out that way. He would dutifully execute every directive concerning an operation, but without adding a single idea of his own, or perhaps without comprehending the subtleties of the Emperor's thoughts. Now, ponder how suitably Berthier met Napoleon's requirements. Napoleon was a commander so knowledgeable and so quick to focus his knowledge that even his apparently spontaneous reactions often emerged as intricate and fully developed ideas. That capacity can paralyze a staff. The interesting work of creation was done for them, and tedium does not stir the imagination. It is likely that many minds sharper than Berthier's, not just Soult's, would have failed precisely because the temptation to bring their fertile imaginations to bear would have been irresistible.

During the 1807–14 reorganization of the Prussian Army, General Gerhard von Scharnhorst ordered reforms many effects of which are still evident today. A regulation issued by Scharnhorst in 1810 was perhaps the most influential. He made the chief of staff a full partner in command decisions. By 1813 all Prussian commanding generals had chiefs of staff with whom they were expected to form effective partnerships. One of the most famous and effective of these teams was that of Gerhard von Blücher and his chief, Count Neithardt von Gneisenau. They were effective because they complemented each other perfectly. Whereas Blücher was a "brave, charismatic, but impatient man," Gneisenau was his polar opposite: cool, methodical, yet courageous and determined.[7] Gordon Craig here elaborates on the inspired collaboration of Blücher and Gneisenau:

> Blücher, who recognized his own shortcomings and the genius of his chief of staff, relied implicitly on Gneisenau's judgment; and he was not wholly joking when—while receiving an honorary degree at Oxford after the war—he remarked: "If I am to become a doctor, you must at least make Gneisenau an apothecary, for we two belong always together."[8]

In contrast to Napoleon and Bethier, in this case the chief developed the plans and the commander executed them. The Gneisenau-Blücher model of teamwork remains the supreme example of its kind for the German Army.

## Montgomery, Patton, and Rommel

Soon after World War II, Field Marshal Bernard Montgomery was asked to enumerate his requirements for a good general. He listed nine items. The first was "have a good chief of staff."[9] And so he did, throughout the war. In his own work, *The Path to Leadership*, Montgomery referred to a good chief of staff as a "pearl of very great price."[10]

As did the other generals mentioned thus far, Montgomery chose the men who worked for him. He insisted upon his right to install soldiers of his own choosing in all key positions. Shortly after Dunkirk, Montgomery described his plan to get the 3rd Division on its feet. He called together his staff and the senior officers in each case. He personally and unilaterally, without waiting for War Office approval, appointed all commanders down to battalion. In Nigel Hamilton's words, Montgomery's "essential drive was to get the 'right man for the right job.' . . . [This was,] together with his unique ability to abstract the essentials of any problem, the touchstone of his genius as a commander. The conduct of battle had borne out how dependent a commander is on his subordinate officers."[11]

Montgomery tried to hold on to the same staff as he progressed in rank through the war; in this endeavor he was reasonably successful. The mainstay of most general staffs, but of Montgomery's in particular, was the chief of staff. The Field Marshal was fortunate to have had Major General Francis de Guingand serve him in this capacity for the better part of the war. De Guingand's comments about his old boss are intriguing in that they explode the usual public image of Montgomery. According to de Guingand, Montgomery naturally tended to be rash and impetuous, not deliberate and wholly rational. The main business of his chief of staff was not to carry out detailed staff work or to make decisions in the absence of the commander, but to "keep Bernard's two great virtues [will and discipline] in tandem."[12] When the War Office thrust an unwanted chief on Montgomery, the invariable result for the command was mediocrity or failure.

Instructively, the single greatest failure with which Montgomery is associated, the Dieppe raid, occurred during a period of flux in his staff. In March 1942 during his tenure as commander, South-East Army, his chief of staff, Brigadier John Sinclair, was transferred over Montgomery's opposition. The commander then turned to the War Office with a personal request for "Simbo" Simpson to replace Sinclair. London refused him not only in this request, but also in his bid for two other staff officers on whom he had depended heavily in earlier assignments. At this time he was denied the strong steadying influence of a de Guingand, and the predictable outcome was a too-quick acceptance of an ill-conceived plan. It seems highly likely that had de Guingand been present, he would have checked Montgomery's essential rashness: "There was . . . a fatal vacuum at this critical moment: and Bernard, as the one soldier—apart from Brooke—who possessed the undisputed prestige and authority to scrap the project, tragically agreed to undertake the raid."[13]

The qualities and talents necessary to be a good staff officer are far different from those necessary to be a good commander. George Patton's career as well as any underscores this point. In the truest sense, Patton was a "general" officer. He abhorred involvement with details; indeed, few great commanders come to mind who felt otherwise. Patton was temperamentally unsuited to the role of staff officer. In his staff assignments he received poor efficiency reports for his performance.[14] The point is that at the operational level, no matter how brilliant the commander, the most glittering conception will go awry if it is not undergirded by the grinding hard work of his staff, which must churn out empirically correct movement tables, time-distance calculations, and logistical data.

Patton demanded that he be permitted to select his staff. Although this mode of operation did not conform to the methods of the U.S. Army replacement system, Patton, for whatever reason, got away with making these decisions himself. When he arrived in England to assume command of Third Army, he shocked the staff then in place by announcing that he was moving them out to make room for his own men. All those he brought on had served with him in North Africa and Sicily; most had backgrounds in Patton's 2d Armored Division. The man who held Patton's staff together, Brigadier General Hugh Gaffey, has been termed "a staff officer of genius."[15] Gaffey held the post as Patton's chief of staff until the early autumn of 1944, when Patton sent him down to command 4th Armored Division, and eventually a corps. Gaffey's replacement was Brigadier General Hobart Gay, a longtime cavalry associate of Patton. According to historian Hubert Essame, "Both were equally competent in the exercise of their intricate craft, . . . both were in the mind of their master."[16]

As one would expect, Patton had an excellent relationship with the staff, making it a personal policy never to interfere with them on matters of minor detail. Like many outstanding German commanders, but unlike some of his American counterparts, Patton promoted an open and frank dialogue between his staff and himself. They did not hesitate to disagree with him. What was best for Third Army came first. George Patton did not play hunches. He had the wisdom to rely on his staff for sound advice, and they consistently gave it to him. His G-2, Colonel Oscar Koch, for example, was felt by many to have the most penetrating mind in the U.S. Army in the intelligence field. Koch always had available for Patton the best, most accurate intelligence estimates to be found at any level of command. Patton's famous 90-degree turn from the Saar bridgehead to the Ardennes has received countless well-deserved accolades in history texts, but seldom are we reminded that at bottom the action was made possible by a dutiful staff officer. It was Koch who persuaded his commander before the fact that planning should commence at once to deal with the situation which would arise if the Germans staged an attack in the Ardennes area.[17] Patton was served equally well by other members of the staff. His primary logistician, Colonel Walter J. Muller, was known throughout the European Theater as "the best quartermaster since Moses."[18]

As for Field Marshal Erwin Rommel's success in North Africa, David Irving suggests six reasons. One pertained to his good equipment, two to Rommel's individual talents, and three took note of the high-quality personnel who worked for him.[19] Like Patton and Montgomery, Rommel "appropriated" his *Panzer* army staff. Without question, this was one of the most remarkably competent staffs assembled in modern times. Siegfried Westphal, later a general officer in command, was the operations officer and a man for whom Rommel had the highest professional respect. F. W. von Mellenthin, destined to wear two stars before the war's end, ran the intelligence section. More than anyone else, Alfred Gause, Rommel's chief of staff, was "in the mind" of the commander. He could anticipate with near-perfect accuracy what Rommel needed and when he needed it. Gause stayed on as Rommel's chief from early 1941 until April 1944, at which time Rommel's wife, as a result of a petty domestic dispute with Gause and his wife, prevailed upon her husband to release Gause. Rommel selected Hans Speidel to succeed Gause. Observe that in this instance, too, the commander chose a man whose temperament, intellect, and personality were nearly opposite his own. The highly literate, sophisticated Speidel was "a useful complement to Rommel's own one-track mind."[20]

Operational leadership is a corporate endeavor, not individual, and it requires full complementarity between the commander and his staff. Sadly, as obvious as this point may appear, it is ignored with frightening regularity by those charged with preparing the U.S. Army's official pronouncements on the subject of leadership.

## The Concerns of War

Getting right down to the basics, what are the essential things that the operational-level commander must cause to happen if he is to be successful in war? There are two in number. First, information must be communicated from the commander to his instruments of war, that is, his troops and weapons. Second, physical force must be applied against the enemy by these instruments of war in a manner calculated to produce the desired result. Let us discuss these two concerns in order.

Before a general can begin to communicate the wherewithal to win victories, he must prepare himself for the task. One of the most difficult parts of such preparation, especially in combat, is to find time to think problems through fully in order to make sound decisions and to plan future operations. Montgomery termed these respites "oases of thought." He believed fervently that the senior combat leader "must allow a certain amount of time [each day] for quiet thought and reflection."[21] He habitually went to bed at 2130, even amid tough battles. Patton as well as Montgomery made time to reflect and think ahead. Each lived apart from his main headquarters in the company of a small group of officers and noncommissioned officers. Each let his chief of staff handle the details and never allowed himself to do so.[22]

Noting that he had seen too many of his peers collapse under the stresses of high command, Sir William Slim insisted that he "have ample leisure in which to think, and unbroken sleep."[23] His permanent order was not to be disturbed unless there arose a crisis no one else could handle. As with any other aspect of combat, commanders must train in peacetime to do well what war will demand. Douglas MacArthur and George Marshall gave this personal training their devout attention. While Superintendent at West Point, MacArthur often worked in his quarters study until 1200 or 1300 instead of going to his office, where he might be distracted. Years later, in the Philippines, he had a standing daily appointment at a Manila movie house for a 2100 showing. He did not care what was playing; he fell asleep as quickly as he sat down. He found moviegoing a convenient way to unburden himself, to undergo a daily psychic housecleaning.

Similarly, during his World War II years as Army Chief of Staff, General Marshall usually left his office by 1500 each day and rarely made any important decisions after that hour. Fully aware that his decisions could make the difference between life and death for large numbers of field combatants, he strove to be as mentally and emotionally prepared as possible to make good decisions. In short, periods of rigorously protected solitude are enormously important to the general in command. If the mind is the key to victory, the general must tend and exercise his mind with a view to its health just as he would his body. This recommendation is not often heard in the U.S. Army.

Combat orders express the commander's desires. History and common sense demonstrate that clarity, conciseness, and rapidity of dissemination are the measures of a good order. At the operational level the general must possess the power, derived from clarity of expression only, to knife through thick layers of command to be understood. Superior commanders at the operational level almost universally have been guided by a concern and talent for clear literary exposition. This does not mean that they must be able to facilely toss off arcane knowledge, but merely that they appreciate the strength of words carefully and economically employed. Even when the commander leaves it to principal staff assistants to actually write out the order, as Napoleon did with Berthier, he still must assure that such orders are prepared in clear, simple language. Commanders who communicate well orally and in writing are likely to have developed this ability over long years of wide reading. Indeed, we may take as axiomatic the proposition that great leaders are great readers.

Conciseness and rapidity of dissemination go hand in hand. More often than not, the unit that acts first wins. This means that time and the saving of it should be at the core of the orders-generating process. Failure in timely issuance of orders is a cardinal error. Fortunately, the leader may avoid this error by following the principle that all orders must be as brief and simple as possible.

Many World War II commanders issued oral orders exclusively. General Heinz Gaedcke, a combat commander with considerable experience on the Russian front, followed the practice of most German generals in giving oral orders. In his opinion, "To actually operate using formal written orders would have been far too slow. Going through the staff mill, correcting, rewriting, and reproducing in order to put out a written order would have meant we would have been too late with every attack we ever attempted."[24] General Gaedcke added that while serving in the postwar German army, he pulled out of the archives some of his orders from the first Russian campaign. He remarked on this occasion that the new generation of officers probably would find inconceivable the running of a field army with such a small staff and on the basis of such simple, brief instructions: "It was a most peculiar feeling to see the orders, all very simple, that I had written in pencil so that the rain wouldn't smear them—and each had the radio operator's stamp to confirm that they had been transmitted."[25]

The Sixth Army commander, General Balck, whom General Gaedcke served for a time as chief of staff, declared that he could present a five-minute oral order which would last a good commander eight days.[26] Asked after the war about his technique for giving orders, General Balck replied: "Even my largest and most important operations orders were [oral]. After all there wasn't any need for written orders. As division commander, I forbade the use of written orders within my division."[27]

The clever commander will discover many ways to reduce the time it takes to communicate direct, unambiguous instructions to his subordinates. Working toward this goal should be a main objective of the operational-echelon commander.

Ironically, one of the toughest tests facing the commander is deciding when *not* to communicate, i.e. in deciding when to control and when not to. If successful fighting units of the 20th century have proved anything, it is that operations must be decentralized to the lowest level possible. Because the operational commander cannot do everything himself (in fact, he rarely will control combat units directly), he must delegate extensively. Commanders might profit from the example of General Ulysses S. Grant, who pledged never to do himself that which someone else could do as well or better. He "trusted subordinates thoroughly, giving only general directions, not hampering them with petty instructions."[28] Sir William Slim spoke for a legion of successful senior commanders when he summarized the compelling case for decentralization:

> Commanders at all levels had to act more on their own; they were given greater latitude to work out their own plans to achieve what they knew was the Army Commander's intention. In time they developed to a marked degree the flexibility of mind and a firmness of decision that enabled them to act swiftly to take advantage of sudden information or changing circumstances without reference to their superiors. . . . This acting without orders, in anticipation of orders, or without waiting for approval, yet always within the overall intention, must become second nature . . . and must go down to the smallest units.[29]

By decentralizing control to low tactical echelons, the operational commander implicitly places heavier weight on his overall intent and lighter weight on detailed orders, thus speeding up the processes of information flow and decisionmaking. The benefits of decentralization are easy to identify. Nonetheless, many in the U.S. Army remain uncomfortable with the practice of issuing mission orders and allowing subordinates broad decision authority within the context of the commander's intent. Among many explanations for this uneasiness, a significant one involves the poor fit of decentralized control with present leadership doctrine. By spotlighting the commander, by exalting his image to the neglect of the follower, the Army subtly and unwittingly has engendered the erroneous notion that the wheel of command will turn only on the strength of the commander.

The final facet of the communication function with which the operational-level commander must be ready to cope is uncertainty, ambiguity, or "noise" (Clausewitz's "friction"). It is astonishing that anyone can perform well as a general in wartime command. Crucial decisions have to be made under "conditions of enormous stress, when *actual* noise, fatigue, lack of sleep, poor food, and grinding responsibility add their quotas to the ever-present threat of total annihilation."[30] Even during the Iranian rescue mission, when some of these conditions did not exist, the sources of friction were plentiful and potent. The Holloway panel investigating the failure of the mission concluded that "the basic weakness displayed by [the Joint Task Force Commander's] staff" was that his "planners were not sufficiently sensitive to those 'areas of great uncertainty' that might have had a shattering impact on the rescue mission."[31] The goal is to be like Grant, "for whom confusion had no terror."[32]

General Archibald Wavell claimed that the first essential of a general is robustness, which he defined as "the ability to stand the shocks of war."[33] The general, Wavell wrote, will constantly be at the mercy of unreliable information, uncertain factors, and unexpected strains. In order to cope in this environment, then, "all materiel of war, including the general, must have a certain solidity, a high margin over the normal breaking strain."[34] He can develop this toughness only by spending most of his peacetime training in the art and science of warcraft. One cannot expect to play a rough game without getting dirty. The Germans played many rough and dirty games during the interwar years, and as a result were generally better prepared than the Allies. In any event, the friction of war, producing a surfeit of "noise" and a welter of incomplete, erroneous, or conflicting data, stresses to the uttermost a commander's ability to keep his thoughts focused and his communications selective and germane.

## Delivering Force on the Objective

After communications, the next fundamental concern in warfighting involves bringing armed force effectively to bear upon the enemy. Force will be applied most effectively if the operational-level commander ascertains, preferably before hostilities begin, the condition he wants to obtain at the end of the conflict. Only if he understands the end he seeks will he be able to prepare a clear statement of intent. No coherent campaign is possible without a lucid vision of how it should conclude. Evidence suggests that planners sometimes do not tend to this crucial first decision.

Students in the School of Advanced Military Studies at Fort Leavenworth participated in an eight-day Southwest Asia wargame. The pertinent part of the scenario portrayed a takeover by anti-American rebel forces of several key cities in Iran, mostly in the southern part of the country. The rebels threatened to seize the Persian Gulf ports, and thereby shut down oil cargo out of the Gulf. Twenty-plus Soviet divisions from three *fronts* entered Iran in support of the rebels. In response to the threat to its national interests as expressed by the Carter Doctrine, the United States deployed a Joint Task Force to assist the loyalist Iranian forces. Ground forces consisted of roughly five and one-half Army divisions under the control of a field army headquarters plus one Marine Amphibious Force.

SAMS students decided early in the planning that their mission, to "defeat" rebel and Soviet forces in Iran and to facilitate the flow of oil out of the Persian Gulf, needed clarification. What was the defeat criterion? Restore Iran's national borders? Destroy all Soviet and rebel forces within the borders of Iran? Or should they emphasize the second part of the mission statement, to facilitate the West's and Japan's access to Persian Gulf oil? Answers to such questions make a mighty difference. In the absence of a National Command Authority player cell, the students judged that NCA intent was to optimize chances for the uninterrupted flow of oil, consistent with means. With this understanding, they concentrated on securing the vital Gulf ports of Chah Bahar, Bushehr, and Bandar Abbas. The ground commander (in this exercise, the notional U.S. Ninth Army commander) determined that he would attempt to drive out, or prevent from entering, any enemy forces in an area centered on Bandar Abbas and circumscribed by an arc running roughly through Shiraz, Kerman, and Bam, some 250 miles away. This decision made sense in three important respects. First, in the ground commander's opinion, the U.S. force was too small to fight much superior enemy forces across the vast entirety of Iran itself. Second, with almost no infrastructure from which to establish supply operations, to move farther than 250 miles inland would have been logistically unsupportable. Third, this course of action permitted friendly forces to exploit the excellent defensible terrain of the Zagros Mountains. Fourth, a secure enclave would be available from which to launch attacks to the northwest should the NCA subsequently decide upon a more ambitious and aggressive course.

The SAMS students' decision is not offered as an approved solution. It did not even provide for securing the Iranian oil fields, at least not initially. Rather, it is used to illustrate the importance of establishing the ends of the campaign. Shortly after the SAMS exercise, the students visited each of the operational-level headquarters actually assigned a comparable mission. Ominously, when questioned about the ends they hoped to achieve, four headquarters responded with four different answers. The reason for their differences was that they had never gotten together to agree on ends before allocating means and drawing up plans.

After he decides the end he seeks, the next question the commander must confront is "How do I sequence the actions of the command to produce the desired conclusion to the conflict?" The short answer is that he must think through a series of battles and major operations which will constitute the campaign. He must weigh probabilities and risks and the challenges of battle management. This is anticipation. Good intelligence analyses will help him immensely, as will an in-depth knowledge of the enemy and his psychological predispositions. Despite the imponderables, he must fashion his thoughts into a convincing, coherent outline for a campaign plan. He presents the outline, representing his vision of how the campaign is to unfold, to the staff for refinement.

Although the commander need not be perfectly prescient, it helps immeasurably if his vision matches reality with reasonable fidelity. Planning at the operational level is tougher than at the tactical level because there is a narrower margin for error. The commander had better make the right decisions most of the time and on the big issues because once large formations are set in motion, it is nearly impossible to cause them to halt or change directions quickly. As Colonel Wallace Franz has written: "Operational (large) units, once set in motion, do not conform readily to later modifications. There must be the fullest realization that any adaptation of means cannot be immediate and instantaneous."[35]

Like a member of a football kickoff team, the forces being employed at the operational level must move downfield at top speed with controlled fury. While charging hard, and under the threat of being knocked off his feet from multiple directions, each player must be capable of moving rapidly out of his assigned lane of responsibility if conditions change radically, for example, if the returner has run past him and is going toward the other side of the field. To carry the analogy a step further, if all has gone well for the kickoff team, they will have disrupted the opposition's timing by clogging all eleven potential running lanes. When this situation develops, the opposition's set play collapses and the runner must freelance. If my team is much smaller than the opponent's, I have to rely on quickness, rapid thinking, hit-and-run tactics, and deceptive moves (all of which together define AirLand Battle doctrine's "agility") to give me the advantage I want.

But all the agility in the world will not be sufficient to guarantee victory. In the real world, it is not unusual for the commander's ideal operational end to exceed his actual operational resources. And it is in recognizing this disconnect that the commander's art must be most acute.

The 18th-century English neoclassicists believed that the antithetical forces of reason and passion struggled for possession of a man's personality. On the actual battlefield the same struggle constantly is being enacted in the mind of the commander. Commanders are sorely tempted to allow emotion to cloud good judgment in decisionmaking. The art lies in realizing when and to what extent to let emotions intervene, to sense when it is proper to discard reason and turn to passion, to let the heart rule the head. Stated differently, the internal conflict is between will and judgment. The force of will usually counsels "can" to the commander while judgment may signal a "cannot."

Nearly every treatise on generalship speaks of the tremendous importance of the will to prevail. The truth of this observation is obvious. The flip side of tenacity, though, is obstinacy. More serious lapses of generalship may have occurred because of a failure to distinguish between tenacity and obstinacy than for any other reason. The general must ever be conscious of the true limitations and capabilities of his forces. As S. L. A. Marshall rightly claims:

> The will does not operate in a vacuum. It cannot be imposed successfully if it runs counter to reason. Things are not done in war primarily because a man wills it; they are done because they are do-able. The limits for the commander in battle are defined by the general circumstances. What he asks of his men must be consistent with the possibilities of the situation.[36]

The way a general understands what his forces can or cannot do is through what Sir John Hackett terms the principle of total engagement. By this he means that the general somehow completely fuses his own identity with the corporate whole of his men.[37] He reaches this state by being a participant in combat, not merely a prompter. In discussing the 1915 Turkish siege of British forces in Kut, India, Norman Dixon furnishes an example of a general who was a prompter and no more. The British commander, Major General Townshend, stayed apart from his soldiers. He had no sense of the true condition of his four weak brigades. As a consequence, his reports lied regarding casualties, food supplies, medical aid, and estimates of Turkish strength.[38] In all, some 43,000 British soldiers needlessly became casualties because their commander lost all physical and emotional contact with his fighting troops. Only when the commander achieves a total moral fusion with his troops will he be able to sense whether they are being asked to do the impossible.

## Leadership in War: Summing Up

Doctrine on leadership ought to talk about leadership in war. This is not the case with present manuals. Field Manuals 22-100 and 22-103 speak mostly about personal attributes desirable in a leader. The problem with so much emphasis on personal qualities is that even if the key ones could be identified, a leader probably cannot adhere to them all at the same time or all the time. Let us also recall that those commonly acclaimed as "great" leaders are not necessarily good men. It is possible to be morally blemished and still be a highly effective combat commander.

There is no simple set of rules by which to establish the pillars of generalship. One rule in any set, though, is that the good general must be adept at the art of choosing competent and compatible subordinates, especially his chief of staff. The Army can modify its personnel system to permit senior commanders to select their own staffs. Surely the devising of such a system is within man's ingenuity. This is a *must-do* requirement if the Army is serious about developing warcraft as something distinct from witchcraft. Every superior combat commander in modern times has relied on the brilliant staff work of men he has hand-picked to assist him. Surely there is a lesson in this observation. Chief executive officers of all large corporations choose their own principal subordinates. No university president in his right mind would attempt to assign the nine assistants to the head football coach, nor for that matter would any head coach worth his salt accept such a proposition. The quality of the great majority of today's Army officers is superb. The issue, then, is not so much whether competent officers will surround the senior commander, but whether he will have officers around him who best complement him. Under the Department of Defense Reorganization Act of 1986, CINCs of unified and specified commands will have veto authority over officers nominated for assignment to their staffs. This is a step in the right direction.

Having selected an able staff, the commanding general in combat must then look to his communicating. He should pay special attention to carving out of his schedule time to think; to issuing simple, unambiguous orders; to decentralizing control to the lowest levels possible; and to developing a tolerance for the uncertain and the unexpected. With respect to the delivery of force, the operational-level commander must furnish a clear-sighted vision of the conditions he wants to obtain at the conclusion of the campaign. Based upon an accurate understanding of the capabilities and limitations of the forces he commands, he must conjure a sequence of actions that will bring to fruition the desired outcome. Finally, the commander must be able to discern with certain knowledge the final distinctions between tenacity and obstinacy.

In the final analysis, U.S. Army operational-level leadership doctrine must step away from preachments on the Boy Scout virtues writ large, and toward the genuine requirements of wartime command. It must also abandon the idea that the general should and can master all the skills practiced by those subordinate to him; that time has long since passed. Instead, he should spend his precious time preparing to make the kinds of decisions war will require him to make, thereby strengthening the pillars of his generalship against the day they must bear the awful weight of war.

## NOTES

1. Gregory Fontenot, "The Promise of Cobra: The Reality of Manchuria," *Military Review* 65 (September 1985): 54. Fontenot credits Lieutenant Colonel Harold R. Winton for this definition of the operational level of war.
2. B. H. Liddell Hart, *The German Generals Talk* (New York: Morrow, 1948), p. 19.
3. David Chandler, *The Campaigns of Napoleon* (New York: Macmillan, 1966), p. 373.

4. Ibid., p. 56
5. Ibid., p. 1021.
6. Gunther E. Rothenberg, *The Art of War in the Age of Napoleon* (Bloomington: Indiana Univ. Press, 1980), p. 210.
7. Ibid., p. 192.
8. Gordon A. Craig, *The Politics of the Prussian Army* (London: Oxford Univ. Press, 1955), pp. 62-63.
9. Harvey DeWeerd, *Great Soldiers of the Second World War* (London: R. Hale, 1946), p. 117.
10. Bernard L. Montgomery, *The Path to Leadership* (New York: Putnam, 1961), p. 247.
11. Nigel Hamilton, *Monty: The Making of a General, 1887-1942* (New York: McGraw-Hill, 1981), pp. 405-06.
12. Ibid., p. 553.
13. Ibid.
14. Hubert Essame, *Patton: A Study in Command* (New York: Scribners, 1974), pp. 23-24.
15. Ibid., p. 121.
16. Ibid.
17. Ibid., pp. 216, 225.
18. Ibid., p. 122.
19. David Irving, *The Trail of the Fox* (New York: Avon, 1978), pp. 170-71.
20. Ibid., p. 406.
21. Montgomery, pp. 249-50.
22. Essame, p. 40.
23. William Slim, *Defeat Into Victory* (London: Cassell, 1956), p. 213.
24. Translation of taped conversation with Lieutenant General Heinz Gaedcke, Battelle Laboratories, Columbus, Ohio, 1979, p. 38.
25. Ibid., p. 37.
26. Translation of taped conversation with General Hermann Balck, Battelle Laboratories, Columbus, Ohio, 1979, p. 26.
27. Ibid., p. 25.
28. J. F. C. Fuller, *Grant and Lee* (Bloomington: Indiana Univ. Press, 1957), p. 74.
29. Slim, pp. 541-42.
30. Norman Dixon, *On the Psychology of Military Incompetence* (New York: Basic Books, 1976), p. 32.
31. Paul B. Ryan, *The Iranian Rescue Mission* (Annapolis, Md.: Naval Institute Press, 1985), p. 76.
32. Fuller, p. 75.
33. Archibald Wavell, *Generals and Generalship* (New York: Macmillan, 1941), p. 41. Reprinted with other works in U.S. Army War College's Art of War Colloquium series, December 1983.
34. Ibid., p.42.
35. Wallace Franz, "Maneuver: The Dynamic Element of Combat," *Military Review* 63 (May 1983): 5.
36. S. L. A. Marshall, *Men Against Fire* (1947; rpt. Gloucester, Mass.: Peter Smith, 1978), p. 175.
37. Hackett, p. 228.
38. Dixon, pp. 95-99.

This article appeared in the Summer 1987 issue of *Parameters*.

# 8

# Command and Control at the Operational Level

By CHARLES G. SUTTEN, JR.

The study of the operational art as one of the principal divisions of military history is a relatively recent phenomenon, although the practice of that art may extend into antiquity. Consensus exists that Napoleon first understood mass warfare and suggests that "his success in raising, organizing, and equipping mass armies revolutionized the conduct of war and marked the origin of modern warfare."[1] Operational art, then, as an integral part of the discipline of military history, can be traced to that French Emperor and his two quarreling students, Clausewitz and Jomini.

With the publication of Field Circular 100-16-1, *Theater Army, Army Group, and Field Army Operations*, the U.S. Army has explicitly recognized the requirement to develop doctrine and organizations at those levels to establish the full range of command and control functions necessary for the conduct of the operational level of war. The existing amplifying literature on the subject of command and control at the corps and division levels and below is extensive. Certainly, the recent publication of Field Circular 101-55, *Corps and Division Command and Control*, represents another positive step in making current doctrine more practicable. However, little published material exists on the subject of command and control at the operational level.

That command and control of large formations has been successfully executed historically is undeniable. Napoleon's conduct of the Jena campaign in the fall of 1806 staggers even the modern imagination. In the space of less than a month, he concentrated his *Grande Armée* of six corps from garrison locations in what is today south and southwestern Germany, joining them with the Old Guard from Paris, and fought two major, simultaneous battles near Erfurt, in what is now southern East Germany, and won both of them. Napoleon then conducted a series of pursuit operations that ranged north to the Baltic Sea, and from present-day western Poland to the city of Hamburg. "In three weeks of unrelenting maneuver, battle, and marching, the French gathered 140,000 prisoners, 250 flags, and 800 field guns."[2] The Prussian

Army was destroyed, and an area that exceeds modern East Germany was occupied.

Martin van Creveld, in his book *Command in War*, thoroughly analyzes the Jena campaign through the conclusion of the simultaneous battles at Jena and Auerstadt. He concludes that Napoleon's command and control system allowed him to issue three different movement orders to his corps commanders in 24 hours and have those orders executed.[3] Napoleon's corps varied in size from 16,500 soldiers in Marshal Augereau's corps to 26,000 soldiers in Marshal Davout's corps during the Jena campaign.[4] The distances between units varied almost continuously, but a figure of between 10 to 20 miles fairly represents the situation while on the march. (The actual fighting at Jena and Auerstadt was separated by a little more than 12 miles.[5]) Even with modern transportation and telecommunications, the flexibility and mobility achieved during the Jena campaign would be no easy feat today.

Detailed study of the Jena campaign serves to illuminate many aspects of command and control. One principal lesson is that the utility and effectiveness of any command and control system must be measured relative to the system of one's adversary. Napoleon's command and control system in its totality was far superior to his enemy's, and by effectively wielding that tool he destroyed the Prussian Army in a single campaign.

That the effectiveness of a command and control system must be evaluated not in isolation, but relative to the system of one's foe, remains as valid today as it was in the Napoleonic era. With the reintroduction of operational art into U.S. Army doctrine, one of the foremost challenges of the true incorporation of that doctrine into practice is the adoption of an appropriate command and control system. The purpose of this article is to examine command and control issues at the operational level with a view toward identifying the philosophic foundations of a system that will provide the U.S. Army with significant relative advantages over potential adversaries.

## Background

On the 6th and 9th of August 1945, U.S. B-29s dropped atomic bombs on Hiroshima and Nagasaki, forever changing the nature of warfare and ushering in a new era in human history. Throughout the 1950s and 1960s, the United States enjoyed overwhelming nuclear superiority, in both quantity and quality.[6] In October 1962, Khrushchev made the decision, possibly because of the Soviet Union's inferiority, to emplace nuclear-tipped missiles in Cuba. President Kennedy ordered a naval blockade and forced the Soviets to back down. During the crisis, "President Kennedy personally supervised the location of each U.S. Navy vessel involved in the blockade."[7] The crisis underscored the perceived need in the nuclear era for the President to exercise firm, absolute control over the military forces to achieve his desired political ends while minimizing the risk of escalation. Since then the incident has been used to justify the establishment of command links extending from the White House to the soldier in the foxhole, and subsequent experience has "further reinforced the tendency toward greater and greater centralization."[8]

While the world was feeling its way through the first decades of the nuclear era, an electronics revolution was taking place which neatly dovetailed with the command and control requirements of the nuclear age. As a result of the rapid technological advances during World War II and in space research, enormous progress was achieved by the early 1960s. The advent of nuclear weapons had created the imperative for those weapons to be tightly controlled at the highest levels of government, and the electronics revolution, with the computer and data processing as a major subset, provided the technical means to exercise the requisite control.

The Cuban missile crisis gave impetus to the fledgling World Wide Military Command and Control System, which progressively extended to the Strategic Air Command and then the conventional forces.[9] The remote control of the war in Vietman from Washington continued the trend toward ever-greater centralization. Additionally, the use of the helicopter as a vehicle for microcommand sometimes created unprecedented situations at the lowest tactical levels. A whole generation of officers matured in an era that taught them exactly the wrong lessons with regard to command and control on the next battlefield.

One of the anomalies of our era is that centralized command and control of nuclear weapons at the highest level is vital to the survival of the human race, but the realities of the battlefield envisioned in FM 100-5 demand that leaders at all levels exercise initiative and aggressiveness to fight and win in a fluid, fragmented environment, very likely with severely degraded command links. The crucial issue is that organizations must continue to function despite the fact that command and control probably will be disrupted. Encouraging signs exist that senior leaders understand this reality. General John Vessey, formerly Chairman of the JCS, clearly recognized this requirement when he assiduously avoided oversupervising Vice Admiral Joseph Metcalf during the Grenada operation. An even more recent example is the freedom of action delegated to Vice Admiral Frank Kelso during the confrontation in the Gulf of Sidra. As *The New York Times* reported:

> Pentagon officials said the rules of engagement, worked out in advance, gave the commander of the Sixth Fleet, Vice Adm. Frank B. Kelso 2d, the authority to attack Libyan missile sites and ships to defend American ships.
> "This Administration is comfortable in delegating authority to the field," a Pentagon official said.[10]

This evidence is clearly a refreshing signal from the highest levels of our government. For training officers, NCOs, and soldiers to exercise their initiative, to take risks, to be aggressive, and to accept responsibility requires the senior trainers of the Army to understand the dichotomy between the pressures toward centralization in the modern world and the decentralizing imperatives of the next battlefield.

To relate this discussion more directly to the Soviet threat, a few points are worth highlighting. The first is that "nuclear weapons, especially at operational and tactical levels of warfare, have become nonrelevant means of seeking the political goals likely to be considered appropriate, especially by First and Second World governments."[11] This state of affairs obtains largely because essential parity exists between the United States and the Soviet Union at both the strategic and theater nuclear levels. Consequently, there has been increased emphasis on strong conventional forces to keep the nuclear threshold as high as possible.

A second point is that whether, in gauging Soviet intentions, one foresees the Soviet-style operational concept of mass, momentum, and continuous combat with echelonment, or the Operational Maneuver Group style, the essential feature of both styles is that they are maneuver-based and designed "to disrupt the operational tactics of the defender."[12] The response to this perceived threat by the U.S. Army and Air Force is the AirLand Battle doctrine, also a maneuver style of fighting.

A third point, repeatedly emphasized in FM 100-5, is that on the next battlefield "opposing forces will rarely fight along orderly, distinct lines."[13] The battle will consist of three fights: the deep, the close-in, and the rear. Exercising command and control will be especially difficult:

> At the very time when battle demands better and more effective command and control, modern electronic countermeasures may make that task more difficult than ever before. Commanders will find it difficult to determine what is happening. Small units will often have to fight without sure knowledge about their force as a whole. Electronic warfare, vulnerability of command and control facilities, and mobile combat will demand initiative in subordinate commanders. The commander who continues to exercise effective command and control will enjoy a decisive edge over his opponent.[14]

## Mission-Oriented Command and Control

The recently published Field Circular 101-55, *Corps and Division Command and Control*, addresses for the first time is U.S. Army doctrinal literature the term mission-oriented command and control: "Mission-oriented command and control promotes clear communication of the commander's intent; coordination of key elements of the deep, close-in, and rear battles; and maximum latitude for subordinates in execution of assigned tasks."[15] The circular goes on to emphasize that the key operative concept stems from a clear statement of the commander's intent.[16] The concept is then illustrated with the historical example of Colonel Joshua Chamberlain's 20th Maine Regiment at the Battle of Little Round Top on 2 July 1863, during the battle of Gettysburg:

> When Colonel Vincent led the 20th Maine to its position, he told Colonel Joshua Chamberlain, its commander, "This is the left of the Union line. You understand. You are to hold this ground at all costs."

After withstanding six violent enemy attacks, . . . Colonel Chamberlain realized his 20th Maine could not repulse another assault. Losses had been high and ammunition was critically short. Chamberlain made the decision to fix bayonets and charge. . . . The 20th Maine swept their entire brigade's front.

Colonel Chamberlains's leadership at Little Round Top demonstrates the kind of creative, thinking leadership needed at all levels to succeed on the modern battlefield. Mission-oriented command and control provides a framework within which subordinates have the latitude to act with imagination as illustrated by the Chamberlain example. Thorough understanding of the higher commander's intent serves as the basis for such independent action.[17]

The origin of the concept of mission-oriented command and control has been traced by Richard Simpkin in his book *Race to the Swift* to an 1806 Prussian regulation.[18] The German Army term for the concept is *Auftragstaktik*, defined as follows in the current German Army regulation:

A command and control procedure within which the subordinate is given extensive latitude, within the framework of the intention of the individual giving the order, in carrying out his mission. The missions are to include only those restraints which are indispensable for being able to interact with others, and it must be possible to accomplish them by making use of the subordinate's forces, resources, and the authority delegated to him. Mission-oriented command and control requires uniformity in the way of thinking, sound judgment and initiative, as well as responsible actions at all levels.[19]

This command and control concept is used at all levels in the German army, both in peacetime and in wartime.[20] The concept is currently enjoying serious attention in the American Army primarily because of renewed interest during recent years in the operational level of war on the Eastern Front during World War II. Many of the more successful German commanders of those battles are still alive, and since 1979 a number of them have been interviewed in tape-recorded sessions and have participated in the Art of War Colloquiums at the U.S. Army War College. All of these German officers subscribe to the concept of *Auftragstaktik*, and their experiences in fighting the Soviets can be enlightening. Many advantages accrue to the army that operates in accordance with the precepts of mission-oriented command and control, not the least of which is that its organizations will continue to function when out of contact with higher headquarters.

Several key ingredients are essential if such a philosophy of command and control is to work. The first prerequisite is that trust and confidence must exist "throughout the ranks, all the way down to the private soldier."[21] There must be confidence that everyone will "exercise initiative to get the mission accomplished."[22] The following remarks by General Hermann Balck are particularly illuminating:

Generally the German higher commander[s] rarely or never reproached their subordinates unless they made a terrible blunder. They were fostering the individual's initiative. They left him room for initiative, and did not reprimand him unless he did something very wrong. This went down to the individual soldier, who was praised for developing initiative.[23]

The second ingredient is an effective officer education system oriented on the concept. The educational process should stress the development of initiative, flexibility, decisiveness, and the willingness to assume responsibility. Mistakes should be corrected without condemnation. Major General F. W. von Mellenthin, General Balck's Chief of Staff, stated, "We found that leaders at any level grow with their experience. . . . [T]heir initiative should be fostered in the case of a division commander as much as in the case of a platoon leader."[24] The German education process also stressed approaching military problems with a common understanding, a common doctrine, and the common determination to execute the commander's intent.[25]

## Soldiers from A Free Society

From a theoretical point of view, one way to approach the subject of command and control would be to characterize the threat, examine one's own society to assess the inherent strengths and weaknesses of its citizens, and then create a command and control system that capitalizes on the strengths of that society to meet the threat. Obviously, the system would also have to have appropriate organizations, processes, and technical means, but attacking the problem from the human side first should lead to a solution that is balanced, integrated, and not the captive of some technological panacea. Although this approach to the problem will not yield a complete answer, it is nonetheless worth examining, particularly in light of S.L.A. Marshall's research into the behavior of soldiers under fire in World War II:

> Wherever one surveys the forces of the battlefield, it is to see that fear is general among men, but to observe further that men commonly are loath that their fear will be expressed in specific acts which their comrades will recognize as cowardice. The majority are unwilling to take extraordinary risks and do not aspire to a hero's role, but they are equally unwilling that they should be considered the least worthy among those present.[26]

While it is true that a small group of infantrymen under fire is several levels removed from the issue of command and control at the operational level, Marshall's results are germane in that they do reveal a primary motivating factor in human beings under extreme stress. Marshall's studies show that American soldiers desire above all else to be held in esteem by their peers. This is true among private soldiers, and it is certainly true among officers who function at the operational level of war. Fiercely independent officers who are held in esteem by their peers are essential to the execution of mission-oriented command and control.

The diversity of American society makes U.S. military training more complicated than training in the European armies, except possibly in the Soviet Army. Despite the heterogeneous nature of American society, however, one trait clearly runs through all segments of our culture: the common determination to improve our lot in life and to better provide for our families. Individuals state that they join the military services for many reasons, but the bottom line is that they perceive it to be in their own best interest. Again, S.L.A. Marshall is worth quoting: "I think that one of the general mistakes made by the military body is that because soldiering is a patriotic calling, it is regarded as somehow base to put self-interest foremost in appealing to the judgment and imagination of the soldier."[27] Officers, particularly those who have risen to positions in the operational-level command and control apparatus, have reached their positions by being ambitious as well as patriotic, and they generally view themselves as decisive, independent, and aggressive.

The way to capitalize on these attributes at the operational level is through the application of the philosophy of mission-oriented command and control in the tradition of the German army's *Auftragstaktik*. The greatest obstruction may be another natural trait, a reluctance of officers "to delegate because, in the intense competition for promotion, a single error by a subordinate could wreck their career."[28] However, in the last several years the American Army has made enormous strides in its training programs to encourage initiative and risk-taking. At this juncture, the Army needs to articulate a philosophy of mission-oriented command and control and to teach young officers, NCOs, and soldiers that initiative, aggressiveness, risk-taking, and willingness to assume responsibility are integral parts of command and control. Those attributes and qualities are prevalent in the soldiers from a free society, and they should be nurtured and honed in training by focusing on the commander's intent and by using common doctrine.

Two points must be made with respect to "leadership." The first is that leadership is inseparable from command and control at the operational level or any other level, although an artificial barrier has been erected between them. It is instructive to note that the German Army regulation that discusses their form of command and control is titled *Truppenführung*. That German word translates as troop-leading or troop-directing or troop-commanding. Simply put, leadership and command cannot be separated.

A second point is that the Army has been focusing on the wrong type of leadership. This point is well argued in an article in *Military Review* titled "Jazz Musicians and Algonquin Indians," by retired Colonel Mike Malone and Major Michael McGee. Malone and McGee point out that there are two basic types of leadership—individual and organizational. The Army has directed most of its efforts to the former, while it should have been concentrating on the latter. Among its central features, organizational leadership promotes "an attitude that emphasizes the relatedness of the unit's subparts and factors that influence unit performance."[29] Similarly, Richard Simpkin argues that the success of *Auftragstaktik* flows from "the acknowledgment and unreserved acceptance of mutual dependence" in traditional Prussian society.[30] The essence of Malone and McGee's article is precisely what Simpkin is describing based on his research and historical evidence.

## Conclusion

The Army does not have a coherent philosophy with regard to command and control. Although many documents exist for the various levels of military operations, no unified, consistent written theory exists. This state of affairs contrasts starkly with the example of the German army, which has a long history of exactly the type of regulation required. The introduction of a mission-oriented command and control philosophy in the doctrinal literature of the operational and tactical levels is specifically needed. Priority must be given to teaching the philosophy to the Army at large.

At present the principal missing element in a consistent theory of command and control has to do with the fact that command and leadership essentially form two distinct disciplines in the Army's Training and Doctrine Command. Leadership is handled at Fort Benning, while command and control is taught at Fort Leavenworth. The two subjects need to be tied closer together through the concept of organizational leadership.

Malone and McGee emphasize in their article that "leadership is a process which must occur within the organization if the organization is to be effective. This process activates, sustains, aims, and synchronizes the smaller parts of the whole system."[31] The great value of organizational leadership is that it focuses on the preservation of the organization. The writings of successful German wartime commanders are replete with specific comments about their actions to preserve their organizations. Focusing on organizational leadership, then, rather than on the infinitely variable individual type of leadership, encourages the growth of a more robust command and control system, increasing the probability that an organization will be effective and will survive.

Many Army programs and initiatives exist that in actuality constitute critical subsets of command and control at all levels, not only the operational. For example, the emphasis by the Army's senior leaders in the last few years on the issue of trust and confidence throughout the chain of command is vitally important. As with all programs, some units and organizations put it into practice while others do not. The importance of trust and confidence to effective command cannot be overstated, and soldiers at all levels should be taught and expected to operate accordingly. The emphasis on mentorship and footlocker counseling, although certainly not promulgated specifically as an element of a command and control training program, contributes to instilling trust and confidence throughout the chain of command. These techniques also contribute to the concept of mission-oriented command and control because, if they are done properly, the subordinate should come away with a better understanding of the senior's intent. Mentorship and counseling can help to eradicate the "them versus us" syndrome that is so debilitating; the techniques can help to establish a unit that executes vigorously because all its members understand the commander's intent. Unanimity of purpose and loyalty to executing the commander's intent are achieved because subordinates understand that they are essential.

The emphasis in recent years on encouraging subordinates to take risks and be innovative and aggressive in the training environment also has contributed to trust and confidence, as well as directly giving units and organizations opportunities to experiment in a no-fault environment. Once again, the senior leadership is committed to the concept; if deviations occur, they are most likely made by colonels or lieutenant colonels who fear having a subordinate make a mistake that would be too visible.

The Army's educational system also is contributing immensely to better command and control. One course that is particularly valuable in that regard is the CAS[3] course for captains at Fort Leavenworth. The course is demanding and it yields an outstanding product. Those captains will be the "doers" in organizations from battalion level to army group if the country gets involved in a major war. Those officers speak the same language and have been through the same tempering process. The CAS[3] course will undoubtedly contribute more to effective command and control than any of the current hardware programs under procurement. A commonality in doctrinal orientation will enable those officers to save their bosses from making grave mistakes.

Despite the presence of these bright spots, the Army remains in need of a coherent and unified philosophy of command and control at the operational level of war. One of the principal lessons emerging from the studies of the Eastern Front during World War II is that with superior command and control, armies can fight outnumbered and win. Only by developing a coherent approach to command and control will our Army achieve the goal for which it must always strive: winning the first battle, and the last.

## NOTES

1. Vincent J. Esposito and John Robert Elting, *A Military History and Atlas of the Napoleonic Wars* (New York: Praeger, 1965), introduction.
2. Ibid., map 68.
3. Martin van Creveld, *Command in War* (Cambridge, Mass.: Harvard Univ. Press, 1985), p. 88.
4. Esposito and Elting, map 63.
5. Ibid., map 68.
6. Russell F. Weigley, *The American Way of War* (New York: Macmillan, 1973), p. 452.
7. Van Creveld, p. 237.
8. Ibid.
9. Ibid.
10. "US Says One Vessel It Hit Had Come Within 10 Miles," *The New York Times*, 26 March 1986, p. A8.
11. General Donn Starry, quoted in Richard Simpkin, *Race to the Swift* (London: Brassey's, 1985), p. x.
12. Ibid., p. ix.
13. US Department of the Army, *Operations*, Field Manual 100-5 (Washington: G.P.O., 1986), p. 1-2.
14. Ibid., p. 1-3
15. US Department of the Army, U.S. Army Command and General Staff College, *Corps and Division Command and Control*, Field Circular 101-55 (Washington: G.P.O., 1985), p. 1-4.
16. Ibid., p. 1-5.
17. Ibid., pp. 1-5 to 1-6.
18. Simpkin, p. 227.
19. "The German Army's Mission Oriented Command and Control," *Armor* 90 (January-February 1981): 12.
20. Ibid.

21. Richard F. Timmons, "Lessons From the Past for NATO," *Parameters* 14 (Autumn 1984): 5.
22. Ibid.
23. General Hermann Balck, in transcript, *Generals Balck and von Mellenthin on Tactics: Implications for NATO Military Doctrine* (McLean, Va.: BDM Corp., 1980), reprinted by the U.S. Army War College for the Art of War Colloquium, April 1983, p. 17.
24. Major General R. W. von Mellenthin, ibid., p. 22.
25. Timmons, p. 7.
26. S.L.A. Marshall, *Men Against Fire* (Washington: Infantry Journal, 1947), p. 149.
27. Ibid., p. 159.
28. Simpkin, p. 219.
29. Dandridge M. Malone and Michael L. McGee, "Jazz Musicians and Algonquin Indians," *Military Review* 65 (December 1985): 53.
30. Simpkin, p. 243.
31. Malone and McGee, p. 54.

This article appeared in the winter 1986 issue of *Parameters*.

# 9

# Strategic Vision and Strength of Will: Imperatives for Theater Command

By MITCHELL M. ZAIS
© 1985 Mitchell M. Zais

While virtual libraries of material have been written on the topic of leadership, nearly all this literature tends to assume that the qualities and attributes which are required for success are the same irrespective of organizational level. Thus, one is left to presume that the most successful battalion or brigade commanders will necessarily perform most effectively at higher levels of command such as corps or army group. It is not the purpose of this essay to debate that premise. It assumes from the start that the reader readily recognizes the fallacy of this argument and accepts as axiomatic the assertion of Clausewitz that

> every level of command has its own intellectual standard; its own prerequisites for fame and honor. . . . There are commanders-in-chief who could not have led a cavalry regiment with distinction, and cavalry commanders who could not have led armies.[1]

In spite of Clausewitz's observation, little has been written concerning the prerequisites, qualities, and attributes required for the leading of armies.

This essay will argue that there are at least two qualities which are essential for the most senior commanders, specifically, theater commanders during wartime. This list is not all inclusive; the cited attributes merely constitute minimum essential conditions for successful wartime theater command.

Further, it is not the intent of this article to prove that the characteristics required in war differ from those required in peace or that the most effective peacetime commanders are not necessarily the best warrior leaders. The reader is presumed to agree with Frank Knox, Secretary of the Navy during World War II, who, in advocating the promotion of aggressive fighters, not peacetime stars, offered the following observation to Admiral Chester W. Nimitz concerning the differences between senior commanders in war and peace:

Most of us, if we had been required to choose at the beginning of the war between the brilliant, polished, socially attractive McClellan and the rough, rather uncouth, unsocial Grant, would have chosen McClellan, just as Lincoln did.[2]

In essence, Knox was simply stating that the qualities required of wartime commanders differ from those valued in peacetime.

Accepting the preceding premises, I would suggest that the two qualities of the wartime theater commander that are most critical can be termed *strategic vision* and *strength of will*.

## Strategic Vision

Strategic vision is the first essential requirement for the theater commander. It constitutes the ability to discern the means for the attainment of the ultimate political objective through the employment of military force. For example, Colonel Harry G. Summers, Jr., in his book *On Strategy*, argues that it was precisely the lack of this strategic vision that led to the ultimate defeat of U.S. forces in South Vietnam.[3] Strategic vision is the single factor that enables the theater commander to act in accordance with national policy to direct the efforts of military force to obtain national goals. If one accepts Clausewitz's dictum that "war is merely the continuation of policy by other means,"[4] then clearly the theater commander must understand the political goals of his government and possess a strategic vision of how those goals might best be attained. For the theater commander, political ends and military means are joined inextricably.

The requirement for strategic vision was, in Clausewitz's eyes, the most important single attribute of the senior or theater commander. He said,

The first, the supreme, the most far-reaching act of judgment that the . . . commander [has] to make is to establish . . . the kind of war on which [he is] embarking; neither mistaking it for, nor trying to turn it into, something that is alien to its nature.[5]

In other words, it is strategic vision which enables the commander to judge the true nature of the war he is fighting and to link the political goals of that conflict to the military means at his disposal. Clausewitz concluded that in directing wars, "*What is required is* a sense of unity and power of judgment raised to *a marvelous pitch of vision*."[6]

Many contemporary writers have observed the importance of vision in directing the activities of large numbers of men undertaking great enterprises. It is the vision of the senior leader or commander, according to Thomas E. Cronin, which provides an organization and its members "a clear sense of direction, a sense of mission." This sense of direction and mission, then, serves to "clarify problems and choices, . . . build morale . . ., and provide a vision of the possibilities and promise."[7] Similarly, Robert Mueller, Chairman of the Board of Arthur D. Little, Inc., saw that "the leader is the visionary providing imminence to the present and a transcendental drive into the future."[8] It is this vision which engages the enthusiasms and energy of subordinates as they strive to make the theater commander's vision a reality.

The theater commander's strategic vision includes the ways and means of obtaining military victory. Both General Matthew Ridgway and General Sir William Slim, in writing about their campaigns in Korea and Burma, respectively, described the vital importance of imparting to all their subordinates their personal visions of victory and the conditions and methods for obtaining it.[9]

Some would argue that tactical or operational genius is a requirement for the successful theater commander in wartime. But this is not entirely the case. At the theater level of war, strategic vision constitutes the essential level of military competence. The theater commander must merely have sufficient understanding of operations and tactics to know generally what lies within the realm of the possible. He can rely upon subordinates to translate his strategic vision into operational and tactical concepts. General Dwight Eisenhower's direction of the European Theater of Operations exemplifies this principle.

As General Omar Bradley noted, Eisenhower's tactical and operational abilities were generally judged to be rather limited. In Bradley's assessment, "Ike was a political general of rare and valuable gifts, but . . . he did not know how to manage a battlefield"[10] Bradley suggested that General George C. Marshall shared the same view of Eisenhower's tactical and operational capabilities. When Bradley was posted by Marshall to serve on Eisenhower's staff in North Africa, Bradley felt that "perhaps Marshall was tactfully seeking a way of reinforcing Ike on the battlefield with professional generals skilled in infantry tactics, without actually saying so."[11] General George Patton held a similar opinion, as Martin Blumenson's *The Patton Papers* revealed.[12] But it did not matter that Eisenhower was unskilled in tactics and operations, for he possessed the strategic vision of the requirements for victory and understood the importance of maintaining a solid alliance for its attainment. Also, Eisenhower coupled his strategic vision with the second imperative for the theater commander, strength of will.

## Strength of Will

It is the commander's strength of will which enables him to impart his vision to his subordinates and to ensure that they adopt his vision as their own. In other words, a strategic vision that exists only in the mind of the commander or his close associates is of no use. His vision must be transferred down through many layers of military organization. This can be accomplished only if the theater commander possesses the necessary strength of will to overcome obstacles to the transmission of his vision and to dominate the wills of those who would obstruct its attainment. In the face of setbacks, casualties, battle losses, and all the vicissitudes of war, there is ample opportunity for subordinates to lose faith, lose enthusiasm, and lose sight of the commander's vision. Strength of will enables the theater commander to maintain his vision as the foremost objective of his subordinates when weaker men around him have cause to abandon hope.

This strength of will has been variously called energy, firmness, staunchness, and strength of character. It is the force which, according to Clausewitz, resists

> the ebbing of moral and physical strength, . . . the heart-rending spectacle of the dead and wounded, that the commander has to withstand—first in himself, and then in all those who, directly or indirectly, have entrusted him with their thoughts and feelings, hopes and fears. As each man's strength gives out, as it no longer responds to his will, the inertia of the whole gradually comes to rest on the commander's will alone. The ardor of his spirit must rekindle the flame of purpose in all others; his inward fire must revive their hope. Only to the extent that he can do this will he retain his hold on his men and keep control. . . . The burdens increase with the number of men in his command, and therefore the higher his position, the greater the strength of character he needs to bear the mounting load.[13]

Other military writers have expressed the same idea, that strength of will is an essential ingredient of the senior commander, particularly the theater commander. Ferdinand Foch, the French theater commander of World War I, shared this view. In his book *Precepts*, he said,

> No victory is possible unless the commander be energetic . . .; unless he possess and can impart to all the resolute will of seeing things through; unless he be capable of exerting a personal action, composed of will, . . . in the midst of danger.[14]

General Sir Archibald P. Wavell, the British theater commander of the Middle East Command in North Africa during World War II, also believed that strength of will was indispensable. He claimed that the "most vital of all" qualities of the commander is "what we call the fighting spirit, the will to win."[15] A related view has been expressed by John Keegan, professor of military history at the Royal Military Academy, Sandhurst, in the landmark work, *The Face of Battle*. According to Keegan, "Mere hardness of character of the sort demonstrated by Zhukov or Model, rather than any particular strategic or tactical flair, increasingly became the principal military virtue as the Second World War dragged on."[16] Similarly, in his article "Leadership as an Art," James L. Stokesbury points out, "Military history is littered with the names of great and good men who were not quite hard enough, and whose disinclination to get their men killed caused only more suffering in the long run."[17] General Hooker's vacillation and timidity at Chancellorsville is a prime example.[18] In essence, what all of these authors are saying, in one way or another, is that strength of will is imperative if the senior commander is to impose his strategic vision on his subordinates.

## Summing Up

Others might argue that different traits, abilities, or characteristics are imperative for the theater commander. Some might suggest that communications skills, or charisma, or any number of other qualities are critical. However, for every example one can find a counter. For every charismatic giant, great orator, or master writer, one can find a theater commander of average ability in these areas. General Grant was a virtual failure at every endeavor he attempted until he assumed command of the Union Army.

Much of the discussion in the current military leadership debate concerns the ethical and moral requirements of our senior leadership. The historical evidence shows, however, that while many theater commanders have been men of high moral character, others, equally successful, have been ruthless, egocentric, inclined to drink too much, or libertine. As Robert Taylor and William Rosenbach remind us in their book *Military Leadership: In Pursuit of Excellence*, "Biographers err in attributing success to what we *want* leaders to be rather than to the realities of the person in time and place."[19] If we look at successful theater commanders of the past as they truly were, and not as we wish them to be, we will find that they possessed a wide assortment of strengths and weaknesses, personalities and temperaments, and skills and abilities. Strategic vision and strength of will seem to be the only attributes which consistently characterize the best theater commanders; it follows that these two attributes, above all others, can be considered imperatives for theater command.

NOTES

1. Carl von Clausewitz, *On War*, ed. and trans. by Michael Howard and Peter Paret (Princeton: Princeton Univ. Press, 1976), pp. 111, 146.
2. Edwin P. Hoyt, *How They Won the War in the Pacific: Admiral Nimitz and His Admirals* (New York: Weybright & Tally, 1971), p. 168.
3. Harry G. Summers, Jr., *On Strategy: A Critical Analysis of the Vietnam War* (Novato, Calif.: Presidio Press, 1982).
4. Clausewitz, p. 87.
5. Ibid., p. 88.
6. Ibid., p. 112. Emphasis added.
7. Thomas E. Cronin, "Thinking About Leadership," in Robert L.Taylor and William E. Rosenbach, eds., *Military Leadership: In Pursuit of Excellence* (Boulder, Colo.: Westview Press, 1984), pp. 195,197.
8. Robert K. Mueller, "Leading Edge Leadership," in *Military Leadership: In Pursuit of Excellence*, p. 146.
9. See Matthew B. Ridgway, *The Korean War* (Garden City, N.Y.: Doubleday, 1967); and William Slim, *Defeat Into Victory* (London: Cassell and Company, 1961).
10. Omar N. Bradley and Clay Blair, *A General's Life* (New York: Simon and Schuster, 1983), p. 130.
11. Ibid., p. 131.
12. Martin Blumenson, *The Patton Papers: 1940-1945* (Boston: Houghton Mifflin, 1974), pp. 139, 418,537.
13. Clausewitz, pp. 104-05.
14. Quoted in Robert D. Heinl, Jr., *Dictionary of Military and Naval Quotations* (Annapolis, Md.: United States Naval Institute, 1966), p. 132.
15. Archibald Wavell, *Generals and Generalship: The Lee Knowles Lectures Delivered at Trinity College, Cambridge, in 1939*, reprinted with other works for The Art of War Colloquium, US Army War College, Carlisle Barracks, Pa., February 1983, p. 43. (Originally printed in *The Times* [London] and subsequently published by the MacMillan Company, New York, 1941.)
16. John Keegan, *The Face of Battle* (New York: Vintage Books, 1976), p. 331.

17. James L. Stokesbury, "Leadership as an Art," in *Military Leadership In Pursuit of Excellence*. p. 17.

18. Bruce Catton, *Never Call Retreat* (New York: Pocket Books, 1967), pp. 138-49.

19. *Military Leadership: In Pursuit of Excellence*, p. 1.

This article is a slightly abridged version of one appearing in the winter 1985 issue of *Parameters*.

# III. CASE STUDIES IN COMBAT COMMAND

# 10

# MacArthur's Fireman: Robert L. Eichelberger

By JOHN F. SHORTAL
© *1986 John F. Shortal*

To millions of people the name Douglas MacArthur evokes the image of a brilliant, confident, and supremely successful commander. In the 41 years that have elapsed since the last campaign of World War II, his victories have come to be viewed as quick, smooth, and simple operations against an impoverished foe. However, hindsight has obscured the tenacity of the Japanese and the immense difficulties MacArthur encountered in the Southwest Pacific. Not all of his victories were quick and easy; the Japanese did not quit upon request. In three major campaigns—Buna in December 1942, Biak in June 1944, and Manila in January 1945—MacArthur suffered initial setbacks from the Japanese. In each case, he was forced to call in a fireman to rally American troops and salvage desperate tactical situations. MacArthur always used the same fireman to handle his most difficult missions, Lieutenant General Robert Lawrence Eichelberger. In each case, Eichelberger's combination of tactical innovation, commonsense training, and personal leadership produced dramatic results.

MacArthur was a legendary field commander. Robert Eichelberger, on the other hand, did not fit the Hollywood image of a general. He was not young, handsome, or tough-talking. He did not wear specially designed uniforms or use theatrics calculated to impress his troops. Rather, by 1944 he was a 58-year-old man who, although in excellent physical condition, was slightly overweight and concerned about his waistline.[1] What Eichelberger did have going for him was an iron will, a strong concept of duty, a warm sense of humor,[2] and an innovative tactical ability. He never failed to conquer any assigned objective.

The story of MacArthur's problem at Buna is well known. His first offensive of the war was in grave jeopardy in November 1942, when an insufficiently trained American division had been stymied and demoralized by the Japanese. Douglas MacArthur, whose pride had been severely wounded in the recent Philippines campaign, had no other reserves in the theater. Furthermore, the poor performance of this division caused the Australians to question the fighting abilities of American soldiers. To salvage this desperate tactical situation and to breathe new life into the American soldiers at Buna, MacArthur summoned Eichelberger from Australia. On the evening of 30 November 1942, MacArthur issued one of the most famous operations orders in American military history. He said:

> Bob, I'm putting you in command at Buna. Relieve Harding. I am sending you in, Bob, and I want you to remove all officers who won't fight. Relieve Regimental and Battalion commanders; if necessary, put Sergeants in charge of Battalions and Corporals in charge of companies—anyone who will fight. Time is of the essence; the Japs may land reinforcements any night. . . . I want you to take Buna, or not come back alive.[3]

Thirty-two days later this American division, whose fighting capabilities had been questioned, conquered Buna. The capture of Buna was MacArthur's first ground victory of World War II. It was a closely fought battle in which he was forced to take on an enemy who held all the advantages in equipment, training, and experience. MacArthur had few troops at his disposal, and the much-discussed industrial capacity of the United States had not yet manifested itself in this theater.[4] The margin between victory and defeat at Buna was the dynamic and inspirational leadership of Robert Eichelberger. An eyewitness later described Eichelberger's contribution as follows:

> You were sent at the eleventh hour to salvage an impossible situation without any assistance except your own intelligence and your own force of character. . . . While I was with you I was convinced that if the troops under your command did not go into Buna, you would have unhesitatingly gone in there alone.[5]

Although Buna is the most well-known example of MacArthur's use of Eichelberger's formidable leadership talents, it was not the only one.

## MacArthur's Second Problem: Biak

The conclusion of the Buna campaign in January 1943 secured the eastern portion of New Guinea for the Allies. In order to carry the Allied offensive into the Philippines, MacArthur had to isolate the powerful Japanese base at Rabaul and then move up the northern coast of New Guinea. Throughout 1943, MacArthur conducted a series of brilliant operations which cut the Japanese line of communication to Rabaul. This enabled him to neutralize completely the Japanese forces at this location without conducting a bloody frontal assault. However, by January 1944 MacArthur had moved only 240 miles north of Buna and still had 2,240 miles to go before reaching Manila.[6] In order to bring the war to a more rapid conclusion, MacArthur decided to conduct a series of deeper amphibious envelopments up the northern coast of New Guinea.[7]

By late May 1944 MacArthur had moved up the northern coast of New Guinea as far as the Island of Biak, which was within bomber range of the Philippines (800 miles), and within fighter range of the Japanese airfields on Palau.[8] MacArthur had cut through the Japanese defenses with skill. The amphibious envelopment at Saidor (2 January), Aitape and Hollandia (22 April), and Wakde (17 May) were great successes. George C. Marshall even called the Hollandia operation a "model of strategic and tactical maneuvers."[9]

At Biak, unfortunately, MacArthur's luck ran out. Biak was important because the Japanese had built three airfields on the island, and MacArthur hoped to use these airfields to launch bombing missions against Japanese bases in the Philippines. Since he expected the task force to have seized and built up at least one airfield by 10 June, he had promised to support Admiral Nimitz's operation at Saipan in the Marianas on 15 June 1944 with aircraft from these airfields.[10]

At 0715 hours on 27 May 1944, Major General Horace Fuller and two regiments (186th and 162nd Infantry) of the 41st Division landed at Biak. The Japanese offered no resistance at the beaches, and the initial landings were a complete success.[11] General Fuller's plan called for the 162nd Regiment to move along the beach road, which ran at the base of a steep cliff, to the three airfields. Meanwhile, the 186th Regiment would move on a parallel route through the mountains.[12] In the first two days General Fuller's forces moved quickly, covering eight miles along the beach road, which brought them within 1,000 yards of the first airfield (Mokmer Drome).[13] Unfortunately, MacArthur's staff had seriously underestimated the Japanese defensive capability on the island. Instead of the 4,380 Japanese troops they had anticipated, more than 11,000 Japanese soldiers were at Biak. In December 1943, the Japanese high command had sent the veteran 222nd Infantry Regiment of the 36th Division to Biak. This unit was commanded by Colonel Naoyuki Kuzume and reinforced with elements of the 221st Infantry and the 2nd Development Unit.[14] Colonel Kuzume was described in an American after-action report as "a soldier of the highest calibre and a tactician compelling respect."[15] For five months he had carefully prepared his defenses.

Colonel Kuzume had astutely assessed the Allied objective as the three airfields along the southern coast of Biak. Therefore, he skillfully emplaced his forces in the coral ridges above the coastal road which ran from Mandom to the Mokmer airfield. He also positioned troops in the compartmented ridge systems 1,000 yards north-northwest of the Mokmer airfield. The terrain, including many caves, complemented the interlocking ridge network which not only dominated the coastal road and three airfields, but provided concealed emplacements for the enemy's artillery, mortars, and machine guns.[16]

On 29 May, Colonel Kuzume counterattacked three times with two battalions of infantry supported by tanks and artillery fire against the 162nd Infantry positions. In the four-hour fight, the American forces neutralized eight Japanese tanks and destroyed the better part of a Japanese battalion. However, the Japanese were successful in driving the 162nd Infantry back two miles east of the Mokmer airfield and forcing them onto the defensive.[17] General Fuller requested and received the 163rd Infantry Regiment to reinforce his task force. With this support, General Fuller was again able to mount an offensive and by 8 June had finally seized his first airfield, Mokmer. However, the Air Corps could not use the field because Japanese gunfire completely controlled it.[18]

On 14 June 1944, the tactical situation of General Fuller's Hurricane Task Force was bleak. In 19 days of combat they had succeeded in seizing only a single Japanese airfield, one that could not be used by Allied air forces. Furthermore, Admiral Nimitz's forces would go ashore at Saipan on 15 June without Southwest Pacific air support because the Hurricane Task Force had failed in its principal mission.[19]

The Biak operation had become a personal embarrassment to MacArthur; he had been caught in exaggerations to the Joint Chiefs of Staff and to the American public. On 28 May, after General Fuller's initial success, General MacArthur had announced that the impending fall of Biak "marks the practical end of the New Guinea campaign." On 1 June, MacArthur's communique announced that Japanese resistance "was collapsing." On 3 June, MacArthur's communique optimistically announced that "mopping up was proceeding on Biak."[20] However, at the same time that MacArthur was announcing to the world the imminent successful conclusion of the campaign, the Australian press was relaying a totally different story. Spencer Davis reported in *Australia Newsweek* that "obviously, it would require additional reinforcements to achieve the resounding victory proclaimed ten days ago by General MacArthur."[21]

MacArthur, aware of the discrepancy between the actual tactical situation and his communiques, became increasingly concerned as time went on. On 5 June he told General Krueger (the 6th Army Commander and General Fuller's immediate superior): "I am becoming concerned at the failure to secure the Biak airfields . . . is the advance being pushed with sufficient determination? Our negligible ground losses would seem to indicate a failure to do so." On 14 June MacArthur cabled General Krueger: "The situation on Biak is unsatisfactory. The strategic purpose of the operation is being jeopardized by the failure to establish without delay an operating field for aircraft."[22]

During the first two weeks of June 1944, as the tactical situation stagnated, MacArth
ur continued to press General Krueger for results. General Krueger recalled that he "dispatched several radiograms to the task force commander directing him to speed up the operation. But it was easier to order this than get it done for . . . the troops were faced by great difficulties."[23]

With the tactical situation stalemated, victory having been proclaimed two weeks earlier and the invasion of Saipan scheduled for the next day, MacArthur and Krueger called for their most able field commander to salvage the situation and put out this fire before it consumed their reputations. At 1800 hours on 14 June 1944, General Krueger summoned General Eichelberger to an emergency conference at his headquarters. At this conference General Krueger "explained that after continuous fighting, coupled with extremely unfriendly terrain, intense heat and scarcity of water, the infantry units within the task force were beginning to tire to a critical degree."[24] General Krueger then told Eichelberger to take command at Biak the following morning.

At 0830 hours on 15 June, Eichelberger and a small staff departed for Biak. They arrived at General Fuller's headquarters at 1230 that day.[25] Eichelberger spent the first two and one-half days at the front familiarizing himself with the tactical situation and the fighting capabilities of his own forces. On 16 June he went to the regimental command posts of the 186th and 162nd Infantry Regiments to assess personally the morale and effectiveness of those units. On 17 June, he observed the conduct of the two units under fire.[26] Eichelberger radioed General Krueger: "Today I have been with General Doe and 186 and 162 Infantry. With the possible exception of the first Bn 162 Inf the troops are not nearly as exhausted as I had expected and I believe they can be made to fight with energy."[27]

On 17 June General Krueger, still under pressure from General MacArthur, radioed Eichelberger to "launch your attack . . . promptly and press it home with the utmost vigor."[28] Eichelberger, however, had a plan for defeating the Japanese and was not going to be pressured into prematurely launching his attack because of MacArthur's and Krueger's embarrassment over previous communiques. Therefore, on 17 June Eichelberger sent this succinct message to General Krueger, outlining his plan of attack:

> Having arrived here forty-eight hours ago in almost complete ignorance of the situation, I have spent two days at the front. Tomorrow [Sunday], I have called off all fighting and troops will be reorganized. On Monday, I propose to put three battalions in the rear of the Japanese, and on Tuesday I propose to take the other two airfields.[29]

After clearly informing General Krueger of his plan and his pace, Eichelberger took two additional actions on 17 June. First, he ordered a reinforced rifle company to occupy Hill 320, which was the dominating terrain feature in the area north of the three airfields, thus providing an excellent observation point.[30] Second, Eichelberger issued his instructions for the 19 June attack. He would not try to directly seize the airfields nor conduct a frontal attack against the Japanese positions. Instead, he would envelop the enemy by going around the Japanese southern flank and seizing the ridgeline north of Mokmer airfield from the rear.[31] Eichelberger's objectives were to eliminate the Japanese ability to fire on Mokmer airfield and to obtain favorable terrain from which to launch future advances.[32] Eichelberger later credited the Japanese with giving him the solution for cracking their defenses. He had carefully examined all their operations in World War II and believed that the Japanese tactics in Malaya would provide the method of ending the stalemate on Biak. In Malaya, each time the British forces prepared a defensive line, the Japanese enveloped it. Once the British discovered that the Japanese were in their rear, the whole defensive line collapsed and the British withdrew to establish another. This process was repeated down the entire peninsula. Eichelberger believed that at Biak the "Japanese troops [would], just like occidental troops, take a very dim and unhappy view of enemy forces in their rear."[33]

On 18 June, Eichelberger repeated a lesson he had learned at Buna and rested his troops before the major attack. As the soldiers rested, Eichelberger gave his subordinate commanders time to reorganize their forces and to ensure that "everybody could find out what they were doing."[34] Eichelberger also sent out patrols to reconnoiter the Japanese positions, and by evening on 18 June his troops were, in the words of an eyewitness, "ready to move hard and fast."[35]

On the morning of 19 June, the 41st Division launched a coordinated attack and moved hard and fast to accomplish Eichelberger's objectives. The 3rd Battalion, 163rd Infantry, and two battalions (2nd and 3rd) of the 186th Infantry Regiment "had enveloped the rear of the Japanese in the west caves and could prevent their reinforcement or escape."[36] Furthermore, this attack secured the Mokmer airfield from hostile ground attack.

Even though the attack on 19 June was a complete success, the situation demanded that Eichelberger continue to press his troops forward. He ordered an attack on 20 June to seize the remaining two airfields, Borokoe and Sorido, and to destroy the Japanese who were emplaced in the west caves (by the 162nd Infantry). By 1030 hours on 20 June, Eichelberger had seized the Borokoe and Sorido airfields.[37] The Hurricane Task Force's original mission had been accomplished. Eichelberger continued to press the attack against the Japanese who were neutralized in caves even though the airfields were secured.

On the night of 21-22 June, the Japanese commander, Colonel Kuzume, recognized defeat. He destroyed the regimental colors and all official documents and then ordered all able-bodied soldiers to attempt a breakout. The Japanese tried three times to break through the lines of the 186th Infantry. At 2100 hours, and then at 2400 hours on 21 June, the Japanese attacked and were repulsed. At 0400 hours on 22 June, the Japanese tried for the final time. All three attacks failed.[38] The last Japanese resistance in the caves was finally mopped up on 27 June.

Eichelberger departed Biak at 0900 hours on 28 June. It had taken him only five days to seize the three Japanese airfields and to break the enemy's main line of defense. It is worth noting that he accomplished this at a cost of only 400 Americans killed, compared to the 4,700 Japanese killed in action.[39] Eichelberger credited his success "to profanity, flattery, offers of rewards, threats, and lady luck."[40] The tactical situation had been solved quickly, and MacArthur's reputation had not been tarnished. MacArthur could move on to his cherished operations in the Philippines without concern for Biak. After this operation, MacArthur rewarded Eichelberger with the command of the new Eighth Army.

## MacArthur's Third Problem: Manila

MacArthur successfully returned to the Philippines on 20 October 1944 when the Sixth United States Army landed on the island of Leyte. On 9 January 1945, MacArthur landed the same Sixth Army, commanded by

Lieutenant General Walter Krueger, at Lingayen Gulf on the main island of Luzon. In 12 months, MacArthur had moved 2,000 miles closer to Japan and had commenced the liberation of the Philippines. With the exception of Biak, all these operations had proceeded like clockwork.

The objective of the Sixth Army forces that landed at Lingayen Gulf was the City of Manila, 120 miles to the south. The assault troops at Lingayen Gulf consisted of the I and XIV Corps and the 40th, 37th, 6th, and 43rd Divisions.[41] General Krueger and his forces encountered no opposition on the beaches and little in the initial advance; however, terrain and logistical problems did slow the pace.[42] On 12 January 1945, only three days after Sixth Army had landed on Luzon, General MacArthur summoned General Krueger to his headquarters to complain of the slow progress. MacArthur believed that since the Sixth Army casualties were light, they had encountered little resistance and could pick up the tempo of their attack. MacArthur was unimpressed with Krueger's arguments for additional troops with which to conduct the dash for Manila.[43]

MacArthur, who felt that the Japanese would not defend Manila, had correctly assessed the intentions of the Japanese commander on Luzon, General Tomoyuki Yamashita. Yamashita, with 275,000 Japanese troops on Luzon, realized that he could not possibly hope to defend the entire island. He knew that he could not confront the overwhelming forces MacArthur could bring to bear against him in the important region of the Central Plains and Manila Bay.[44] Therefore, he planned a fighting withdrawal into the mountainous strongholds in northern Luzon, which would tie up large amounts of allied shipping, troops, and aircraft. He hoped that this defense would delay the inevitable invasion of the Japanese homeland.[45] General Yamashita specifically ordered Lieutenant General Shizuo Yokoyama, the Eighth Division Commander, not to defend Manila but rather evacuate the city.[46] However, due to bureaucratic disagreements between the Japanese Army and Navy, Vice Admiral Denshichi Okochi, the naval commander in Manila, decided to conduct a full-scale defense of the city against Yamashita's wishes.[47] Admiral Okochi's decision later caused a great deal of friction between General MacArthur and General Krueger.

By mid-January 1945, as the Sixth Army moved on Manila at a snail's pace, MacArthur grew more and more obsessed with the capture of the city. Manila Bay was of vital importance, but MacArthur's reasons were more than simply logistical and strategic.[48] It was almost as if his personal military reputation depended on liberating the city as quickly as possible. Therefore, throughout the month of January, the slow progress of the Sixth Army was a great irritant to General MacArthur. On 23 January, a newspaper correspondent, Lee Van Atta, informed Eichelberger that "General MacArthur had been laying down the law to Krueger about the slow advance at Lingayen and that he had given him an ultimatum to be in Manila by the 5th of February."[49] On 30 January 1945, General MacArthur personally went to the front to investigate the reason for the Sixth Army's slow advance. According to the official Army historian for this campaign, MacArthur found the pace of the advance "much too leisurely."[50] MacArthur then informed General Krueger that the 37th Division had demonstrated "a noticeable lack of drive and aggressive initiative."[51] General MacArthur in frustration said that the Sixth Army was "mentally incapable but if given tremendous forces they [were] able to advance ponderously and slowly to victory."[52]

This standard of performance was unacceptable to MacArthur and, as had become the routine when his reputation was at stake, he called on Eichelberger. To speed up the pace of operations on Luzon, MacArthur directed Eichelberger to conduct an amphibious landing on 31 January at Nasugbu, 45 miles southwest of Manila. The assault troops for this operation were the 11th Airborne Division, commanded by Major General Joseph Swing, and the 511th Parachute Regimental Combat Team.[53] MacArthur intended the Nasugbu landing to be a "reconnaissance in force to test the enemy defenses in southern Luzon."[54] Eichelberger was directed to land only one regimental combat team (188th Glider Regiment) initially. However, he was given the discretion to land the 187th Glider Regiment and to push north toward Manila if he met no opposition. In addition, Eichelberger had the authority to airdrop the 511th Parachute Regiment to exploit success, it the situation warranted it.[55] General MacArthur hoped that this operation would divert Japanese forces from north of Manila and prohibit them from concentrating all their defenses against the Sixth Army.[56]

At 0815 hours on 13 January 1945, Eichelberger landed his first assault force (the 188th Regimental Combat Team) at Nasugbu Beach. This regiment encountered light resistance from the Japanese and by 0945 had seized the town of Nasugbu and the Nasugbu airport.[57] At 1030 hours Eichelberger, aboard the USS *Spencer*, made the decision to exploit the initial success of the 188th Regimental Combat Team. He ordered General Swing to land the rest of the 11th Airborne Division and to push on as rapidly as possible toward Manila. By noon the rest of the division had landed and was driving inland.[58]

Eichelberger went ashore at 1300 hours and immediately proceeded to the front to confer with General Swing.[59] Eichelberger, who was not without personal ambition, had as his objective to drive rapidly toward the capture of Manila.[60] Eichelberger later reflected that this operation was successful because "speed was emphasized and contact once gained was maintained until the enemy was either dispersed or annihilated." Eichelberger's tactics, which demanded rapid penetration by his infantry in order to avoid the stalemate that would ensue if the Japanese had time to establish their defenses, had been developed at Buna and Biak, where he had found that the infantry had a tendency to go slow and wait for the artillery to defeat the enemy.[61]

Eichelberger's emphasis on speed was rewarded when lead elements of the 188th Regiment seized the important Palico River Bridge, eight miles inland, at 1430. The 11th Airborne Division's after-action report stated that "the

Palico River Bridge had been prepared for demolition, but the Japanese were surprised by the rapid advance of our troops, and were caught on the far side of the bridge. Our fire prevented them from reaching the bridge and they withdrew toward Tagaytay Ridge.''[62] This bridge was important because it allowed Eichelberger's forces to use the Nasugbu-Tagaytay road, which was an all-weather highway, and considerably shortened their supply line.[63]

After the bridge was seized, Eichelberger ordered General Swing to continue the advance through the night because he believed that the ''enemy troops were confused and retreating,'' and a halt at dark would have permitted them to reorganize.[64] At midnight, the 187th Regiment passed through the 188th and continued the advance toward Manila. The 11th Airborne Division pushed on throughout the night. The following morning Eichelberger went to the front to inspect and exhort his men and soon found himself moving with the lead company in the advance.[65] His emphasis on speed had paid great dividends in his first 28 hours ashore. The 11th Airborne Division not only had established a port and an airfield in this time, but also had penetrated the main line of Japanese resistance and had advanced 19 miles.[66] To exploit this success, Eichelberger alerted the 511th Parachute Regiment to be prepared for an airborne drop in the vicinity of Tagaytay Ridge.[67]

By 2 February 1945, the 11th Airborne Division had fought its way through two Japanese defensive positions and by dusk had reached the third and most powerful Japanese position in the vicinity of Tagaytay Ridge.[68] Tagaytay Ridge was the most important military position held by the Japanese in southern Luzon. It was a formidable obstacle because its 2,400-foot height dominated all the terrain in the region. Also, there was a two-lane concrete highway which led from Tagaytay Ridge straight down (30 miles) into Manila.[69] Therefore, as General Eichelberger and General Swing personally moved forward with the lead elements on 2 February, Eichelberger made the decision to envelop the Japanese positions on Tagaytay Ridge by air-dropping the 511th Parachute Regiment behind the Japanese. The Japanese would then be in a crossfire between the U.S. elements.[70]

At 0730 on 3 February 1945, the 188th Regimental Combat Team assaulted the highest hill on Tagaytay Ridge, known as Shorty Hill. At 0815 the 511th Parachute Regiment jumped behind the Japanese position on Tagaytay Ridge.[71] Eichelberger was again under fire as he observed the critical assault from two directions, which finally reduced the Japanese positions on Tagaytay Ridge. By 1300 hours the Japanese positions had been destroyed and the 511th Parachute Regiment had linked up with the 188th Regiment. As soon as Tagaytay Ridge was secure, patrols were sent down the highway toward Manila.[72]

In accordance with General Eichelberger's tactical emphasis on speed, General Swing loaded the 511th Parachute Regiment on trucks on the night of 3-4 February and ordered them to proceed ''toward Manila until resistance was encountered.''[73] The rest of the division followed on foot.[74] The Eighth

Army after-action report describes the success of this tactic: "So rapid was our advance that the enemy had neither the time nor the presence of mind to detonate mines they had previously prepared along the route of march. Consequently, demolished bridges did not slow our advance until we reached [the town of] of Imus."[75]

At 1000 hours on 4 February 1945, Eichelberger had reached Imus and was moving with the forwardmost elements of the 511th Parachute Regiment. The main highway bridge at Imus had been destroyed by the Japanese, and an alternate crossing bridge, 500 yards to the west, was heavily defended. However, the 511th with Eichelberger leading soon found a small crossing site and destroyed the Japanese positions from the rear.[76] Eichelberger's emphasis on speed in this action almost cost him his life, as he recorded in his diary: "[I] moved forward to the south end of the bridge and was pinned down by sniper fire which could not be located."[77]

After this action the 511th Parachute Regiment pushed on toward Manila. Eichelberger again positioned himself at the most dangerous and crucial point of the operation, as evidenced by the following diary entry: "I continued on down the road keeping abreast of the leading elements until [we] reached Las Pinas."[78] The speed of this attack continued to surprise the Japanese. The 11th Airborne after-action report stated that "once again the Japanese were found asleep, and the Las Pinas bridge was secured before the demolitions were set off."[79] The 511th had reached the southern suburbs of Manila and continued their drive until 2130 hours, when they were halted by well-prepared Japanese positions at the Paranque bridge. By 4 February the 11th Airborne had traveled 45 miles and had reached Manila.[80]

During this operation Eichelberger seemed to be everywhere at once. After the 511th Parachute Regiment crossed the Las Pinas bridge, Eichelberger found that the truck shuttling system was not functioning properly; therefore, he "returned to Tagaytay Ridge to do what [he] could about speeding up this advance."[81] The next morning Eichelberger again displayed great personal courage and moved with the advance elements of the 511th Parachute Regiment across the Paranque bridge. However, this was the end of the rapid movement by the Eighth Army. The Americans had reached the Genko-Line which had been designed to protect Manila from an attack from the south.[82] The Genko-Line was held by the Japanese 3rd Naval Battalion. Robert Ross Smith, the U.S. Army official historian for this campaign, described the 3rd Naval Battalion position as "the strongest in the Manila area, having the virtue of being long established. Reinforced concrete pillboxes abounded at street intersections in the suburban area south of the city limits, many of them covered with dirt long enough to have natural camouflage."[83] Against these positions, the 11th Airborne was able to move only 2,000 yards in two days.[84]

On 7 February 1945, Eichelberger received word from MacArthur that the 11th Airborne would soon come under the Sixth Army control. Eichelberger departed Luzon before Manila was captured, on 9 February 1945, in order to prepare for the southern Philippines campaign.[85]

MacArthur had two reasons for ordering Eichelberger to conduct the Nasugbu landing, and Eichelberger had successfully accomplished both of them. The official objective was "to disrupt the Japanese lines of communication [and] create a diversion to support the main landing at Lingayen [by Sixth Army]."[86] However, Eichelberger understood that MacArthur had another motive: "I realize that placing me with a small force south of Manila was the MacArthur way of stirring up Krueger into action and speed. He succeeded when the newspapermen reported that troops that had been able to go only yards a day had begun to go miles after hearing that I was en route."[87] Eichelberger's estimate of the Sixth Army was verified by an eyewitness; Major General William C. Dunckel wrote Eichelberger: "When you were pushing on Manila so rapidly, I visited Sixth Army Headquarters and found them greatly agitated over the fact that you would be in Manila before they were, and I believe to this day that we could have saved more of Manila if they had given you the means to come in by way of Nasugbu."[88] The result of MacArthur's prodding of General Krueger, Eighth Army's siphoning of Japanese troops from the north of Manila, and General Krueger's jealousy of Eichelberger was that by 4 February 1945 the Sixth Army had two divisions, the 1st Cavalry Division and the 37th Division, on the outskirts of Manila.[89]

In 104 hours, Eichelberger had pushed his troops 45 miles from Nasugbu to Manila. He had once again salvaged the tactical situation for MacArthur.

In the 41 years that have elapsed since World War II, the difficulties encountered by MacArthur in the Southwest Pacific have been glossed over and in some cases all but forgotten. His victories have been made to seem automatic. This is terribly unfair to the soldiers who fought for MacArthur. He had problems in the Southwest Pacific and his victories were far from automatic. In three cases, Buna, Biak, and Manila, his reputation as a brilliant strategist was almost tarnished. In each case he called on Lieutenant General Robert Eichelberger to salvage the situation. Eichelberger never failed him. A combination of innovative tactics, personal courage, and commonsense leadership made Eichelberger an effective, trusted field commander.

## NOTES

1. Eichelberger was 6'1" and weighed 190 pounds. R. Eichelberger to E. Eichelberger, 13 January 1944 and 3 April 1945. Contained in the Eichelberger Papers, Duke University, Durham, North Carolina.
2. Fred Brown to R. Eichelberger, 4 August 1961. Eichelberger Papers, Duke University; Jay Luvaas, *Dear Miss Em: General Eichelberger's War in the Pacific, 1942-45* (Westport, Conn.: Greenwood Press, 1972), p. xiv.
3. Robert Eichelberger and Milton MacKaye, *Our Jungle Road To Tokyo* (Washington: Zenger, 1949), pp. 21-23. The division was the 32nd Infantry.
4. Ibid., pp. 18-19.
5. Luvaas, p. 58; D. Edwards to R. Eichelberger, 11 January 1943, Eichelberger Papers.

6.   Eichelberger and MacKaye, p. 101.
7.   Ibid.
8.   Eichelberger and MacKaye, p. 138; Harold Riegelman, *Caves of Biak: An American Officer's Experience in the Southwest Pacific* (New Yord: Dial, 1955), p. 137.
9.   D. Clayton James, *The Years of MacArthur, Vol. II, 1941-1945* (Boston: Houghton-Mifflin, 1975), p. 453.
10.  George Kenney, *General Kenney Reports: A Personal History of the Pacific War* (New York: Duell, Sloan and Pearle, 1949), p. 289; James, p. 459; Luvaas, p. 125.
11.  R. G. 407-201-2: B. 3028, "G-2 Summary of the Biak Operation: 27 May-29 June 1944," p. 2, Federal Research Center, Suitland, Md., hereinafter cited as "G-2 Summary of Biak."
12.  James, p. 458.
13.  Spencer Davis, "Slaughter on Biak," *Australia Newsweek*, 12 June 1944; Eichelberger Papers.
14.  "G-2 Summary of Biak," pp. 2-4, 7-9; Robert Ross Smith, *Approach to the Philippines* (Washington: Dept. of the Army, Office of the Chief of Military History, 1953), p. 299.
15.  "G-2 Summary of Biak," p. 9.
16.  Ibid., p. 4.
17.  Ibid., p. 5; Davis; Eichelberger Papers.
18.  Eichelberger and MacKaye, p. 139; Smith, *Approach*, p. 325.
19.  Smith, *Approach*, p. 341.
20.  James, p. 459.
21.  Davis; Eichelberger Papers.
22.  James, pp. 459-60.
23.  Walter Krueger, *From Down Under to Nippon* (Washington: Combat Forces Press, 1953), p. 101.
24.  Allied Forces, Southwest Pacific Area, "I Corps History of the Biak Operation," p. 3; Eichelberger Diary, 14 June 1944, Eichelberger Papers.
25.  Eichelberger Diary, 15 June 1944; Eichelberger Papers.
26.  Ibid., 16-17 June 1944.
27.  R. Eichelberger to W. Krueger, 16 June 1944; Eichelberger Papers.
28.  W. Krueger to R. Eichelberger, 17 June 1944; Eichelberger Papers.
29.  Eichelberger and MacKaye, p. 146.
30.  Allied Forces, "History of the Biak Operation," pp. 5-6; Eichelberger Papers.
31.  Ibid.
32.  Smith, *Approach*, pp. 368-69.
33.  Eichelberger and MacKaye, p. 146.
34.  R. Eichelberger to E. Eichelberger, 19 June 1944, Eichelberger Papers.
35.  Riegelman, p. 142.
36.  Smith, *Approach*, p. 372.
37.  Eichelberger Diary, 19 June 1944; Allied Forces, "History of the Biak Operation," p. 8; Eichelberger Papers.
38.  R. G. 407: 341-INF(186)-0.1 B.10641, pp. 25-26, Federal Records Center, Suitland, Md.; Allied Forces, "History of the Biak Operation," p. 12; Eichelberger Papers.
39.  James, p. 460.
40.  R. Eichelberger to E. Eichelberger, 3 June 1944, in Luvaas, p. 135.
41.  Krueger, p. 218.
42.  Ibid., p. 225.
43.  Ibid., pp. 227-28.
44.  Robert Ross Smith, *Triumph in the Philippines* (Washington: Dept. of the Army, Office of the Chief of Military History, 1963), p. 94.
45.  James, p. 625.
46.  Smith, *Triumph*, pp. 96-97.
47.  Ibid., pp. 240-41.
48.  James, p. 631.
49.  Eichelberger Diary, 23 January 1945; Eichelberger Papers.
50.  Smith, *Triumph*, p. 212.
51.  Ibid.
52.  Eichelberger Diary, 23 March 1945; Eichelberger Papers.
53.  "Report of the Commanding General, Eighth Army, on the Nasugbu and Bataan

Operations," p. 9. Robert Eichelberger, "The Amphibious Eighth," p. 4, both contained in the Eichelberger Papers.

54. "Report After Action with the Enemy Operation Eikevi, Luzon Campaign, 31 January-30 June 1945," p. 3. R. G. 407: 7.311-0.3 Box 7583, National Records Center, Suitland, Md. Hereinafter cited as "Operation Shoestring."
55. Smith, *Triumph*, p. 14; "C.G. Report on Nasugbu and Bataan," p. 14; Eichelberger Papers.
56. Eichelberger, "Amphibious Eighth," p. 4; Eichelberger Papers.
57. "Operation Shoestring," p. 1.
58. Ibid.; Eichelberger and MacKaye, p. 190.
59. Eichelberger Diary, 31 January 1945; Eichelberger Papers.
60. "Report of C.G. Nasugbu and Bataan," foreword; Eichelberger Papers.
61. Ibid.; R. Eichelberger to E. Eichelberger, 20 June 1944, Luvaas, p. 133.
62. "Operation Shoestring," p. 1.
63. "Report of C.G. Nasugbu and Bataan," pp. 6, 16; Eichelberger Papers.
64. Eichelberger and MacKaye, p. 190.
65. R. Eichelberger to E. Eichelberger, 2 February 1945, Luvaas, p. 208; "Operation Shoestring," p. 2.
66. "Operation Shoestring," p. 2.
67. "Report of the C.G. Nasugbu and Bataan," p. 16; Eichelberger Papers.
68. Ibid.; 'Operation Shoestring," p. 2.
69. Eichelberger and MacKaye, p. 194; "C.G. Report on Nasugbu and Bataan," p. 6; Eichelberger Papers.
70. "Operation Shoestring," p. 2.
71. Ibid., p. 3.
72. Edward M. Flanagan, *The Angels: A History of the 11th Airborne Division, 1943-1946* (Washington: Infantry Journal Press, 1948), p. 76; Eichelberger Diary, 3 February 1945, Eichelberger Papers.
73. "Operation Shoestring," p. 3.
74. Ibid.
75. "Report of the C.G. Nasugbu and Bataan," p. 22, Eichelberger Papers.
76. Ibid.; Eichelberger Diary, 4 February 1945, Eichelberger Papers.
77. Eichelberger Diary, 4 February 1945, Eichelberger Papers.
78. Ibid.
79. "Operation Shoestring," p. 4.
80. Ibid.; "C.G. Report Nasugbu and Bataan," p. 22; Eichelberger Papers.
81. Eichelberger Diary, 4 February 1945, Eichelberger Papers.
82. "Operation Shoestring," pp. 4-5; "C.G. Report Nasugbu and Bataan," p. 24; Eichelberger Papers.
83. Smith, *Triumph*, p. 265.
84. Ibid.
85. Eichelberger Diary, 7-9 February 1945, Eichelberger Papers.
86. "Report of C.G. Nasugbu and Bataan," foreword; Eichelberger Papers.
87. Eichelberger Dictations, 4 November 1960; Eichelberger Papers.
88. Major General Bill Dunckel to R. Eichelberger, 3 March 1945; Eichelberger Papers; James, p. 634.
89. James, pp. 632-33.

This article appeared in the autumn 1986 issue of *Parameters*.

# 11

# General William Hood Simpson: Combat Commander

By THOMAS R. STONE

In late March 1945, Lieutenant General William H. Simpson focused the efforts of his U.S. Ninth Army, now numbering more than 300,000 troops, on the impending crossing of the Rhine.[1] Ninth Army headquarters, smoothly managing the buildup for the crossing, was no longer the green organization that had become operational in France the previous August. As General Omar Bradley observed after the war, Ninth Army had been "ambitious and impressively eager to learn,"[2] and it had achieved success after success in battle on the Continent. Simpson and his now combat-seasoned senior staff officers had brought Ninth Army to maturity.

Simpson's skills as an army commander, though not highly publicized during the war, were recognized by many senior officers, including General of the Army Dwight D. Eisenhower. In *Crusade in Europe*, Eisenhower wrote that he was aware of no mistake the Ninth Army Commander had made. "He was," in General Eisenhower's fitting words, "the type of leader American soldiers deserve."[3]

Controlling an organization as diversified as a field army is difficult at any time, but under combat conditions the challenge is especially great. At Ninth Army headquarters, General Simpson set the tone, and under the close supervision of his Chief of Staff, Brigadier General James E. Moore, headquarters functions were conducted according to well-established Army principles. Many on the staff at army level and in subordinate units had attended the Command and General Staff School, and it was ensured that the lessons learned at Leavenworth were followed in practice.[4]

That this system worked has been attested to by Ninth Army soldiers of various ranks. Major General Robert C. Macon, whose 83d Infantry Division served in several armies, recalled after the war that he had had a problemless relationship with the Ninth Army staff, while a former sergeant recollected that once his division joined Ninth Army he received patrol instructions early enough to plan, an advantage he had not enjoyed when his division was in two other armies. Another veteran of service in several armies,

Brigadier General John H. "Pee Wee" Collier of the 2d Armored Division, also remembered Ninth Army for its preeminently smooth operation. Of course, Simpson's subordinate commanders and his staff officers did not always see eye-to-eye, but when a disagreement did arise—as, for example, when the Army G-3 changed a corps boundary during the advance to the Rhine—Simpson and Moore saw to it that the problem was resolved in a professional manner.[5]

Ensuring that the efforts of this large army staff were unified and that subordinate units received proper support required careful coordination. Staff conferences were held virtually every morning; at these, Simpson and his key officers were updated on the military situation, following which the Commander gave appropriate guidance. Often problems raised or actions discussed during the briefing would cause Simpson to adjust his plans for the day. General Simpson was easy to brief. Even-tempered and composed, he refrained from interrupting and allowed the briefer to complete his presentation before questions were asked.[6] Following the regular staff meeting, Simpson often met with his air commander and G-3 to discuss air support plans. When artillery ammunition was short, the artillery officer joined the group.[7]

General Simpson and other properly cleared officers also routinely received Ultra briefings in which decoded material from intercepted German messages was presented. Following analysis of such intelligence for the ground forces, a representative of the XXIX Tactical Air Command would discuss the air situation. After the first Ultra briefing, General Simpson talked to those present concerning the need for absolute secrecy. Reminders were issued occasionally, and there were no reportable security breaches.[8]

While formal briefings were important, informal discussions also contributed to the feeling of camaraderie and mutual understanding which marked the Ninth Army staff. Each evening at about 1800 hours, General Moore assembled his G-staff and his deputy for a half-hour informal look at what had happened during the day and what was on tap for the next. Routine actions, which would eventually reach Moore's desk through the papermill, were not discussed; rather, this early evening meeting was reserved for an airing of important decisions the staff officers had made during the day. Moore wanted to be fully involved, not only so that he could answer any questions that might arise, but so as to be able to respond to General Simpson's insistence on being kept up to date on key staff matters.[9]

Later, the senior staff members would join the Commanding General at the evening meal. On occasion, a unit commander in from the field would be a part of the group. The atmosphere was cordial, with the conversation serving not only to keep Simpson and Moore informed, but also helping to tie the staff together. Simpson's junior aide, Major John H. Harden, recalled that the informal atmosphere of these gatherings permitted the airing of matters that would ordinarily not come to an army commander's attention.[10]

After dinner, another officer would come in and update the group on the war situation. The Army Commander would then telephone each of his corps commanders to see how things were going and to ask them how they felt about what was expected to take place the next day. It was generally his practice then to discuss the calls informally with a small group, usually the Chief of Staff, G-2, G-3, G-4, and sometimes the Deputy Chief of Staff. Later, to relax, General Simpson might watch a movie or talk with a visiting USO artist; then he would take a brisk walk, perhaps review the situation map maintained in his quarters, and retire for the night.[11]

The staff worked together to implement Simpson's directives, keep him informed, and handle routine duties. More was involved than office work, since the Army staff officers, often headquartered far from the scene of combat, made frequent trips to units closer to the front as well as to higher and adjacent headquarters. While forward, they not only observed the situation, but also saw for themselves the problems faced by their counterparts in subordinate units. These visits were encouraged by the Army Commander. Simpson believed that staff officers should center their attention on activities one and two echelons below. Thus, the focus of Ninth Army Staff officers was on the corps and division level, though smaller units were often visited as well. Such visits allowed staff officers to resolve some problems on the spot and pass others along with vital information back to Ninth Army headquarters. Further, as General Simpson well realized, the mere presence of Army staff officers in the forward area demonstrated to those assigned to subordinate headquarters that the Army staff cared about them and their troubles.[12]

Planning was a major staff function, of course, and both Simpson and Moore stressed that regular military staff planning procedures be scrupulously followed. Simpson usually discussed each major mission, such as the attack to the Roer River or the crossing of the Rhine, with the Army Group Commander before a directive was issued. When the mission arrived. Simpson would give only general guidance. The staff then set to work preparing an estimate of the situation. Heads of each staff section directed study of their appropriate areas, with the engineer making a terrain analysis, the G-3 preparing possible courses of action, the G-1 and G-4 calculating whether the plans could be supported with sufficient men and material, and special staff officers making comments when appropriate.[13] All but about three courses of action were normally discarded.

As had been taught at the Command and General Staff School, early in the planning sequence the staff took a careful look at the final terrain objective and at what operations would probably have to be conducted after its seizure. With the probable subsequent objective in mind, troop dispositions were envisioned and whenever possible plans were designed so that each operation would end with troops properly disposed for a rapid kickoff of the succeeding attack. Swift, deep, and decisive combat was habitually planned for and anticipated; provisions were always made to exploit success. As a means for Simpson to influence the action at critical battle junctures, a division was normally kept in Army reserve. When the reserve was committed during an operation, it was reconstituted by withdrawing a tired division from the line.[14]

Viewed from the perspective of those close to the battle, Simpson's insistence on detailed preparations paid great dividends. "Pee Wee" Collier recalled that Simpson's operations were well known for their perfect timing.[15]

Simpson was a great believer in the necessity of adequate logistical support, and before he approved any plan he wanted to ensure that it could be supported. Consequently, the G-4's contribution was a key factor in all planning. When the staff work was completed, the finished product was briefed to the Army Commander, who usually approved the staff recommendation.[16]

Key to the successful operation of this system was the relationship between the Commanding General and his Chief of Staff. Simpson and Moore had worked together in several units, and they understood, trusted, and admired each other. Moore usually could anticipate Simpson's reactions, while Simpson gave Moore a great deal of latitude. Often when Simpson was in the field, Moore would issue orders in the commander's name, then tell Simpson later. So closely did the two work together that in many instances it is impossible to sort out actions taken or ideas conceived. Moore was an intelligent, thorough, dedicated, and loyal staff officer; he well complemented General Simpson, a down-to-earth troop leader.[17]

Simpson was careful to enhance Moore's position by using the staff through the Chief. When the Army Commander was in his office, he either passed his guidance and questions through the Chief or had Moore sit in on his discussions with staff officers. Both Simpson and Moore realized that just as there could be only one Army Commander, only one man should be in charge of the staff. Thus, even when Simpson was contacted by another general officer—for example, when Brigadier General Sibert, Bradley's G-2, called concerning personnel changes in the Ninth Army G-2 section—Simpson referred him to Moore. The team of Simpson and Moore was extremely effective, earning the respect and praise of those with whom they worked.[18]

General Simpson had the knack for eliciting the best from his staff, and working for him was enjoyable in many ways. He let staff officers do their jobs, appreciated and praised good performance, and provided encouragement as necessary. When he spoke with staff officers, his understanding smile led them to feel that he was interested and was sincerely listening. Though even-tempered, and never a ranter or raver, he could make his displeasure plainly known when necessary. Armistead D. Mead, Simpson's wartime G-3, remarked that there was "an iron fist in the velvet glove." Mead recalled, for instance, a time when Simpson became enraged and pounded a table so hard that everything on it was flung into the air. This uncharacteristic demeanor was in response to one of his division commanders who had been offering excuses about why his unit was not advancing. Simpson's order to the division commander was unambiguous: "Get off your tail and get out there and command your troops. I want you on your objective before nightfall.'' Mead remarked that the officer "was running when he grabbed his helmet, moved out from his CP, and was on his objective that night."[19]

Much of Simpson's time was spent visiting subordinate units. He was concerned about the welfare of his troops, realizing that soldiers in the front lines would often not be aware of the work being done to solve the problems they faced. Without any theatrics, he moved about the Army area asking questions. He listened closely to his soldiers when they talked about their problems, but he did not overreact. His standard reply was that he would look into the situation, and he *would* later do so. His aide made notes; when Simpson returned to his headquarters, he and his aide discussed their trip with the Chief of Staff. General Moore saw that staff action was initiated when necessary, but more often than not he was able to tell General Simpson of work that was already being done to resolve the various problems.

By moving in this deliberate manner, Simpson benefited from the broadest of perspectives. He could make decisions based on what he thought was best for the entire Ninth Army and at the same time ensure that staff efforts were focused where he and Moore thought they should be.

Mead later summed up Simpson's ability to deal with the staff:

> General Simpson's genius lay in his charismatic manner, his command presence, his ability to listen, his unfailing use of his staff to check things out before making decisions, and his way of making all hands feel that they were important to him and to the army. . . . I have never known a commander to make better use of his staff than General Simpson.[20]

Staff officers can make plans and see that war material is available when needed, but it is the combat elements which must ultimately close with and defeat the enemy. During heavy fighting Simpson felt that he needed to maintain a perspective of his entire front and be easily available by telephone or radio in case a critical decision had to be made. Thus, he believed he could do the most good by working through his corps and division commanders. He did understand the front-line situation, of course. Aside from his own front-line visits, his service in the Philippines in 1910-12, in Mexico in 1916 as a member of Pershing's Punitive Expedition against Pancho Villa, and as a divisional staff officer in World War I, when he won the Silver Star, had given him a feel for the situation of the infantrymen and tankers who were daily in face-to-face contact with the enemy. While assuring that the Ninth Army attained its objectives, he took great care to see that battles were won with a minimum of casualties. His guiding principle seemed to be: "Never send an infantryman where you can send an artillery shell."[21] Whenever Simpson visited the front, his presence had a noticeably positive effect. In fact, when it seemed to Moore and Mead that an advance of a couple of miles was needed from a somewhat sluggish division, they would suggest that the "old man" drop in for a visit—and that method never seemed to fail.[22]

Simpson's corps commanders actually directed the tactical battle, and his relations with John B. Anderson (XVI Corps), Alvan C. Gillem, Jr. (XIII

Corps), and Raymond S. McLain (XIX Corps) were exemplary. General Simpson routinely solicited the views of each of his corps commanders, then gave due attention to their thoughts before final orders were written. When he was planning an operation, Simpson would explain his concept early, frequently orally, so that as much time as possible was available for discussion and corps-level planning. True to American preference, he told his subordinates what he wanted accomplished, then left it up to them to devise a way to attain the objective. During the corps planning process, small conferences between corps and army level officers would be held. Once all corps plans were prepared and submitted to Ninth Army Headquarters, Simpson convened a larger conference at which he and his corps commanders discussed and modified plans as necessary. By so intimately involving his subordinate commanders, he hoped that they would accept the plan as partly their own. His system worked. Brigadier General I. D. White, who commanded the 2d Armored Division, recalled: "When the orders were finally issued, each subordinate commander felt a compelling personal interest to effectively carry out his assignment."[23]

Much like a head football coach and his assistants work out a game plan, Simpson, his corps commanders, and sometimes his division commanders wargamed an upcoming operation so that they could anticipate contingencies and agree on what action should be taken in each case. Before troops were committed to battle, Simpson wanted mutual understanding, maximum preparation, and resolution of difficulties. In recalling Operation Grenade, during which Ninth Army crossed the Roer River and closed on the Rhine, Simpson described his method of operation: "I've often said that the way that fight developed and went on through until we reached the Rhine was very much like a series of successful football plays. These drives start way back and just keep going and pretty soon . . . touchdown. Everything went pretty smoothly and I think a large part of it was the result of my having three corps commanders in with my staff."[24]

Once combat began, Simpson kept a close watch on the situation. He made it a practice, however, not to interfere with a subordinate's conduct of the battle. Should an occasion arise which had not been foreseen in the planning sessions, Simpson was prepared to modify his plans or influence the action by using the resources he could summon. Corps commanders appreciated this flexibility and also Simpson's cool, calm manner of operation. When Simpson felt that things were not going as he wanted, he did not bypass a corps commander to give orders to a division or regimental commander, but worked through the senior commander.[25]

Reflecting after the war, Gillem expressed his recollection of how Simpson worked with his corps commanders:

> The relationship maintained between the Army commander and his corps commanders
> . . . was pleasant, very personal, understanding, and cooperative. I had a high regard for
> his professional ability, his integrity, his knowledge, and his general human qualities . . . .

He was eminently fair. . . . I could not wish for a more desirable relationship, both personal and professional. . . . He reflected the highest ideals of service and always respected the advice [of] his corps commanders. . . . General Simpson represented the type of leadership which inspired subordinates and stimulated all ranks to work with him and for him.[26]

Simpson's treatment of his Ninth Army staff and his corps commanders was influenced by his study of the successful command styles of leaders of previous wars. As a cadet at West Point, Class of 1909, he had read of Napoleon's counsel to study the great commanders of the past. Accordingly, Simpson had made it his practice to read military biographies.

Early in the war, for example, Simpson read Archibald Wavell's *Allenby: A Study in Greatness*. Reflecting on Allenby's performance during World War I, Simpson noted that the British General "didn't devil his staff to death. He laid down the general policy he wanted them to follow, gave them all instructions, and then let them go ahead and do it without sitting on top of them and trying to do it all himself, like lots of commanders do or have done."[27] Allenby had realized that it was impossible to achieve a maximum effort if the commander became immersed in minor details and tried to run everything himself. That Simpson learned these lessons well was evident in his dealings with his own staff.[28]

After Simpson took command of Ninth Army in 1944, he was given a copy of Douglas Southall Freeman's *Lee's Lieutenants*. The son of a Confederate veteran himself, Simpson was an instinctive admirer of Lee, and his admiration had grown through the years as he learned more about the Virginian. One of Lee's techniques particularly impressed Simpson, who observed: "After he got going and had a pretty good team of corps commanders, he gave them orders and it was up to them to perform the duties. He only intervened when it was necessary."[29]

Simpson's manner of command was also shaped by the lessons he had learned in nearly 35 years of commissioned service. When he was a staff officer in the 33d Infantry Division in World War I, for example, Simpson noted how General John J. Pershing, immediately prior to the Meuse-Argonne offensive, visited each assaulting division to ensure that the attack plan was understood. Simpson, as Ninth Army Commander, did not feel that he had to visit each division, but he took pains through conferences and telephone calls to be absolutely sure that his subordinate commanders had no doubt in their minds concerning the army plan and objectives.[30] Wise in the ways of soldiers and soldiering, he tried to build the confidence of his subordinate commanders and ensure that they knew that everything possible was being done to support them.

Simpson's experience also helped him deal with a delicate security problem. When one of his corps commanders confessed to Simpson that he had violated security regulations during a telephone conversation, the army Commander paused to recall a similar situation in World War I. At that time, despite a clear no-patrolling order, a patrol from Simpson's division was in fact dispatched from which, embarrassingly, some soldiers were captured. When Simpson's division commander reported the incident, his senior considered that the act of candid reporting was reprimand enough and took the incident no further. Over 15 years later, Simpson did likewise in the case of his own corps commander, telling the offender that the incident was closed. That corps commander went on to give distinguished service throughout the rest of the war.[31]

This sincere, caring demeanor was a key to Simpson's ability to maintain rapport and elicit maximum efforts from his subordinates. Should a staff officer stumble during a briefing, Simpson attempted, without cussing or raising his voice, to draw him out. When it became obvious that an officer could not handle the pressure and would have to go, Simpson was known to arrange for the man to be admitted to the hospital, then quietly shifted to a job he could handle. Such an approach was appreciated, for while it was no secret that the officer was moved, he was spared the indignity of a highly prejudicial relief in combat. In at least one case an individual so treated later recovered to the extent that, during another assignment, he was promoted to the rank of general officer.[32]

Simpson proved that a senior officer can be sympathetic and feeling while still being a winner. And Simpson looked the part of a general; he was a self-confident, lean, and fit Texan, with a warm smile, a shaven head, and always a sharp-looking regulation uniform.

Though Simpson was not always highly visible and did not stand out as a personal spectacle in a theater where officers named Patton and Montgomery served, his quiet competence nonetheless became progressively more evident, as did the disciplined and orderly operation of the Ninth Army.[33] As a comparative late-comer to the ranks of high command in the European war, it took time for Simpson to win in the eyes of Bradley and Eisenhower the esteem enjoyed by the veteran commanders who had been in the thick of the fighting since Overlord. For example, when, just before the Battle of the Bulge, Bradley compiled for Eisenhower a list of officers who had contributed importantly to the war effort, he placed Simpson only 16th of the 32 mentioned.[34] But as the war progressed, Simpson rose to a far more imposing position.

In late August 1944, the Supreme Commander had told General Marshall that if Ninth Army was not committed soon, a corps commander experienced in handling large numbers of troops might be put in command in place of Simpson. Owing to the peculiarities of the prevailing system of promotions and billets, no provision had been made for the Ninth Army Commander to be a lieutenant general, so that Simpson held his three stars only tenuously. On 1 October, Eisenhower wrote the Army Chief of Staff recommending that Simpson be nominated to the Senate for confirmation in the grade of lieutenant general. If Marshall recommended Simpson, and if his recommendation was approved, the aberration would be corrected by an appropriate increase in the number of three-star billets.[35] In mid-January 1945, Marshall asked Eisenhower if he still felt that Simpson should be a lieutenant general. Eisenhower replied: "By all means. . . . He is excellent in every respect."[36]

On 27 January, Marshall, en route to the Yalta Conference, stopped at Marseilles to meet with Eisenhower. After that meeting Eisenhower prepared a memorandum in which he ranked 38 senior wartime general officers according to their contribution to the war effort. Simpson was listed 12th, preceded only by Bradley, Spaatz, Smith, Patton, Clark, Truscott, Doolittle, Gerow, Collins, Patch, and Hodges. In a column which called for outstanding characteristics or qualifications, Eisenhower wrote of Simpson: "Clear thinker, energetic, balanced."[37] Simpson was appointed lieutenant general on 6 February, and in early March Eisenhower wrote to Marshall that Simpson was one of only six officers whom he eventually planned to recommend for a fourth star.[38]

Thus, when Simpson moved on 10 March 1945 to München-Gladbach, the first Ninth Army headquarters site located on German soil, his superiors had come to a full realization of the net worth to the war effort of this unflashy but superbly competent officer. Nor was such recognition confined to Simpson's American comrades, for his value had become evident to Field Marshal Montgomery as well. Ninth Army was under Montgomery's operational command. On the same day that the army moved forward, Montgomery wrote to Simpson:

> I would like to tell you how very pleased I have been with everything the Ninth Army has done. The operations were planned and carried through with great skill and energy. It has fallen to my lot to be mixed up with a good deal of fighting since I took command of the Eighth Army before Alamein in 1942; and the experience I have gained enables me to judge pretty well the military calibre of Armies. I can truthfully say that the operations of the Ninth Army, since 23 Feb last, have been up to the best standards.[39]

Considering the letter's source, this was high praise indeed.

When Montgomery's letter was received, the Rhine still lay ahead and beyond it was the Elbe and Berlin. On 24 March, Simpson took his Ninth Army across the Rhine. Soon the dash into the heart of Germany began. By the time that General Eisenhower halted further advance, Simpson had his lead elements across the Elbe and was planning his move on Berlin.

Ninth Army had done its work well. William Hood Simpson's combat leadership, featuring a unique blend of strength and humanity, would remain a model for those who aspire to higher command.[40]

## NOTES

1. For more information about Simpson and his Ninth Army from arrival in England to the taking of the west bank of the Rhine, see Thomas R. Stone, "He Had the Guts to Say No: A Military Biography of General William H. Simpson" (unpublished Ph.D. dissertation, Rice University, 1974). A portion of this dissertation which deals with General Simpson's decision to postpone Operation Grenade has been published under the title, "1630 Comes Early in the Roer," in *Military Review*, 53 (October 1973), 3-21. The official U.S. Army history series, *United States Army in World War II: The European Theater of Operations*, contains much material concerning Ninth Army. Particularly important are Martin Blumenson, *Breakout and Pursuit* (Washington: Office of the Chief of Military History, 1961) for operations on the Brittany Peninsula; Charles B. MacDonald, *The Siegfried Line Campaign* (Washington: Office of the

Chief of Military History, 1963) for the movement into the line south of First Army, the shift to the north, and the November offensive; Hugh M. Cole, *The Ardennes: Battle of the Bulge* (Washington: Office of the Chief of Military History, 1965) for operations during the Bulge; and Charles B. MacDonald, *The Last Offensive* (Washingon: Office of the Chief of Military History, 1973) for the period from January 1945 to the reaching of the Rhine. Another valuable source is the committee-authored history, *Conquer, the Story of the Ninth Army, 1944-45* (Washington: Infantry Journal Press, 1947). *Conquer* is a comprehensive work and is, according to MacDonald, "one of the most objective of the unofficial histories" (*Last Offensive*, p. 136).

2.  Omar N. Bradley, *A Soldier's Story* (New York: Henry Holt, 1951), p. 422.

3.  Dwight D. Eisenhower, *Crusade in Europe* (Garden City, N.Y.: Doubleday, 1948), p. 376.

4.  Personal interviews with James E. Moore on 17 and 29 June 1971, with Armistead D. Mead on 9 June 1972, with Theodore W. Parker on 18 June 1971, and with Charles D. Y. Ostrom Jr. on 7 June 1972. Mead had been G-3 of Ninth Army; Parker, G-3 Operations Officer; and Ostrom, Ninth Army Ammunition Officer.

5.  Telephone interview with Robert C. Macon on 22 February 1972; personal interviews with John H. Collier on 27 April 1972, with Bernard J. Leu Sr. on 23 March 1973, with William H. Simpson on 23 June 1972, and with Moore on 30 May 1972; letter received from John H. Harden, undated (approximately 14 February 1972); MacDonald, *The Last Offensive*, pp. 174-75. Macon had been Commanding General of the 83d Infantry Division; Collier, Commanding General, Combat Command A, 2d Armored Division; Leu, a sergeant in Company I, 291st Regiment, 75th Infantry Division; and Harden, one of Simpson's aides.

6.  Personal interviews with Simpson on 23 June 1972, and with Rowland F. Kirks on 28 June 1971; letter received from Daniel H. Hundley, 14 February 1972. Kirks, as Chief of Combat Intelligence, G-2, had briefed Simpson almost daily. Hundley had been G-1 of the Ninth Army.

7.  Mead interview, 9 June 1972.

8.  Loftus E. Becker, "Use of Ultra by Ninth US Army," 27 May 1945, pp. 2-3, in *Reports by US Army Ultra Representatives with Army Field Commands in the European Theater of Operations* (n.p., n.d.) (copy in U.S. Army Military History Institute [hereafter referred to as MHI], Carlisle Barracks, Pa.); Ronald Lewin, *Ultra Goes to War* (New York: McGraw-Hill, 1978), pp. 245-46.

9.  Moore interviews, 29 June 1971 and 30 May 1972; Harden letter.

10.  Harden letter; personal interview with Maurice J. D'Andrea, 2 July 1971. D'Andrea had been Simpson's physician.

11.  Moore interviews, 29 June 1971 and 30 May 1972; Mead interview, 9 June 1972; Harden letter; letter received from George A. Millener, 4 February 1972. Millener had been Deputy Chief of Staff, Ninth Army.

12.  Personal interviews with Charles P. Bixel on 28 June 1971, and with Harry D. McHugh on 16 February 1972; Hundley letter; letter received from William E. Shambora, 17 February 1972. Bixel had been G-2 of Ninth Army from 22 May 1944 to 22 February 1945; McHugh had held several positions in Ninth Army, including commander of an infantry regiment; Shambora had been Ninth Army surgeon.

13.  Moore interview, 29 June 1971; Hundley letter.

14.  Mead interviews, 24 June 1971 and 9 June 1972.

15.  Collier interview, 27 April 1972.

16.  Personal interviews with Moore on 29 June 1971, with Simpson on 27 January 1972, and with Parker on 18 June 1971; letter received from Simpson, 12 August 1970; letter received from Parker, 8 April 1973.

17.  Personal interviews with Jacob L. Devers on 13 June 1971, and with Moore on 17 June 1971 and 30 May 1972; Millener letter. Devers, who commanded the 6th Army Group in Europe during World War II, was a West Point classmate and long-time friend of General Simpson.

18.  Personal interviews with Moore on 17 June 1971, and with Bixel on 28 June 1971; "Resume of Telephone Conversation between General Simpson and General Sibert, Time: 271040 Feb 45," General Simpson's Personal Calendar [prepared by General Simpson's aides—Simpson did not keep a regular diary], vol. IV, William H. Simpson Papers, San Antonio, Tex.; telephone interview with William A. Harris on 23 June 1971; letter received from Isaac D. White, 23 February 1972. Harris had been a member of the 12th Army Group G-3 Section. White, who had been Commanding General of the 2d Armored Division,

recalled that he had heard many war correspondents remark that Ninth Army Headquarters was the most professional of all army headquarters.

19.  Mead interviews, 24 June 1971 and 9 June 1972.

20.  Mead interview, 24 June 1971. Sources of comments on Simpson's visits to the field and relations with his staff are: personal interviews with Mead on 9 June 1972, with Moore on 17 June 1971 and 30 May 1972, with Kirks on 28 June 1971, with Perry L. Baldwin on 26 June 1971, and with John G. Murphy on 23 June 1971; Hundley letter; and John Toland, *The Last 100 Days* (New York: Random House, 1966), p. 98. Baldwin had been Inspector General, Ninth Army, Murphy had been the Ninth Army Antiaircraft Officer.

21.  Leu interview, 23 March 1973.

22.  Personal interviews with Simpson on 27 January 1972, 16 February 1972, and 23 August 1977; with Moore on 17 June 1971 and 30 May 1972; and with Harold D. Kehm on 25 June 1971. Kehm became G-2 of Ninth Army on 3 March 1945.

23.  White letter. Sources of comments on Simpson's relations with subordinate commanders are: personal interviews with Simpson on 16 February and 17 March 1972, and with Moore on 17 and 29 June 1971; Alvan C. Gillem Jr., letter to Louis Truman, 26 February 1954, Simpson Papers; Hundley letter; letter received from Richard W. Stephens, 25 March 1972. Gillem had been Commanding General of XIII Corps. Stephens had been Chief of Staff of the 30th Infantry Division.

24.  Simpson interview, 16 February 1972.

25.  Mead interview, 24 June 1971. Also, Gillem letter to Truman; letter received from Gillem, 8 June 1971; and personal interviews with Simpson on 17 March 1972, with Moore on 29 June 1971 and 30 May 1972, and with John B. Anderson on 23 June 1971. Anderson had commanded XVI Corps.

26.  Letter received from Gillem, 8 June 1971. Anderson remembered his experience as XVI Corps Commander as "the most pleasant service during my career" (letter received from Anderson, 30 May 1971). Raymond S. McLain, Commander of XIX Corps, died before the research for this article was begun. In a letter to Simpson, McLain wrote "I consider it a great honor to have been a part of the great Ninth Army, and I will always remember the kindness with which I was received by you and your staff and will always be sensible of the confidence and faith you reposed in me as Corps Commander of your great army" (Raymond S. McLain, letter to William H. Simpson, 23 June 1950, Simpson Papers).

27.  Simpson interview, 26 January 1972.

28.  Simpson interviews, 22 April 1971 and 26 January 1972.

29.  Simpson interview, 26 January 1972; "War Correspondent Frank Conniff's Interview with General Simpson for Press Release," filed with 27 February 1945 entry, Simpson's Personal Calendar, vol. IV, Simpson Papers.

30.  Simpson interview, 5 January 1971.

31.  Ibid.

32.  Personal interviews with D'Andrea on 8 August 1971, with Mead on 9 June 1972, and with Parker on 18 June 1971; Harden letter.

33.  Letter received from Robert H. York, 20 May 1972. York, a regimental commander in a division which had also been assigned to another army, remarked that though he never met Simpson, he could see Simpson's personality coming through.

34.  "Memorandum For: General Eisenhower, SUBJECT: List of Officers Contributing to War Effort," 1 December 1945, Omar N. Bradley Papers, MHI. Bradley's memorandum read: "The following list is submitted in accordance with your recent letter in which you asked me to submit to you a list in order of priority of those officers whom I considered had contributed the maximum to the war effort. I have placed certain officers who have had great opportunity to contribute to the war effort below others who have had less opportunity, because, reading over your letter carefully, I felt that that was what you wanted; in other words, a Corps commander who had less opportunity than an Army commander and still contributed much more when his opportunity is considered." The names on the list were: 1. W. B. Smith; 2. Carl A. Spaatz; 3. C. H. Hodges; 4. Elwood R. Quesada; 5. L. K. Truscott Jr.; 6. George S. Patton Jr.; 7. J. Lawton Collins; 8. L. T Gerow; 9. Mark W. Clark; 10. Harold R. Bull; 11. A. M. Gruenther; 12. W. B. Kean; 13. L. C. Allen; 14. Troy H. Middleton; 15. Alexander McC. Patch; 16. W. H. Simpson; 17. James H. Doolittle; 18. M. S. Eddy; 19. Wade H. Haislip; 20. Charles H. Corlett; 21. Jacob L. Devers; 22. Ira C. Eaker; 23. W. H. Walker;

24. Edward H. Brooks; 25. R. S. McLain; 26. Hoyt S. Vandenberg; 27. R. McG. Littlejohn; 28. John C. H. Lee; 29. C. R. Heubner; 30. Ernest N. Harmon; 31. Matthew B. Ridgway; 32. J. A. Van Fleet.

35. Letter received from Omar N. Bradley, 8 May 1971; Dwight D. Eisenhower, letters to George C. Marshall, 31 August and 1 October 1944, in *The Papers of Dwight D. Eisenhower*, ed. by Alfred D. Chandler (Baltimore: Johns Hopkins Univ. Press, 1970), IV, nos. 1925 and 2016; Simpson interview, 26 January 1972; John D. Horn, "War Diary," entry of 28 January 1945, John D. Horn Papers, Darien, Conn. Horn had been Simpson's senior aide.

36. Dwight D. Eisenhower, letter to Marshall, 14 January 1945, *Papers of Eisenhower*, IV, no. 2238. Marshall's message of 12 January 1945 is mentioned in n. 1.

37. Memorandum dated 1 February 1945, *Papers of Eisenhower*, IV, no. 2271 and n. 1. Eisenhower's meeting with Marshall is mentioned in Eisenhower's letter to Marshall, 9 February 1945, *Papers of Eisenhower*, IV, no. 2276. In this message Eisenhower explained that he had prepared a list of "outstanding" general officers, and that the list was composed after he had reviewed similar lists submitted by Bradley and Smith. He offered to send a copy to Marshall. The names on the list were: 1. & 2. Bradley and Spaatz (equal); 3. Smith; 4. Patton; 5. Clark; 6. Truscott; 7. Doolittle; 8. Gerow; 9. Collins; 10. Patch; 11. Hodges; 12. Simpson; 13. Eaker; 14. Bull; 15. Cannon; 16. & 17. Ridgway and Brooks (equal); 18. Walker; 19. Lee; 20. Gruenther; 21. Vandenberg; 22. Haislip; 23. Quesada; 24. Devers (Eisenhower had not definitely made up his mind concerning where to place Devers); 25. Eddy; 26. Rooks; 27. Crawford; 28. Larkin; 29. Weyland; 30. Norstad; 31. L. Allen; 32. McLain; 33. Littlejohn; 34. Fred Anderson; 35., 36., & 37. Huebner, E. Harmon, and J. A. Van Fleet (equal); 38. Nugent.

38. Horn, "War Diary," entry of 28 January 1945; "Orders, SEC/WAR DIRECTS," 7 February 1945, Simpson 201 File, Simpson Papers; Eisenhower, letter to Marshall, 2 March 1945, *Papers of Eisenhower*, IV, no. 2307. The six officers Eisenhower planned to recommend for promotion were Bradley, Spaatz, Devers, Patton, Hodges, and Simpson.

39. B. L. Montgomery, letter to Simpson, 10 March 1945, Simpson Papers. Eisenhower's forwarding letter to The Adjutant General for inclusion in Simpson's official record contained the following paragraph: "The commendation from Field Marshal Montgomery has been fully earned. In the entire operations of the Ninth Army, Lt. General Simpson has performed in a superior manner. This includes the operations for crossing the Rhine, just initiated yesterday" ("Memorandum to: The Adjutant General, United States Army," 25 March 1945; Eisenhower Papers 1916-62, James A. Ulio folder, Dwight D. Eisenhower Library, Abilene, Kans.).

40. General Simpson died at the age of 92 at Brooke Army Hospital in San Antonio on 15 August 1980. For a brief recapitulation of his life, see Wolfgang Saxon, "Gen. William Hood Simpson, 92: From Pancho Villa to World War II," *The New York Times*, 17 August 1980, p. 44.

This article appeared in the June 1981 issue of *Parameters* under the title "General William Hood Simpson: Unsung Commander of the U.S. Ninth Army."

# IV. THE ETHICAL DIMENSION OF LEADERSHIP

# 12

# Defining Character in Military Leaders

By PHILIP LEWIS, KARL KUHNERT & ROBERT MAGINNIS

To a degree that is often surprising to people outside the military, decisionmakers and planners in the armed forces have an abiding interest in the character and integrity of military leaders and their subordinates. The service academies view as one of their primary goals the development and reinforcement of high moral and ethical standards in future military leaders. The Army's basic leadership training manual, Field Manual 22-100, identifies character as an essential attribute of military leaders and includes an entire chapter on the definition, importance, and development of character.[1]

Character may also be an important component of combat readiness. British General Sir James Glover has argued that a man of character in peace is a man of courage in war. He goes on to tell us that character is "a moral quality that grows to maturity in peace and is not suddenly developed in war."[2] We share a similar developmental view of character. In this article we argue that character is an inner quality that develops over the course of one's life and that its development in adolescence and adulthood can be understood as progressing through three relatively distinct phases or stages. At the completion of each successive phase, there is an increase in a person's ability to reflect upon and disengage from a prior way of understanding the dynamics of human relationships. Each successive developmental shift enables the individual to view personal and organizational life from a broader and more encompassing perspective. This process facilitates both an increase in ethical decisionmaking and an ability to take account of more of the complexity of human and organizational experience in making decisions.

## Leadership and Character

The Army's leadership training and development efforts recognize that the requirements for effective leadership change as one advances in rank and responsibility. Recently, leadership experts have identified three distinct levels of leadership in the Army: direct-level leadership, senior-level leadership, and

121

executive-level leadership.[3] As one moves up through these three levels there is a relative decrease in the use of personal or direct leadership and a corresponding increase in organizational and strategic (conceptual) leadership. While the skills and knowledge required to make the transitions from direct to senior to executive leadership are many, we would argue that one vital component is the level of character development that has also occurred. In short, there must be changes in the inner qualities of the military leader that parallel and support changes in the leader's technical competence in order for him to function effectively at increasingly higher levels of leadership. Without these inner qualities, technically competent senior- and executive-level leaders will not be able to use their technical competence effectively.

Although the view of an individual's level of character development as a critical feature of leader effectiveness is an appealing one, attempts to promote character development have been handicapped by the absence of a coherent view of exactly what character is. Despite the fact that character is usually considered to be an inner quality of the person, until recently social scientists have had little to say about what it actually is or how it develops. Fortunately, in the past few years psychologists working at Harvard University have proposed a radically new way of looking at and understanding the development of the person, a way which we think provides a powerfully persuasive view of the nature of character and its development.[4] In this article we will present a brief summary of this new view and some of the conclusions from our research with Army and Air Force officers that illustrate it in the context of military leadership.

Most people readily recognize the presence of character when it is demonstrated in a person's actions. The account of the conduct of Second Lieutenant Cleo W. Buxton in the 34th Infantry Division during World War II provides one such example.[5] As a rifle platoon leader, Lieutenant Buxton indoctrinated his men with regard to their responsibility for prisoners; they searched prisoners to be sure they had no weapons, then protected them from those who might attack or injure them. Early in the fighting in Italy, his platoon captured three German soldiers. They were escorted to the battalion headquarters, where one of the prisoners refused to give his name, rank, and serial number (as required by the Geneva Convention of 1929). The battalion commander became angry and slapped the prisoner. The prisoner spat back. The commander was furious and ordered his troops to kill the three prisoners.

Lieutenant Buxton's men returned from battalion headquarters with this story. Buxton immediately walked back to headquarters, thereby risking charges of desertion in the face of the enemy. There he found the prisoners digging what appeared to be their own graves. Buxton confronted the battalion operations officer with the question, "What are the prisoners doing?" Told in effect that they were indeed digging their own graves, Lieutenant Buxton then engaged his superior officer in a heated discussion of national and Army values. Lieutenant Buxton later learned that the prisoners were not killed.

Unfortunately, our military history also includes instances where character and integrity did not prevail—witness My Lai in Vietnam. These lapses in moral and ethical decisionmaking have been attributed to a number of factors, including poor command climate, battle stress, and the callous nature of warfare itself. Whatever the external reasons may have been, it is also likely that the inner qualities of character, integrity, and moral courage (or their lack) were also implicated.

What is it in a person that enables him to demonstrate the sort of integrity and strength of character shown by Lieutenant Buxton? Surely it is important that one uphold the military virtues of loyalty (to one's unit and to the nation), personal responsibility, and selfless service. But how can we be sure that at times of extreme stress a person will act on these values?

## The Three Faces of Military Character

In our interviews with military officers, our emphasis has been on how and why each officer holds particular values and beliefs, with less emphasis on what those values actually are. In choosing to focus on the inner source of each officer's values rather than on the content of those values, we have been able to identify three distinct types of officers, all of whom may espouse the same values but who, under the surface, are strikingly different. The approach that enabled us to identify these different types of leaders was a structured interview focused on the deep structure of the personality, the internal frame of reference that each officer used to impart meaning to his experiences. Before attempting to clarify the nature of these critical character differences, let us glance at the three types of military leaders we have identified. Again, each type is defined not so much by what values he endorses as by the extent to which the individual is able to take a critical and disinterested perspective toward his own value system.

### *The Operator*

The first leader type we identified can be called "the operator." This label usually brings to mind a person who has a personal agenda which he pursues without any real concern for the welfare of others. People don't trust operators because they believe that the operator will go beyond permissible bounds to meet his own needs and also because they sense that operators can't really be trusted. Commonsense wisdom about operators is that they are secretly "looking out for number one" despite appearances to the contrary. In our opinion this negative view of operators is too narrow. In fact, our interviews suggest that many individuals who fit this personality type are positive, productive, and interested in being good military officers. For example, an operator could be very interested in keeping himself in top physical condition, helping his nine-year-old daughter earn a starting spot on the neighborhood softball team, and insuring that 90 percent of the transport vehicles under his command are combat-ready at all times. These are all acceptable goals in a military officer, yet the operator pursues them in a particular way, a way that reflects a characteristically one-sided view of the world. What distinguishes these officers is not that they have self-serving personal agendas. Rather, their critical attribute is that they can't take a perspective on their goals or agendas. And it is this inability to take a perspective on, to make secondary, their goals and agendas that leads to the operator's fatal flaw. *That flaw is an inability to internalize another person's perceptions of them.*

The ability to think about another person thinking about you is the basis of all the connections that people feel for one another, including such unifying experiences as mutual trust, loyalty, and even guilt. To use an old expression, you have to be able to put yourself in the other fellow's shoes before you can truly feel a connection to him. Operators lack this ability. The closest they can come to seeing the other guy's point of view is to realize that others may have their own separate agendas and goals. When the operator puts himself in your shoes, he is imagining or thinking about what your agendas are. He's trying to figure out what you are hoping to accomplish or get out of your joint situation. This will allow him to maximize his own payoffs. But what he can't do is think about how you may be experiencing or thinking about him. Lacking such empathy, the operator, in one very important respect, is not trustworthy. Trust for the operator means that if I help you get what you want, you'll help me get what I want. But trust is a great deal more than that for most of us. It's a commitment to doing what is necessary to maintain a certain feeling for one another, a feeling that is not directly connected to the accomplishment of individual goals. This is the way in which operators cannot be trusted; they are unable to be sensitive to shared meanings or shared perceptions. Real trust means being able to place confidence in the motives and actions of one another in the absence of external sanctions and rewards. That confidence occurs only with others who have gotten past a concept of relationships based on the exchange of mutually beneficial rewards.

Because of this lack of empathic ability, the operator is unable to participate fully in those collective processes that are so essential to effective leadership: mutual respect, team spirit, and mutual trust. One officer we interviewed who fit this pattern viewed his leadership role as consisting entirely of helping his subordinates identify personal goals that they could attain if they also took care of Army business (taking care of Army business was this officer's personal agenda). He was good at clarifying for his subordinates the consequences of their actions and specifying what was expected of them. Although he had done well in a staff position, he was much less effective when he was promoted to a position where he was in command of a combat unit. As a commander this officer seemed unable to inspire his men, and he never seemed able to capitalize on esprit de corps as a motivational tool. Although he did earn the respect of some of his men—owing to his determination and hard work—his own view remained that his men appreciated him because he was able to help them meet their own goals. Lacking was the deep bond of shared respect that can be so critical in combat situations. We labeled him an operator because of his single-minded focus on concrete payoffs (both his own and others') as opposed to thinking about how others were viewing him. This particular focus was the critical determinant of his identity as a military officer.

## The Team Player

Our second type of military officer is the one we refer to as the "team player." The team player's stock in trade is his connection to others. Unlike the operator, the team player is highly sensitive to how others *feel* about him. This contrasts with the operator, who is most concerned about what others will do to or for him. For the team player such actual outcomes or consequences are important only for what they reveal about how the actors feel about him. More accurately, what is critical for the team player is how people simultaneously feel about each other. Is there a special feeling? Do they perform out of a feeling of mutual respect? Is there a satisfactory degree of team loyalty?

Having this ability to engage in the world of interpersonal connections, the team player has some enormous advantages over the operator, who is effectively oblivious to the fact that a world based on mutual trust or loyalty even exists. True, the team player can use the concrete "You scratch my back and I'll scratch yours" strategy of the operator with his men. But he also can use his personal connections to them; that is, he can capitalize on their mutual feelings of trust, respect, or affection in the exercise of his leadership. If we think of the operator as solely a fastball pitcher, the team player has the advantage of also having a curve. He can use whichever pitch is going to get the job done. He has a broader perspective than does his operator counterpart. Whereas the operator is constrained to view the world as a place where everyone is out to get the best deal he can for himself, the team player sees another way that things often work. He understands that at times some people will forgo their individual interests to pursue group goals, achievement of which will engender shared trust and loyalty.

Despite the broader perspective and added power possessed by the team player in comparison with the operator, team players also have a critical flaw. *Team players are unable to take a perspective on their connections and loyalties.* They are, quite literally, prisoners of the ways in which they are viewed and experienced by others. Consider how one Army captain described his current assignment as a field instructor. In response to a question about what his reaction would be if his men thought he was a phony, he replied: "I'd feel rejected; I'd feel a lowered sense of self-worth because I base my sense of self-worth primarily on my ability to be real to my men. And even though I can rationally accept the fact that there are some men I just cannot lead, I still try, because you have to."

The team player doesn't decide to be a team player. He is one. Being part of a team is a basic part of the way he defines himself. He is the officer who, were he to "turn" as a POW, would do so by becoming a part of the enemy's team. He would never do it just for the personal gain. It's the operator, who defines himself in terms of his ability to accomplish his goals, who would defect purely because of the advantages he sees for himself.

Yet it is important to realize that team players are often seen as good officers. Listen to the following dialogue involving another Army officer whom we found to be a team player:

*Officer:* "For that time that I have a man, I'm responsible for him. No matter what I think of that man or what his background is, what his values are, I'm responsible to *make* him a better person."
*Interviewer:* "What makes you responsible?"
*Officer:* "Well, the position you're in as a leader. Those men are under your control, so you're responsible in that sense."

This officer espouses the somewhat appealing idea of responsibility to others. But, as this and other parts of the interview revealed, he was not able to allow others to take responsibility for themselves. He's not saying that he *takes* responsibility for his men. He says he *is* responsible for them. And why is he responsible? Not because of some personal conviction, but because of his position on the Army team.

## The Self-Defining Leader

If the operator is defined by his goals and agendas and the team player by his relationships with others, then our third type is defined by his personal commitment to certain internalized values and ideals. This is the officer who is able to forgo certain personal payoffs and, when necessary, risk the loss of his men's respect and affection to pursue actions that he is convinced are right.

Here is the officer whose sense of worth is self-determined. Unlike the operator, who depends solely on the accomplishment of certain goals to maintain his sense of worth, or the team player, who needs to feel accepted or at least respected by his men to maintain his self-esteem, the self-defining leader makes his own judgments about his worthiness. He is of the group in which Lieutenant Buxton would probably be classified. Buxton's actions in Italy seemed to be a function of his own deep commitment to humane values. He was able to risk loss of his own command and his place as a good junior officer because he didn't, ultimately, define himself either by the accomplishment of certain goals (as the operator does) or by being a good team player. Aware of these risks and pressures, he could, nonetheless, follow his own conscience. And this, we think, is what largely defines the person of character.

It is important to note that the pursuit of personal goals and a reverence for team play are not themselves discarded as one moves up the scale of development to become a self-defining leader. Obviously, all human beings do—or should—pursue goals and cultivate human connections. But the self-defining leader keeps these desirable human impulses in their proper perspective, always subordinating them to the dictates of his internalized sense of right and wrong.

## A Developmental Framework

Even if you have been able to recognize officers of your experience, partly or wholly, in the three officer types outlined above, you may find yourself thinking, "So what? How does this classification of different types of leaders equip me to be a better leader?" It wouldn't except for the fact that *the three types of military officer depicted represent successive stages in the potential development of every person.*[6] This being so, they have some important implications for the development of character in military officers and, more generally, for the development of leader effectiveness.

One important implication of the developmental view is that it provides a powerful way of understanding personality differences in those whom we lead, a view that permits the leader to look past the surface to the core of each individual's way of approaching and understanding himself and the world. For example, this view can help us understand why a focus on the team, team spirit, and team morale just doesn't work with some subordinates. It's not because they don't care about the rest of the unit. Rather, it's because they have not yet reached that phase of their own character development where they are able to understand and participate in the world of shared perceptions. To motivate these subordinates, the leader may have to appeal to their personal interests, not to their status in a mutually supportive unit. As another example, this developmental view can shed light on the agony of a junior officer who feels torn between loyalty to his men and loyalty to his family. If he is a team player, then he is literally caught between the conflicting demands of two interpersonal worlds that collectively provide his sense of identity. To tell him merely that he has to set priorities may be of no use to him at all, because the ability to set priorities in his connections to others (his men vs. his family) is exactly the developmental step he has failed to take. In the short run, it will be much more effective simply to help him find a solution to his dilemma that he can see as preserving his standing with both his men and his family. In sum, an appreciation of the psychological dynamics of the three character types may assist the commander in devising short-term leadership tactics tailored to the individual needs and peculiarities of his subordinates.

A second implication of the developmental view concerns the longer-range responsibility of leaders to promote character development and maturation. Leaders aspire to more than just getting others to follow. They also have a commitment to the character development of their subordinates. It's here that the developmental view has the most utility. It's not enough to be able to motivate the operator to be a good officer. We also want the operator to learn how to be a part of the shared commitment and mutual respect of a good combat unit, and we want him to be able to live by good military values in those rare situations where there are pressures to betray those values. Of course, one can't take an operator and make him a man of character directly. First, he's going to have to learn how to be a valued member of a team. Operators don't become self-defining leaders without first coming to an understanding of the world of mutual loyalties. When trying to inculcate military values, leaders who fail to recognize this fact may find their words falling on deaf ears.

Indeed, our view is that the only way to help subordinates grow is to tune into the way they currently view their world (i.e., as operators or team players) and then help them experience the limitations of that view. No single approach is going to work with all three types of subordinates. In dealing with self-defining leaders, the task becomes one of exploring the compatibility of Army values with the personal values they already hold dear. For the team player, the same approach would likely fail because team players, in one sense, don't have values that are wholly their own. The values of team players always turn out to be shared values, values that derive from their connection to, or membership in, a group—i.e., their own unit. And even though you can get the team player to embrace Army values by making those values the standards of his current reference group, you must remember that if the team player perceives a growing divergence between the interests of his own unit and those of the Army at large, the higher values are likely to be dropped. There's not the same risk with the self-defined leader because his values were developed personally through an internal process of character development. Only repeated personal experiences that call into question the validity of those values are likely to lead to their abandonment. No single event, however stressful, is likely to have such an effect, and so the self-defined leader can stand by his values despite enormous pressures to abandon them.

## The Next Step

In its ongoing efforts to prepare officers for leadership responsibilities at the direct, senior, and executive levels, we think it critical that the Army include training that focuses on the character development of its officers. As one progresses up the leadership ladder in rank and responsibility, his ability to disengage from immediate situational constraints is likely to become increasingly important. As a first step toward equipping senior officers with this ability, the Army should support research that explores the links between the officer's developmental level (operator, team player, or self-defining leader) and his peformance in critical decision-making situations. Also critical will be a careful exploration of how the officer's character interacts with his experience as he progresses through his military career. Though the outlines of our developmental view of character are now fairly well established, it remains to flesh out and refine this view in the context of devising specific training strategies to achieve desired results.

Meanwhile, we would caution against premature attempts to use this framework to select officers for promotion or other important assignments based on their developmental level. In the first place, assessment of an officer's developmental level can be complicated by exigencies of the moment. Thus, some situations demand leader behaviors (e.g., "You'll do it because I'm giving you a direct order!") that may not reflect the leader's highest level of functioning. In addition, the links between developmental level and performance in various leadership contexts have yet to be established. Still, we remain convinced that eventually such linkages will be established and will confirm what most of us have known in our hearts all along, that good leadership requires leaders who are persons of maturity, vision, character, and integrity.

## NOTES

1. U.S. Department of the Army, *Military Leadership*, Field Manual 22-100 (Washington: G.P.O., 31 October 1983).
2. Sir James Glover, "A Soldier and His Conscience," *Parameters*, 13 (September 1983), 53-58.
3. Cecil Calloway and Keith Kettler, "Leadership: A Multidimensional Framework," Excel Net Concept Paper 75-86, 1986.
4. Robert Kegan, *The Evolving Self: Problem and Process in Human Development* (Cambridge, Mass.: Harvard Univ. Press, 1982); Robert Kegan and Lisa Lahey, "Adult Leadership and Adult Development: A Constructivist View," in *Leadership: Multidisciplinary Perspectives*, ed. B. Kellerman (Englewood Cliffs, N.J.: Prentice-Hall, 1984); Robert Selman, *The Growth of Interpersonal Understanding: Developmental and Clinical Analysis* (New York: Academic Press, 1980).
5. Cleo W. Buxton, "Morality in Combat," *Command*, 17 (Spring 1975), 37-38.
6. We did not develop arguments in this article for our assertion that the three kinds of character represent successive stages along a developmental continuum. These arguments are set forth most cogently in Kegan, *The Evolving Self*. A longitudinal study is currently underway at Harvard to test the theory.

This article appeared in the summer 1987 issue of *Parameters* under the title "Defining Military Character."

# 13

# Doing What's Right: Shaping the Army's Professional Environment

By LEWIS SORLEY

Professional studies often include exposure to the ideas of the classical philosophers, and that is all to the good. It is important to know the ethical touchstones that have guided the great civilizations, the great societies, of the past. It is important to know that men have agreed upon standards of conduct, have established mores and sanctions to encourage observance of those standards and to punish transgressions against them, and have thus sought to determine the ethical character of their lives.

It is perhaps more important, with those studies as background, to think hard and seriously about the ethical standards that soldiers choose to guide their lives, both personal and professional. This is because there cannot be a lack of congruence between personal and professional standards, between the private man and the public man in value terms, without devastating harm to one's ability to perform professionally.

This essay concentrates on one further essential step—beyond understanding the great value systems that have guided men over the generations, and beyond establishing a commitment to a value system that will guide one's actions. It deals with the final, difficult, and all-important tasks of translating those values into guidelines for day-to-day activities and then, after adapting them and manifesting them in our own lives, teaching them to those who are entrusted to our leadership, and gaining their willing acceptance and ultimately their own wholehearted commitment to those same values.

This last step is at the heart of professional leadership. Such leadership is, in its essence, the task of establishing and transmitting values. Certainly there are many other desirable attributes of leadership. Technical competence, energy, physical bravery and moral courage, intellectual capacity, commitment—all these and more are undoubtedly desirable attributes of the successful leader. None of the great leaders, of course, has manifested all these in equal parts. Men are, after all, both fallible and infinitely diverse.

But these attributes, however important, are secondary to the capacity to set and impart values. Professionalism is, after all, the hewing to a set of values postulated as the ideal of performance in the profession at hand. It is important to remember, in thinking about these matters, that they all take place within a given cultural and societal context. Thus what constitute the canons of ideal professional behavior for the leaders of American soldiers in the 20th century may vary substantially, even radically, from the imperatives to which other leaders, at other times, were expected to respond.

Thus I argue that the essence of professionalism is character. Character may be defined as the commitment to an admirable set of values, and the courage to manifest those values in one's life, no matter the cost in terms of personal success or popularity. One writer referred to "those hard outcroppings of character that determine a life." It is no accident that one of the key phrases in the prayer taught to cadets at West Point concerns the need to "choose the harder right instead of the easier wrong."

Now "those hard outcroppings of character," as I understand them, refer to those key situations—ethical crises, we might say—in which we have the opportunity to stand up and be counted, to weigh in on the side we believe to be right, regardless of the consequences. Such crises, fortunately for us all, only seldom confront us. But that does not mean that we are only rarely faced with the necessity to manifest values in our daily actions. Quite the contrary, as I see it. Virtually everything we do has a value component to it, and—whether we like it or not, whether we realize it or not—we are revealing our values, and teaching our values to others, in an almost constant stream of words and deeds throughout each day.

This realization is both daunting and encouraging. It means that we carry an enormous responsibility as leaders, perhaps greater than we ordinarily realize (and here I am not speaking of the self-evident heavy burden of those who lead troops in combat). It means that we are constantly being observed, and our actions are constantly being assessed, by those we lead (and, of course, by our seniors and our peers as well). The dean of George Washington University's business school once observed, tellingly, that "management is one of the performing arts." He was quite right, and the corollary is that the leader, or manager, is never off stage. But while that is a heavy responsibility, it is also a magnificent opportunity. It means that literally hundreds of times a day the leader has an opportunity to touch the people he comes into contact with, and to shape their approach to duty and responsibility.

One of our finest soldiers, Lieutenant General Arthur S. Collins, Jr., wrote a superb book called *Common Sense Training*.[1] In it he pointed out how virtually everything a unit does in the course of a day may be used for training by a wise commander. And it was not just training in specific techniques or tasks he had in mind, but indoctrination in such fundamental attributes as discipline, patriotism, responsiveness to command, initiative, and unit cohesion. General Collins held that training is all-encompassing, with the result that "individual training is designed to improve the whole person." "Improve the whole person"—think of it, and what that says about the trainer (the leader) and his responsibility to set and impart values.

A shared commitment to professional values, and to service, transcends the individual and constitutes the basis for our Army's corporate persona, its central values. We teach these values to our young leaders, who in turn inherit a responsibility to see that they are preserved and passed on. In this way we maintain the continuity and solidarity of our profession.

When new officers leave their basic schools and training centers and enter the Army at large, they have a major adjustment to make. Things are different, and radically so, in this larger world, where practice takes over from theory. They must be prepared to go out and deal with the problems which those differences can cause, differences which have the capacity to undermine the very essence of the Army—its ability to carry out its mission. An important part of being prepared to deal with such differences is understanding just how much influence a leader can have.

Most men, it seems to me, are inherently neither good nor evil. Each has within himself the capacity for actions that are admirable or reprehensible. What brings out the best or worst in us is often the organizational climate in which we find ourselves. In the Army there are units and posts that, at particular times and under particular commanders, come close to living up to the ideal standards to which we aspire. There are others which fall lamentably short.

It is not that the one post or unit happened to have assigned to it a high proportion of principled soldiers, while another had many of lesser quality. Rather it is that in one case the leaders were able to build an environment supportive of the kind of behavior (in ethical terms) they professed to want, while others elsewhere failed to do so (and perhaps even failed to understand their responsibility for doing so). The late General Bruce C. Clarke, a renowned Army commander in Europe in the early days of the Cold War, told his commanders that "the outstanding officer is the one who gets superior results from average soldiers." There is much wisdom in that. There are units in the Army which, because of the high priority of their mission or other factors, get more than a fair share of the talent and assets the Army has to pass around. But most units get a representative cross-section of talent, and do a better or worse job of making use of it.

What this brings us down to is building an environment in which people (soldiers) are encouraged and enabled to live up to the highest standards of professionalism. The Army's declaratory policy on ethical standards has always been of the highest order. Its operational policy, unfortunately, has not always matched those high declaratory standards. Perhaps the best example is the distortions of the body count as a measure of operational success in Vietnam, a measure widely acknowledged even by senior commanders to be both corrupt and corrupting. In that case our operational standards failed to come up to our declaratory ones, and the integrity of the whole enterprise suffered as a result.

Many similar problems come up in the course of professional service. But there are many practical things that the individual leader can do to enhance the climate for professionalism. Some of the most important are these:

• First, and by all odds the most important, is to set the example in terms of personal and professional conduct by demonstrating commitment to the highest standards of professionalism and diligent efforts to live up to those standards.

• Second is communicating to all subordinates what your standards are, and that you expect them to live up to those standards as well. Be sure that they understand what you mean, and what you expect; then help them appreciate how that translates into day-to-day behavior.

• Third is ensuring that the professional environment (to the extent you have any control over it) is supportive of ethical behavior, and not supportive of behavior that is ethically flawed. This entails ensuring that in all aspects of your leadership (evaluation of subordinates, competition with other units, methods of motivating subordinates, etc.) you operate in a way that encourages and rewards ethical behavior on the part of your subordinates, and discourages unethical behavior (by not rewarding and, where necessary, punishing it).

• Fourth is recognizing that you have more control over the professional environment than you may realize. If you communicate your commitment of high standards to your fellow officers, they will be more likely to respect those standards in their dealings with you. If you form alliances with like-minded peers, the solidarity of your joint commitment to high standards can improve the organization's professionalism. If you detect unethical practices, and devise other—more acceptable—ways to get the mission accomplished, you can change undesirable patterns of behavior. If you are generous in recognizing highly professional performance, even (or especially) on the part of those with whom you are in professional competition, you can build new bonds of shared commitment to high standards. And if, when it may become necessary, you stand up to be counted in refusing to compromise your standards, you set an example that seniors, peers, and subordinates alike can take counsel from.

Undeniably, there are risks in such a course of action, especially if the command of which you are a part is not at the moment distinguishing itself in terms of professional behavior. No one could possibly argue that adherence to ethical standards, and the responsibility to leaven the officer corps in terms of its ethical norms, is free of risk, or even easy. It is just essential.

It is as simple as that. Doing what is right yourself, teaching what is right to your troops, and encouraging all with whom you come in contact (including peers and seniors) to do what is right—that is what we are training officers to do, what the Army needs them to do, and what the nation relies on them to do. On this all else depends.

134       *Lewis Sorley*

## NOTES

1.  Arthur S. Collins, Jr., *Common Sense Training: A Working Philosophy for Leaders* (Novato, Calif.: Presidio, 1978). General Collins retired from the Army in 1974 and died in 1984.

This article appeared in the March 1989 issue of *Parameters*.

# 14

# Ethics and the Senior Officer

By CLAY T. BUCKINGHAM
© 1985 Clay T. Buckingham

Army officers are devoting a lot of thoughtful consideration to the subject of ethics. The purpose of this article is to present a firsthand appreciation of various ethical tensions that confront senior Army officers. To accomplish this I will briefly explore the foundations of our ethical system, offer some thoughts about how this ethical system should apply specifically to the military profession, and finally take an empirical look at the tensions in the military society that provide fertile grounds for ethical abuses.

The term ethics is used to mean the study of human actions in respect to their being right or wrong. Whether we like it or not, ethical reflection has seldom been carried out in isolation from theology. Ethical values generally reflect our view of human life as it is embodied in the teachings of the prevailing religion, because all human conduct, essentially, takes place in relationship to other human beings. Therefore, if I believe that human life, that is, *all* of human life, without exception, has equal and infinite value, then my concept of right and wrong conduct will reflect this conviction. If I believe that human life has limited value, let's say limited by what it can contribute to the common good, then my concept of right or wrong conduct will reflect this conviction. If I believe that some forms of human life have more worth than others—that, say, males are more valuable than females, or whites are more valuable than blacks, or Americans are more valuable than Cambodians, or the rich are more valuable than the poor, or Jews are more valuable than Arabs—then my concept of right and wrong conduct will reflect whichever of these convictions I hold.

Our Western value system of right and wrong is based primarily on what Jesus taught concerning the origin and value of human life, augmented by the Old Testament lawgivers and prophets. This is what we commonly call the Judeo-Christian tradition. Although these teachings have been eroded and in some cases prostituted radically through the centuries, they still strongly influence the attitudes of Americans and other Westerners and form the core of our ethical concepts. In the Judeo-Christian view, man was created by God in

135

His image; that is, with awareness, with purpose, with personality, and with inherent worth. All forms of human life are equally endowed by God with worth and dignity. There is no distinction between male and female, between black and white, rich and poor, aristocrat and peasant, Americans and Cambodians, Jews and Arabs, old and young, born and unborn, smart and dumb, with regard to inherent worth and dignity. All are created with equal dignity, with equal status, and with equal rights within the human race.

From this basic belief has come the thesis that whatever protects life is good, and whatever destroys or degrades human life is evil. Thus, our whole moral and ethical concept of right and wrong stems from this thesis-antithesis of good and evil, and I believe that we cannot consider right and wrong within the military profession outside of this framework; that whatever protects and enhances life is good, and whatever destroys and degrades life is evil. The great concepts of justice, mercy, compassion, service, and freedom are immediate derivatives of this central distinction between good and evil as received from our Judeo-Christian heritage.

Before addressing ethics within the military profession, I will deal briefly with the ethical basis for our profession. The moral justification for our profession is embedded in the Constitution—"to provide for the Common Defense." We are that segment of the American society which is set apart to provide for the defense of the remainder of that society. The word defense is key. We are to defend our territory, because that is where our people live, but in an expanded sense, we are defending our value systems, our way of life, our standard of life, our essential institutions, and whatever our government declares to be our national interest. Our Founding Fathers were realists. They knew that most of the rest of the world did not share our view of the value and worth of human life. They recognized that we lived in and would continue to live in a dangerous world, one in which only the strong, or those allied to the strong, can remain free. Only the strong can influence whether peace will be preserved or broken, because strength deters aggression and discourages conflict, and weakness invites aggression and encourages conflict.

Those who provide for the common defense, who protect the lives of our citizens, can best do so by creating a stong, effective deterrent to would-be aggressors. As military people our objective is "not to promote war, but to preserve peace" and to protect life. Even if deterrence fails and we go to war, our final objective is peace. Ours is an honorable profession with an ethical purpose entirely consistent with our basic view that whatever protects and enhances life is good.

I will now turn to ethics as they specifically apply to the military profession. In essence, professional ethics is that body of written or unwritten standards of conduct by which that profession disciplines itself. One writer said, "Professional ethics are designed to assure high standards of competence in a given field." In the general case, then, that conduct which contributes to the attainment of the purpose of that profession is good. The conduct which detracts from the attainment of the purpose of that profession is bad. Various professions have adopted either written or unwritten codes. Doctors, nurses, engineers, journalists, lawyers, businessmen—all have established standards of right and wrong for their respective profession. For instance, the written code of Hippocrates states that the medical profession is dedicated to the preservation of life and should be of service to mankind. Certain practices inimical to that goal are forbidden in the Hippocratic code.

In the military profession we do not have an all-inclusive code of ethics, although we do have documents which contain broad and compelling standards of professional conduct. Some would say that the West Point motto of "duty, honor, country" is all that we really need. But those values, as good as they are, do not give a conceptual basis for their implementation. What is duty? What is honor? What do we mean by country? Lieutenant Calley probably considered that he was doing his duty at My Lai. Our code of conduct for POWs sets forth right and wrong conduct under those limited but extremely trying conditions. Can we think of the Oath of Allegiance as a document of ethics? It is—of sorts. "I will support and defend the Constitution of the United States against all enemies foreign and domestic." That sounds great. But whose interpretation of the Constitution? The latest Supreme Court decision? And who are those domestic enemies? Anyone who disagrees with our interpretation of the Constitution? And what is the role of the Department of Defense in fighting domestic enemies? I thought that was the role of the FBI. And further, the Oath states, "I will obey the orders of the officers appointed over me." Well, yes, assuming they're legal, assuming they're consistent with my moral standards.

But back to my earlier statement: If that conduct which contributes to the attainment of the purpose of the profession is good, and that which detracts from the attainment of the purpose of that profession is bad, then for the military profession, whatever enhances the common defense essentially is good, and whatever diminishes the common defense is essentially bad. But this must be tempered by the larger issue, that whatever protects and enhances human life is good and whatever destroys life or diminishes the quality of life is bad.

This consideration leads, of necessity, to a brief discussion of means and ends. I think it should be an absolute rule among military people that ends do not justify means. Nor that means justify ends. Both ends and means must be consistent with our fundamental values. Honorable ends cannot be achieved by dishonorable means, nor do honorable means justify dishonorable or unethical ends. Although the general welfare of our nation is an honorable and ethical purpose, the selective elimination of nonproductive members of society, although it would contribute to the general welfare, cannot be tolerated. Domestic tranquility, although an honorable purpose, cannot justify police brutality or unlawful detention. Common defense is an honorable purpose, but misrepresentation of an enemy threat before a congressional committee cannot be justified by the belief that it is necessary in order to acquire funding for an important weapon system.

So can we make any general rules for ethical conduct within the military profession? I think so. Essentially, what is right is that which enhances the accomplishment of our basic purpose, the common defense, provided that it is consistent with our overall view of the value and dignity of all human life and that the means to accomplish it are acceptable. Or, ask these questions: Does the action we are about to take or the policy under consideration contribute to the national defense? Is it consistent with the protection and enhancement of life? Are both ends and means consistent with our national values?

Given these thoughts, I will now turn to the empirical aspects of the subject, the tensions within the Army which provide fertile grounds for ethical abuse. All military officers have experienced these tensions, and they will continue to characterize the environment in which senior officers will serve. The higher the position, the more complex and less precise are the issues. The last job I really understood was being tank platoon leader in combat. As I progressed upward, the ethical environment became more murky, less clear, less subject to specific rules and simple solutions. However, an officer's usefulness to the nation and overall credibility will be fundamentally affected by his ability to enter an environment where absolutes are hard to find, and still make wise and ethical decisions. These tensions will require of the senior leader a bedrock of ethical values.

The one tension that will be most consistently with the officer involves the ethical use of authority. The authoritarian structure of our profession, even though essential, is the natural breeding ground for the unethical use of authority. The power and influence of a colonel are greater than that of a lieutenant colonel. The influence of a general officer is truly awesome. This fact requires a clear understanding, first, of the meaning of rank.

Within our hierarchical, authoritarian structure, there are various levels of responsibility. Each level of responsibility is assigned a commensurate degree of authority. Rank is simply a badge of the authority vested in a person to carry out a specific level of responsibility. Company-level responsibility requires company-level authority, and the rank of captain is associated with that level of authority. So lieutenant colonel rank represents the authority necessary to carry out battalion-level responsibilities; colonel, brigade-level responsibilities; major general, division-level responsibilities. When authority is used in the fulfilling of responsibility, it is used legitimately and ethically. When authority is used for purposes not directly associated with carrying out assigned responsibilities, it is being used illegitimately and unethically. Conversely, if I fail to use my authority to carry out my responsibilities, my negligence is itself unethical, and someone who will use that authority should be given my job. The question is: Am I using my authority, my rank, fully but solely for the purpose of carrying out my responsibilities?

As one goes up in rank, those of lower grade tend more readily to assume that he is using his authority legitimately and ethically, because of the high regard with which juniors hold very senior officers. Thus, the general who directs his pilot to arrange a flight plan on an authorized TDY visit so as to remain overnight at a city not specifically on the most direct route, so that the general can visit his mother who is in a nursing home, will be assumed by the pilot to be fully authorized to do so. The Pentagon colonel who calls an action officer in from leave because the colonel thinks his general might ask a question which the action officer is best qualified to answer will be assumed to be using his authority ethically. Think about that.

This gets to the guts of the use of authority. In my opinion, one of the most widespread and patently unethical uses of authority is the exploitation and degradation of subordinates, which is a generally accepted institutional practice. It is an encouraged institutional practice, and it is wrong. We have fostered the image of the successful leader as the one who doesn't get ulcers, but gives ulcers; as the one who is hard, unfeeling, even vicious.

Some may disagree, but I think that is true. Whom do we admire? We admire the man with "guts." What do we really mean by this? We mean the man who drives his people hard, who has the reputation for firing subordinates, who goes for the jugular, who works his people 14 hours a day, and who takes his objective in spite of heavy and possibly unnecessary casualties. We set these people up and idolize them. Even in industry. We like the kind of guy who moves in as the CEO and fires three-fourths of the vice presidents the first week. He gets things done! He's got guts! But what about the perceptive, cool-headed leader who takes a group of misfits and molds them into an effective, highly-spirited team? Or the colonel who can see the great potential of a young commander who is performing only marginally and, through coaching and encouraging, turns him into a first-rate performer? Or the leader in combat who takes his objective with no casualties? Or the brigade commander who has the guts to resist the arbitrary, capricious order of a division commander to fire a faltering battalion commander because the colonel believes that with the proper leadership that battalion commander can be made into a successful one? Or the Pentagon division chief who defies the norm and refuses to arrive in his office before 0730, or to require his action officers to do so, and who manages the workload of his division so that every man gets a reasonable amount of leave, seldom has to work on weekends, and gets home every evening at a reasonable hour?

We seldom hear about those people. We don't hold them up as examples as we should. The higher we go, the more important it is to be careful that our impact on the lives and careers and families of our subordinates is positive and not negative. I can think of a division artillery commander in Germany who ruled by fear, who was hated by his subordinates, and who was the proximate cause of a number of serious domestic crises. I can think of a lieutenant general in the Pentagon who purposely intimidated his subordinates and associates in order to get his own way. I can think of a colonel, the executive to a former Chief of Staff, who blossomed like a rose to his superiors, but who was vicious, demeaning, and bullying to his subordinates. I can think of a colonel in the Pentagon who never showed appreciation and voiced only criticism and whose subordinates gradually became discouraged and frustrated and unproductive.

In contrast, I can think of an Army lieutenant general whose modus operandi was to make his subordinates successful in their jobs. He said, "I'll have no problem with my job if I can make all of my subordinates successful." I think of a division commander in Germany with whom I was closely associated, who spent countless hours talking with subordinates at every level, coaching them, encouraging them, teaching them. I think of a Pentagon division chief who looked for opportunities to push his action officers into the limelight, who volunteered them for prestigious positions as secretarial-level "horse-holders," who worked in the background to cross-train his people so that no one would ever have to be called back from leave, who personally took the rap when things went wrong, and who, in my opinion, ran the best division in the Pentagon. It all gets back to how they looked at people, their value, their dignity, their fundamental worth, their potential.

The higher you go, the easier it is to misuse authority. The checks that we were subject to as junior officers become less evident and less compelling. We gradually begin to believe that we really don't need to seek the counsel of others. We are at first surprised by and then pleased by the freedom of action accorded us.

For instance: "I really have to visit Germany, but should I do so this winter? No, I'll wait until the weather's better. Let's see, where can I go this winter? I really need to visit Panama and Hawaii. Let's visit Panama or Hawaii this winter."

We begin to rationalize small personal indiscretions that we would never accept in a subordinate, like having our personal car worked on by a division mechanic during duty hours, or allowing our wife to bully the post engineer into refurbishing the kitchen of our quarters out of cycle. Sometimes we begin to believe that we are somehow above they law—they really didn't have a person of our status and responsibility in mind when they wrote it, did they?—and we divert funds, appropriated for barracks maintenance, to refurbish the interior of a rod and gun club, or piece several segments of minor construction money together to accomplish some major construction projects that were disallowed in the last appropriation cycle. These examples are taken from my personal knowledge. As a rule, and this is very important I think, general officers do not get relieved for incompetence. They do get fired for indiscretions, which is simply another way of saying that they've used their authority unethically.

A former Inspector General of the Army for whom I have great regard and who was, in a sense, the conscience of the Army for the four years that he was the IG, told me that at any one time about ten percent of the general officers in the Army were under investigation of some kind or another. Most of those charges turn out to be either false or simply a matter of perception, i.e. where the general did something which others perceived to be unethical but really was not. As General Creighton W. Abrams, Jr., once said, "The higher you go on the flag pole, the more your rear-end shows."

The second great tension involves the ethical use of military force. The higher you go the more you'll be called on to exercise judgment in this arena, although some with relatively moderate rank in key positions have great influence on such matters. For instance, a U.S. Marine Corps major on the National Security Council staff wrote the point paper that convinced the President to send Marines into Lebanon. The Weinberger-Shultz debates often fell into the category of this tension regarding the ethical use of military force. When should it be used? Under what circumstances? In what strength? In defense of U.S. territory only? Or in defense of U.S. interests? Or in defense of our allies? What are our interests? Grenada? Lebanon? The Straits of Hormuz? How about Vietnam?

Our involvement in Vietnam was purely ethical in the sense that the United States had no really compelling self-interest. We simply wanted to prevent 16 million South Vietnamese from becoming slaves to a totalitarian neighbor. But what about the level of force used? Was it ethical *not* to saturate-bomb Hanoi in an effort to force the North Vietnamese government to call off the invasion of South Vietnam? How about Czechoslovakia, Hungary, Afghanistan, the Iranian rescue operation? Should force be used only if there is a reasonable chance of effecting a desirable outcome? General Matthew Ridgway, then Chief of Staff, went to President Eisenhower in the summer of 1953 and personally talked him out of sending American ground troops to Vietnam after the French defeat at Dien Bien Phu at the hands of the Viet Minh. Was he more ethical or less ethical than the Chairman of the Joint Chiefs of Staff who failed to intercede ten years later to prevent combat troops from being sent into South Vietnam? Could *failure* to use military force in the defense of freedom be unethical? That's a good question

And what of the Bay of Pigs? Was it moral for the President to call off the air strikes at the last minute, thus practically insuring failure? Was it moral for the Chairman of the Joint Chiefs of Staff to agree to the calling off of those air strikes? Did the operation in and of itself have an ethical purpose?

And now today, what of the use of military power to accomplish our purposes in Central America? What are our purposes in Central America? Is the use of military force the only way to accomplish these purposes? If so, how much force? In what form?

In addition to these two prime ethical tensions, there are others that every senior officer will confront, although the forms might vary. I will briefly cite several. One ethical tension is that what is just and fair to an individual may conflict with a policy that attempts to correct long-standing injustice. One of the major problems here is that an open and frank discussion is not only discouraged but virtually impossible due to the emotionally explosive nature of the issue. I'm speaking of course about establishing quotas or their look-alikes for minorities and women in various selective processes like promotions, schooling, command, and other visible assignments.

Another ethical tension is loyalty to the organizational position or policy versus adherence to personal conviction when the two are in conflict. In testimony before a congressional staff, how can you present the OSD or Army position if you personally disagree with it? The same ethical dilemma confronts a Chief of Staff who personally disagrees with the President's chosen strategy. Another ethical tension involves the conflict between ambition and selflessness. What is legitimate ambition? We preach selflessness as a sterling quality of character and then we tend to reward ambition. It is ironic that one Chief of Staff who talked a lot about selflessness was, in his rise to that position, one of the most openly ambitious officers I know.

Another ethical tension is between people and mission. Does the goal of having combat-ready units justify neglect of families? Conversely, does the proper care and nurture of families excuse having noncombat-ready units? Can we achieve both? Should dependents accompany their sponsors overseas? Does it detract from readiness, or contribute to it? Is it ethical to separate families from their sponsors in peacetime under any circumstances? What are the effects of separating families? We've muddled through this one, perhaps not very successfully.

A final ethical tension involves the difference between honesty and deception. Decisions at every echelon in our structure are made based upon the information available to the decisionmakers. If that information is inaccurate or incomplete, the decision may well be faulty. The decision may be faulty even if the information is accurate and complete, but it is more likely to be faulty if the information is inaccurate and incomplete. Therefore, it is essential that information provided to our superiors, to our subordinates, and to our peers be accurate and complete. The oath of a witness in a trial to tell "the truth, the whole truth, and nothing but the truth" should be the oath of a professional officer.

This was brought home to me as a tank platoon leader in the Korean War. It was nighttime. The tank battalion of which I was a part had been heavily engaged during the day in support of an infantry regiment in a river-crossing operation. Now we were defending against a flank attack by a Chinese force on the near side of the river. There was a lot of mortar and artillery fire, including illumination and white phosphorus; many casualties; and general confusion. The friendly force was withdrawing and I ended up with my tank platoon fighting sort of a rear-guard action in pitch dark along a road. About the time I got my platoon past a certain checkpoint, I got a radio call from my battalion commander asking if I was the last friendly force to cross the checkpoint. Since we were in close contact with the advancing Chinese force, I said yes, we were the last. Shortly thereafter a long and intense American artillery barrage was laid down in the area I had just vacated. The next morning my battalion commander came to me in our assembly area. He told me he had called the artillery into that area because of my statement that I was the last unit out. In fact, I was not. A friendly infantry unit somehow had been intermingled with the Chinese force and had sustained casualties in the artillery barrage. Gently, but clearly, the battalion commander said, "Buck, you made me tell a lie."

I've never forgotten that. I had told him what I perceived to be true, but was not. I should have qualified my answer, explaining that in the dark and confusion I could report only that my tanks had crossed the checkpoint. That was the only thing I knew for sure. The rest was speculation. Many times since then I've been tempted to speculate beyond what I knew and was certain to be true and I have sometimes yielded to that temptation.

As DCSOPS of USAREUR during the Turkish invasion of Cyprus, I was reporting to CINCUSAREUR on the situation so far as we knew it. The actual invasion was of less importance to us than the threat to our nuclear weapons in both Greece and Turkey stemming from intense animosity by both sides toward Americans for failing to take a clear stand with either country on the invasion. I was discussing the threat to our nuclear weapons with CINCUSAREUR and unconsciously began to drift away from known facts into speculation about what might be true. The CINC looked squarely at me and said, "General, stop bugling. I can't make decisions on speculation. You're intermingling facts with possibilities."

In many situations at high levels of command, the issues of honesty and deception are not recognized as such. One of the most common deceptions is the exaggeration of need in order to get what is really needed, knowing that the initial request is certainly going to be reduced. Money is usually the object, at least in the Pentagon environment. In fact, the whole program budget procedure, in my view, is essentially deceptive and unethical. The annual requests for operations and maintenance funds come in from the major commands over four-star signatures claiming that the request is the bare minimum they can live with. The DA action officers in the planning and budgeting arena don't believe a word of it. They look at what the command got the previous year, do some puts and takes, and come up with their own figures. The whole process at the major command level was a waste of time, energy, and money. Commanders' statements are given about as much credence as a Dan Rather commentary on the objectivity of the news media. Then the Programming and Budgeting System, in crunching together the Program Objective Memorandum, inflates those requests which are the "pet rocks" of influential Pentagon pachyderms, and submits them to OSD knowing full well that OSD will cut some of these programs back, knowing they have been inflated by the Army. Of course, OSD may take the money thus "saved" and add it to other programs based on what some assistant secretary of defense perceives to be important, of what the current wind of opinion thinks will sell on the Hill and what won't.

Another blatantly unethical practice in the programming and budgeting arena is what I call the "multiple stampede effect." Newly assigned Lieutenant General A or Assistant Secretary A comes along with Project A which has been his obsession for years. It requires major multi-year funding. He forces it into the program, stampeding the appropriation directors to get on the team, and so the program is funded at the expense of other ongoing programs. Lieutenant General A is then promoted and made a MACOM commander where his influence in the central programming and budgeting procedure fades considerably. Now Lieutenant General B arrives on the scene with Project B, his personal "pet rock," and he is able to push his project through the Program Budget Committee and into the next year's Program Objective Memorandum. And where does the money come from? From Program A. So Program A and all the other Program A's are cut back to make way for Program B and all the other Program B's sponsored by the powerful new Lieutenat General B's who will be replaced the next year by Lieutenant General C's with their projects.

Thus we have programs by the dozens, originally spawned by the stampede effect of strong-willed, powerful proponents, which are distorted from their original purpose and deflated by inadequate funding, and flop around from year to year due to changes of emphasis and priority at DA level. The people assigned to manage these programs in the field never know from year to year what they can expect in the way of support. Over the course of my last 12 years on active duty, I was involved in the programming and budgeting procedure for ten of those years, eight of them at the DA level and two at the MACOM level. I used to leave Program Budget Committee meetings in the Pentagon feeling unclean, polluted, like I needed to go to confession. The whole system is wasteful of the money our citizens have entrusted to us for their common defense. And most of the senior programming and budgeting participants recognize this. Almost every year that I was in the Pentagon, the Director of PA&E or the Director of the Army staff or the DCSOPS or the Vice Chief of Staff vowed to implement reform and instituted new and different procedures—none of which, as of 30 June 1982, when I retired, had fundamentally improved the system in my opinion.

Another aspect of the honesty/deception tension involves readiness reports. First of all, even the most accurate unit readiness report is a deception unless it is considered in the context of the Army's capability to sustain that unit in combat. The tooth-to-tail, combat-support ratio debate is a case in point. Combat divisions in Europe with C-1 ratings give our national leaders a false sense of confidence if these divisions cannot be sustained in combat past the first few weeks. The readiness of the whole force is what is important. If you are in the force structure business you are contributing to a massive deception if you fail to provide adequate combat support and combat service support to our combat divisions. If you are in the programming and budgeting business you are contributing to a massive deception if you fail to program sufficient ammunition or repair parts to sustain our divisions in combat. The readiness reporting system is not and cannot be purely objective. Subjective judgment always enters in, but the intent, the motive, is what is important.

Consider a new division commander in Europe who has been in command about a month. His predecessor, a young, ambitious major general, is the new USAREUR Chief of Staff. The new division commander makes his assessment and gives his division a C-3 in training, a drop from C-2. As USAREUR DCSOPS, I review the reports. All the other divisions report C-2. I discuss the reports with the Chief of Staff. He takes strong exception to the C-3 rating of his old division, recognizing that if the report is accurate, his own leadership, judgment, and candor are in question. The Chief of Staff challenges the judgment of the new division commander, indicating to him that he's using an unrealistic standard to measure the training status of the division. The new division CG holds his ground. The Chief of Staff then questions the motive of the division commander, saying that he obviously wants to show a lower rating on his first reports so he can show improvement later on. The division commander holds his ground. The Chief of Staff then begins a subtle campaign to discredit the division commander in the eyes of the CINC. Time passes. The Chief of Staff moves rapidly on to a three-star job and is promoted to lieutenant general. The division commander, who is highly respected both by his peers and by his subordinates, completes his tour and transfers to a job in the Pentagon, and eventually retires as a two-star with 35 years of service. In retrospect, the division commander's subjective judgment on the training status of his division may have been too severe, although I do not in any way question his motive. As DCSOPS, I would have judged all divisions essentially the same in training. Maybe they all should have been C-3. Who was right?

The officer efficiency report system is even more complex. Here the ethical principle of fairness conflicts directly with the ethical principle of honesty. Am I being fair to my people to rate them honestly in accordance with the intent of the OER regulation when I know that across the Army my contemporaries are inflating the reports of their people? Am I justified in waging a one-man campaign for strict honesty when it comes at the expense of my people?

Another aspect of honesty involves what you show your boss when he comes to visit. Conversely, what you should be looking for when you visit your subordinates may be inferred.

The scene is Fort Hood. I am Chief of Staff of the 2nd Armored Division. The Army Chief of Staff is coming to visit the post and wants to see tank gunnery training in progress. Recently the division has received a large number of infantrymen rotating back from Vietnam combat duty. Department of the Army has directed us to convert these infantrymen quickly into tankers, and to integrate them into our tank battalions. Most of these Vietnam veterans have only a few months to go before leaving the Army. They are not at all interested in becoming tankers, and as a matter of fact, they're not really interested in anything but getting out of the Army. We have developed a strenuous, four-week TBT (to be tankers) program, which includes familiarization firing on ranges 1 through 5 of the tank gunnery course. The TBTs will be firing Table 4 main gun when the Chief of Staff visits. All indications are that they will be doing poorly, considering the extreme brevity of their preliminary gunnery training, their record on the subcaliber ranges, their general lack of technical aptitude, and their negative attitude.

A senior adviser suggests to the division commander that we should take our best NCO gunners and have them firing when the Army Chief of Staff visits the range. The point is made that an Army Chief of Staff usually visits any given division only once during the tenure in command of a division commander. Our division is a fine division. It has a good reputation. We have some great battalions. Field training has been going well. Maintenance is up. To show the Chief of Staff what we know would be subpar marksmanship will give him a distorted view of the overall standards of the division and will be a disservice to the Chief of Staff. An alternative is put forth. Why not simply change and reprint the training schedule with attendant back-dating, bringing one of our better-trained tank battalions off of maintenance cycle and putting them on the range on the day the Chief visits.

As division chief of staff, I opposed these proposals, stating that the Army Chief of Staff needs to know the trauma we are undergoing resulting from a DA decision to convert short-term Vietnam infantrymen into qualified tankers in four weeks. After all, I argued, the Chief of Staff is an experienced commander with a reputation for fairness and will understand our situation, and anyway, it would be deceptive to alter the training schedule and substitute training in which he might be more pleased. We owe it to him to tell it like it is, to show him what he needs to see, not just what he may want to see.

The division commander sides with me, and we make no special arrangements to change the schedule. The Chief of Staff visits the range. The outward appearance of the range—that is, the police, the ammunition stack, the communications, the flags, the condition of the tanks, the saluting, the uniforms—is superb. But the gunnery is atrocious. Few rounds hit the targets. Although the CG had carefully briefed him on the whole situation enroute to the range, the Army Chief of Staff is incensed. He calls the firing to a halt, dismounts the TBTs, the NCOs, the officers, and gathers everyone around him. He berates everyone for such a rotten example of gunnery, for the waste of ammo, for the poor NCO instruction, for inadequate officer supervision. Then he takes the CG aside, mercifully out of hearing of the troops, but in their full view, and proceeds to tear the division commander apart; he thereafter leaves the range without a single word of appreciation for anyone. The division commander is philosophical. "The Chief of Staff is in a foul mood today," he says. "Nothing would have pleased him. He is exhausted from a killing schedule. He has been under severe attack by the press in recent weeks. He will calm down and the whole episode will pass away."

The Army Chief of Staff never visited the division again during the CG's tenure of duty. And the CG, until then considered to be a rising star, eventually moved on to another major general's position, well out of the mainstream of the Army, from which he retired.

Before I left the division, the CG gave me a superb efficiency report, and I was selected for brigadier general just a year later. Was I right or wrong in recommending that we not change the schedule or substitute experienced gunners for the TBTs? Did my decision contribute to the common defense? Was it consistent with our basic value systems? It certainly ruined a great division commander's career, and the influence of his character and competence was lost to the Army. On the other hand, I got away unscathed, except for a deep sense of continuing sadness at what I had done to my boss.

In conclusion, I can give no easy answers regarding these ethical tensions. I can, however, from my experience, conclude that an officer's ethical framework for addressing each of them needs to address the three fundamental questions: Does the action contribute to the national defense? Is it consistent with the protection and enhancement of life? Are the means to accomplish it acceptable? Standing firm ethically can exact a cost, perhaps a steep one. As professionals, as leaders, as commanders, we must be willing to pay it.

This article appeared in the autumn 1985 issue of *Parameters* under the title "Ethics and the Senior Officer: Institutional Tensions."

# V. MILITARY LEADERSHIP—
# THE LARGER VISION

# 15

# The "Modern Major General"

By DONALD F. BLETZ

What will be the role of military force in future domestic and international environments? What will the U.S. military profession likely be called upon to do? In what sort of world will the military be called upon to do it? What kind of military professional will be needed to employ military force? The last question is the one which will be examined here. But to get to the last question, the first three must be considered in at least general terms. For it makes little sense to discuss the qualifications that a "modern major general" must possess, if what he is expected to do is not considered first.

Over a century ago, Sir William Gilbert and Arthur Sullivan produced the delightful light opera, "The Pirates of Penzance," a satire on the modes and mores of Victorian England. The title of the present article is borrowed from a song of that opera in which Major General Stanley sings happily and confidently that

> I am the very pattern of a modern Major-General,
> I've information vegetable, animal, and mineral,
> I know the kings of England, and I quote the fights historical,
> From Marathon to Waterloo, in order categorical;
> I'm very well acquainted too with matters mathematical,
> I understand equations, both the simple and quadratical;
> About binomial theorem I'm teeming with a lot o' news,
> With many cheerful facts about the square of the hypotenuse. . . .
> In short, in matters vegetable, animal, and mineral,
> I am the very model of a modern Major-General.

He continues, extolling the vast breadth and depth of his knowledge, and then admits graciously to some minor shortcomings:

> In fact, when I know what is meant by "mamelon" and "ravelin,"
> When I can tell at a sight a Chassepôt rifle from a javelin,
> When such affairs as sorties and surprises I'm more wary at,
> And when I know precisely what is meant by "commissariat,"
> When I have learnt what progress has been made in modern gunnery,
> When I know more of tactics than a novice in a nunnery,
> In short, when I've a smattering of elemental strategy,
> You'll say a better Major-General has never *sat* a gee—

151

For my military knowledge, though I'm plucky and adventury,
Has only been brought down to the beginning of the century;
But still in learning vegetable, animal, and mineral,
I am the very model of a modern Major-General.

The tragedy was not that Stanley was a well informed man, but that he was well informed only on matters that were irrelevant to his profession. The contemporary "modern major general" who does, in fact, know "more of tactics than a novice in a nunnery," but who fails to understand the role of military force in the affairs of state would make Stanley's shortcomings appear pale by comparison.

All of us can enjoy a laugh or two at the expense of the fictional Major General Stanley. Some serious reflection is in order, however, as we wonder how many Major General Stanleys may have been produced in our own armed forces, and what we would like our model modern major general to be.

In this article, the expression "modern major general" is essentially generic. It does not equate to a specific military rank but to a level of military professionalism that could include the ranks of lieutenant colonel/commander through general/admiral.

As a professional military officer progresses through his career from commissioning to the end of his service—some thirty or so years later—the tasks change that he can logically be called upon to perform. In the early years of his service, he may have to perform tasks that emphasize technical proficiency in a fairly narrow military skill—the "how to do it." As the officer continues with his career and has attained higher rank, the tasks he may have to perform emphasize professional competence on an infinitely broader scale. The mature professional's contribution to the nation is more in his understanding of the nature of military force and its utility and application in the overall domestic and international environments. The professional military officer, at both levels, is defined as the career officer who possesses the necessary education, training, experience, and intellect to carry out those tasks that he is likely to be called upon to perform.

At some imprecise time around mid-career (15-20 years of service), and probably slightly beyond, the tasks that the professional officer may be required to perform fall more into the second of the two levels identified above. It is within this higher level of professionalism that my modern major general is to be found.

It should be apparent that not all senior officers could expect logically to be required to perform precisely the same tasks. It is not logical for an Army brigadier general to expect to be assigned command of a carrier task force, or for a Navy rear admiral to expect to be given command of an army separate brigade or division. It is not at all illogical, however, for either of them to expect an assignment on the Joint Staff or on the staff of the National Security Council, to cite only two examples. Our military professionals are not normally called upon to perform the more technical military tasks for which they are not trained, but they are expected to be educated well enough so that they can range beyond their narrow military proficiencies in other areas.

What our modern major general should know will be examined from three points of view. What should he know about U.S. civil-military relations? What should he know about U.S. political-military relations? What should he know about the utility of military force in the evolving domestic and international environments?

## Civil-Military Relations

The term civil-military relations has both a broad and a narrow connotation; it is used here in the narrow sense to mean the relationship between U.S. domestic and military policies. This is the general area of interest of academicians who identify themselves with the sub-discipline of military sociology. The expression "the military in society" has appeared frequently in recent years in the titles of books and articles to describe the relationship of the military professional with the domestic social and political system of which he is a part.

It is important that our modern major general understands the constitutional and historical underpinnings of U.S. civil-military relations. He must appreciate the general historical distrust of the American body politic for regular military forces, and realize that this apprehension is rooted very deeply in our colonial heritage. While our modern major general may at times be distressed by the realization that his profession is not held in particularly high national esteem, he may find some comfort in the realization that, except in times of clearly perceived national peril, it never has been much appreciated. He might also reflect that if it were otherwise, it might be at the peril of the very democracy he defends.

The Vietnam experience has caused some of our military professionals to yearn for the "good old days" of World War II when returning military men were greeted as heroes by a grateful nation—not as villains or unthinking stooges who implemented what was to become an exceedingly unpopular foreign policy. Today's senior leaders fought in Vietnam, and somehow they long for the hero's welcome that was extended to another generation of military men. They also long for society to "understand" them, but this is unrealistic and naive thinking. To believe otherwise is to misunderstand democratic societies in general and American history in particular.

It is essential that the military professional understand the make-up of the society he serves, as well as the political system that the society has produced. While I do not feel it is true that the armed forces of the United States are a mirror image of American society—and I don't really believe they should be—I fully accept the proposition that the armed forces of any nation are more or less a reflection of the parent society.

One of the surest ways to acquire a lack of understanding of the political process is to fail to participate in it. In the past, many military professionals did not exercise their right to vote. Forty years ago this might have been attributed to the lack of absentee voting mechanisms in some states. Many officers, however, felt strongly that voting while on active duty was improper involvement in domestic politics, and they did not exercise their franchise even when the machinery existed to do so. I am convinced that far fewer officers now hold to this view.

The military professional cannot serve his society if he is not aware of its strengths and its weaknesses, its fears and its aspirations. He needs intelligently to be aware of the major social and political issues in the nation. He needs to know something about the problems of poverty, urbanization, pollution, education, minorities, the role of women, youth, law and order, and inflation, to name but a few. Creighton Abrams, the late Chief of Staff of the United States Army, was an example of the modern major general during a tense July in 1962 as the Army Chief of Staff's representative in Mississippi, when federal troops were standing by during racial unrest, and in May 1963 in Alabama. He earned a reputation as a remarkably perceptive, politically astute figure; and he won the acclaim of the highest officials in government and his military colleagues because, in addition to being a proven leader of men and an expert at the "management of violence," he proved in those exceedingly sensitive situations that he fully understood the society he served.[1]

We do not need many military professionals who are primarily sociologists, but we do need military professionals who understand the society of which they are a part. We do not need many military professionals who are primarily political scientists, but we do need military professionals who are sensitive to the political system they defend. Above all, we do not need military professionals who are politicians, but we do need military professionals who fully understand the dangers inherent in politicizing the military profession of a democracy. It is concern for this latter point that caused consternation among some military professionals when it was announced that General Alexander Haig would be recalled to active duty to assume the duties of Supreme Allied Commander, Europe. This, of course, after he had made the decision, only a relatively short time before, to retire from military service to assume a sensitive political post.

Finally, the military professional must fully understand the concept of civil control of the military as it is practiced in the United States. While there is no doubt that, at times, the military professional finds the control exercised by some civilian leaders to be less than inspiring, I have never heard a senior military officer even so much as question the concept. Civil control of the military is an accepted element of the American system, and it is fully and unquestionably accepted by the military professional. The last great test of the concept was the Truman-MacArthur controversy during the Korean War. If there ever was any real question about who was "in charge," it was settled quickly, for the general was properly relieved by his civilian Commander-in-Chief.

Civil-military relations have little meaning in isolation; it is their relationship with political-military affairs that gives them substance. Stanley Hoffman has pointed out that domestic legitimacy is essential if the armed forces of a democracy are to have any value as an instrument of foreign policy. He said, "An army which is domestically illegitimate can have no efficiency in international relations; precisely because we are dealing with democracies, there is no substitute for domestic support."[2]

While the legitimacy of the American military profession in the eyes of the body politic was eroded seriously by the war in Vietnam, there are ample indications that this has changed. In the frequent surveys among Americans today concerning their confidence in various U.S. institutions, the military is consistently rated among the leaders.[3]

The Vietnam experience provided an excellent example of a legitimate military establishment losing its public support because of its association with what became an extremely unpopular foreign policy. One might argue from another viewpoint, and suggest that an unpopular or illegitimate military establishment participating in the execution of even a popular foreign policy may turn the nation against that policy. A democracy must have a legitimate foreign policy, or both will suffer and likely fail. In Vietnam, it was probably the foreign policy that lost its legitimacy first, and, by association, the military became tarnished.

There are a number of very strong ties between a nation's foreign and domestic policies, and one of the most apparent is the acceptance of the military by society and its use as a legitimate instrument of foreign policy. Indeed, the key to successful civil-military relations is acceptance of the military by society. This is not necessarily love, affection, high esteem, endearment, adoration, infatuation, or any number of like expressions of fondness, but simple, practical acceptance as a legitimate instrument of national policy. The military professional, however, cannot hope to be understood and awarded legitimacy by society if he does not understand that policy.

## Political-Military Relations

As with civil-military relations, the term political-military relations has both a broad and a narrow connotation. Again, in this discussion the expression will be used in its narrow sense. It means the relationship between U.S. foreign and military policies.

Most of our 20th-century generals will claim acceptance of the Clausewitz dictum that war is but an extension of policy by other means. A few of them may even entertain the proposition that the reverse is at least equally true in the contemporary international environment, and that diplomatic policy is but an extension of war by other means. The first thought suggests that, in the final analysis, war deals with those issues that diplomacy failed to resolve. The second raises the proposition that diplomacy is the final arbiter and deals with those issues that war has failed to sort out. I would argue that the two thoughts are not mutually exclusive, but both are perfectly legitimate expressions of the relationship between diplomacy and military force. That relationship is more pronounced in today's environment, and political-military relationships are understood by a growing number of political and military leaders. The modern major general must fully understand that military force has no meaning as an end in itself, but takes on "legitimacy" only in the context of the political objective it is intended to achieve.

It now appears broadly accepted that the United States "lost" the war in Vietnam. But one modern major general—a senior one in this case—has stated categorically that this idea is ridiculous. He argued that we won the war militarily but lost it politically, and somehow this hocus-pocus seemed to satisfy him. The fact that the nation had not achieved completely the political objective it apparently sought, even though we had won the military battles, did not disturb him. He could not comprehend the idea that the only justification for the use of military force as an instrument of foreign policy is the achievement of some political objective. Although he is a senior military officer, he does not fit my concept of a modern professional.

The military professional has a valid question when he asks what foreign policy objectives he may be called upon to pursue, and in what international environment he may be required to use military force. Especially since the onset of the cold war, the American military profession and the civil leadership came to think in terms of the "threat." This was not only convenient but also it was eminently practical. In the bi-polar configuration that evolved after 1947, the threat was generally agreed upon and the unquestioned task of the American military profession was to defend against it. Commencing in the late 1940s and extending into the mid to late 1960s, there was a widely accepted political-military policy explained best by the word "containment." It can be argued with some persuasiveness that our involvement in Vietnam by the Kennedy-Johnson administrations in the 1960s was the last great surge of the containment policy. For practical purposes, the military establishment was domestically legitimate in implementing that policy.

In a very real sense, it was a simple world model from the political-military point of view. The threat was clear, and not only the need for military force but also the nature of that force was clear and broadly accepted. The American military establishment had legitimacy to spare. The world changed, however, and observers began to talk in terms of a multi-polar world with up to five major centers of power. Pentagonal models appeared and models of overlapping and intertwining triangles followed. The debate continues, and clearly will for some time, as to exactly what kind of international system we are likely to have. To the extent that anything resembling a consensus exists, it might be found in the proposition that the world is no longer bi-polar as it was considered for the past forty years, and that multi-polarity is quickly becoming a reality. It would seem, then, that we are somewhere in limbo between the comfortable (because we thought we understood it) bi-polar world and the uncomfortable (because we don't understand it) multi-polar world. The never-never land between the two is the terrain upon which some kind of a political-military consensus must be constructed. The military professional finds this ground uncertain and unsteady; the civilian policymaker finds it equally troublesome, while the public finds it even more difficult to comprehend.

It is indeed difficult to defend before the Congress a large military budget designed to maintain forces whose task is to cope with some unidentifiable threat centered on the unpredictability of an international system that cannot even be described in reasonably precise terms. A strategic nuclear force to deter the Soviet Union is understandable and accepted as legitimate. Beyond that, the nation asks: How much and what kind of force do we need to defend against this amorphous threat—whatever it may be? What kind of foreign policy makes sense in this evolving world, and what sort of military force and military policy do we need to serve as an instrument of that policy? Perhaps most important of all, how does one legitimize military force in such an environment?

The modern major general must understand the world in which he lives—to the extent anyone can understand it. He must realize that this is not the same world in which he served as a junior officer. He must also realize that the threat is no longer so clear and precise, that the perceptions of the American people have changed considerably in recent years, and that the legitimacy of military force is no longer to be taken for granted. The military professional tends to think of himself as a hard, cold realist who understands the threat and knows what the nation should do to deal with it; he frequently fails, however, to consider the changing perceptions of the domestic and international scene by the body politic.

## The Utility of Military Force

If one accepts the proposition stated earlier that military force is legitimate only if it serves as an instrument of a legitimate foreign policy, a logical question must be: What is the utility of military force in the contemporary and projected international environment? Although the American armed forces are concerned with war and must be ready to fight, their most important function now and in the foreseeable future is to make war less likely. The armed forces contribute to making war less likely in five distinct ways.

The first way is deterrence. It has been the foundation of American national security policy for the past forty years; it was an essential element of the containment policy, and is equally important in contemporary national security thinking; it is the least questioned—the most legitimate. There is every reason to believe that it will remain an essential part of our defense thinking for the foreseeable future.

Historically, western military thought has been based on the assumption that military forces existed for the express purpose of fighting the next war, which was certain to come. The concept of deterrence was not a part of military thought, and the notion of maintaining expensive forces to achieve a standoff—even before their use—would have been considered ludicrous. But the new idea that a military professional is successful, even if he never has to fight a war, is a fact of life that the modern major general must accept. It is part of deterrence—of the contemporary balance of power.

Deterrent policy has been concerned largely with avoiding nuclear war; as a result, the popular conception of deterrence is almost one of nuclear force. In actual fact, the question is infinitely more complex than that. Deterrence must be an operative concept at all levels of force, and be applicable before, during, and after an armed conflict. The idea of preventing small local wars from spreading and growing into worldwide confrontations is an essential aspect of the concept of deterrence.

A reasonable deterrent posture, then, would appear to include the "capability," as well as the perceived "intention," to fight a conventional as well as a nuclear war; a limited, as well as a total war; and an unconventional, as well as orthodox war—whatever those terms may mean. All of this capability exists to deter—to prevent any conflict from breaking out, if possible, but at least to keep local conflict truly local and to prevent nuclear Armageddon. The forces that make this deterrence credible must be operational so as to deter an adversary from expanding an incident, from intensifying an ongoing conflict, or from initiating an action of any description. Perceived mutual vulnerability at all conflict levels is an important element of deterrence, and some argue that it is indeed the very cornerstone of our national security. Senator Edward Kennedy has argued that this cornerstone is "the mutual vulnerability of Soviet and American societies, and that each superpower is now partly responsible for the security of the other."[4] How many modern major generals have even toyed with the concept that the utility of American military force may have to be explained to the Congress and the public as contributing to the security of the Soviet Union?

The second way in which military force has utility is to provide options. Varied forces provide a major increase in the number of options open to the United States in implementation of a deterrence strategy, in support of foreign policy, and in defense of the United States. Conventional forces make additional options available below the threshold of nuclear warfare. If the nation were to preoccupy itself with nuclear strategic forces, it would be in the position of having no options other than the strategy of massive retaliation which was discarded some 25 years ago.

The nation might adopt a deliberate policy of "no more Vietnams," but potential conflict situations may arise regardless of such declarations. In these circumstances, such a policy may embolden other nations to take greater risks and aggressive actions against their neighbors. Moreover, if a policy of no more Vietnams is construed to mean that an effective armed force is no longer required, the absence of conventional forces capable of responding to a conventional attack may actually reduce the risks a prospective enemy must weigh in deciding whether to undertake provocative military actions.

Some form of "flexible response" is therefore required; although the world has changed, the basic requirement to have a balanced force in existence has not. The basis for the concept of "flexible response," as it was developed in the early 1960s, remains intellectually sound. As a result of the Vietnam experience, the concept has lost credibility with much of the American public. It has also lost credibility with many military professionals because it has been confused with the operational concept of gradualism that was applied in Vietnam. By whatever new name it receives, providing a range of military options to the decisionmaker remains important—it is a central element of the rationale for armed forces.

Third, military forces play an important—although difficult to define—political and psychological role in international affairs. Specifically, military forces provide strong evidence, to friends and adversaries alike, of national commitment and determination. In an era of negotiations and of complex relations among the major states, the political and psychological significance of deployed forces is heightened. Military forces have played such a role in the past; a significant level of American forces in Europe should continue to be convincing evidence to Western Europeans of the importance the United States attaches to a politically stable Europe, free of excessive Soviet pressure and untroubled by serious intra-European conflict. Similarly, deployment of forces to an area, or reinforcement of an already deployed force, indicates dramatically to the world the importance of that area to the United States.

Deployed forces are not the only evidence of national commitment. It is difficult, however, to identify an instrumentality of foreign policy that can perform this role as a substitute for military forces. Forward deployed forces can best provide the politically and psychologically significant elements of control in dealing with people, as well as the assurance of national resolve stemming from the apparent inextricability of deployed ground forces.

Fourth, since announcement of the Truman Doctrine after World War II, military advisory and assistance activities have played an important role in American foreign and military policies. These activities are clearly consistent with the partnership concept of the Nixon Doctrine. The military's partnership responsibilities, assuming the necessary Congressional support for these activities is forthcoming (an admittedly tenuous assumption), will focus largely on improving the capabilities of indigenous forces in the developing areas. Since these nations have little genuine need for technologically advanced air or naval forces, the principal burden of military partnership should fall upon the army.

The fifth reason is a hedge against uncertainty. The critical thrust of current U.S. foreign policies is negotiations, and the desired outcome of these negotiations is improved relations with former adversaries and continued good relations with current allies. If it were certain that this policy thrust would continue as projected, it would be reasonably simple to design military forces that would contribute usefully to American objectives during each phase of the negotiations. Yet the most striking features of the envisaged international system are ambiguity and uncertainty. The 1973 Arab-Israeli war and the Iran-Iraq war are examples of the uncertainty and unpredictability inherent in international affairs. Given these characteristics of the international system, it is prudent to hedge against them. Military forces provide insurance against the unexpected; in particular, forces in being reduce the time required to make an appropriate response, whether the response is reinforcement of an existing force, deployment of forces to a threatened area, or a credible ultimatum presented to another power. In this sense, armed forces are the nation's fire department—they can help prevent fires from breaking out and fight them if they do occur.

I have listed five ways—deterrence, additional decision options, increased political and psychological importance, partnership activities, and a hedge against uncertainty—to which the utility of military force can be linked. Note that none of these five uses of military force involves combat operations, although proven combat readiness is an essential ingredient in each. And if, for whatever reason, war is not avoided, the armed forces must then be prepared to undertake combat operations and to bring them to a successful conclusion.

## Putting It All Together

I am asking a great deal of my modern major general. I expect him to understand the society that he serves, to be knowledgeable of the world in which he lives, and to have a firm grip on the very complex concept of the utility of military force within the context of the assumed domestic and international environment. At the same time, I expect him to be a true expert in the conduct of military operations, so that he has credibility in the deterrent role and the ability to lead his forces so as to "win"—to achieve the political objective—if force is eventually brought to bear.

In the 1930s, Harold Lasswell described the job of the military professional as "the management of violence." That remains an extremely descriptive phrase, but I would argue that today it is much too narrow in scope.[5] About thirty years later, General Sir John Hackett described it as the "ordered application of force in the resolution of a social problem."[6] Most would agree that Hackett's expression is more descriptive of the expanded role of the military professional. His description does not exclude the management of violence but suggests something much more than that. The best description, in my opinion, is that constructed by Amos Jordan when he was head of the Social Science Department at the U.S. Military Academy. He described the role of the military professional as "the management and application of military resources in deterrent, peacekeeping, advisory, and combat roles in the context of rapid technological, social, and political change."[7] This is clearly the broadest and most inclusive description, and it best describes the wide variety of tasks the modern major general will probably be called upon to perform.

How does a nation go about getting or developing military professionals who can even approach the model that is evolving? The short answer is the military education system, including the professional military schools and complementary civil schooling. It is not my purpose here to deal with the educational system, except to comment that it is a very complex, comprehensive system that is constantly undergoing close examination by the Services, the Department of Defense, and the Congress to determine whether it is indeed producing the kind of military professional who will qualify as a modern major general.

For several years, the Army has sent selected brigadier generals and promotable colonels to the Center for Creative Leadership in Greensboro, North Carolina. For two weeks the officers undergo an extensive evaluation exercise. On the basis of results from one of the earliest groups, it was determined that they could be categorized rather clearly into three distinct managerial types.[8]

The first category was the "dependable, cautious, managerial type." The strengths of those in this category lie in their high-level capabilities, their dedication to mission accomplishment, and their dependability or predictability. The weaknesses lie in their lack of innovativeness, and lack of people-related concern and effectiveness. Half of the group fell into this category.

The second category was the "outgoing managerial type." The strengths here lie in the ability to get things done quickly and efficiently. The weaknesses lie in frequent failure to perceive in detail the possibilities inherent in various leadership situations. A quarter of the officers fit this group.

The third category was the "potentially creative managerial type." These officers scored highest on measures of intelligence and creative ability, and performed best in unstructured roles and vague situations. The strengths lie in performance in situations where discovering the best way to proceed is a major part of the problem. Weaknesses lie in situations requiring moving ahead quickly along well-defined pathways without deviation. A quarter fit this category.

This limited analysis is inadequate to provide a basis for far-reaching conclusions, but it does provide some interesting hints. Offhand, it would seem that category three best describes the modern major general who will be needed to operate in the highly unpredictable domestic and international environments hypothesized above. But only one-fourth of the group falls in that category. Is there something that should be done to ensure that the education, training, and experience of the modern major general will develop the necessary flexibility of intellect to operate effectively in the 1990s?

The fictional Major General Stanley was a product of the Victorian era. Today's modern major generals are a product of the cold war era, and a very large percentage of them are, more specifically, products of the most tragic part of the cold war era—Vietnam. Their experience is narrow and their understanding of the society they serve, and the world in which they live, is in many cases limited and heavily colored by the Vietnam era. One can hope that, because there is an operative educational system, they will be capable of performing those tasks they will be called upon to peform. In the simplest terms, they are to see to the security of the United States in an era where the major threat is the unpredictability of the international system. The demands on the military professional today are greater than they have ever been in our history and there is no sign that these demands will lessen in the future.

With apologies to Messrs. Gilbert and Sullivan, I shall improvise a few lines that describe, at least in small part, my modern major general, vintage 1990:

> When I comprehend my role in a world of rapid change,
> And think of my profession in its very broadest range;
> When deterrence I understand, and all that it implies,
> And on the meaning of detente I am among the wise;
> When the nation that I serve is better known to me,
> And the world in which I live is less a mystery;
> When "utility of force" is a concept I can grasp,
> And multi-polar politics no longer make me gasp;
> When the rhetoric of hawks and doves I've really found the clues to,
> And puzzled out the meaning of the loons and cockatoos;
> In short, I'll be the very model of a creature incredible,
> That widely-trained professional, the modern Major-General.

## NOTES

1.  "Abe—A Tribute," *Army* (October 1974): 6.
2.  Stanley Hoffman, "The Acceptability of Military Force," *Adelphi Papers 102* (1973): 11.
3.  "Religion, Military on Top in Winning Public Trust," *Washington Times*, November 27, 1987, p. E-6.
4.  Edward M. Kennedy, "Beyond Detente," *Foreign Policy* (Fall 1974): 4.
5.  Samuel P. Huntington, *The Soldier and the State: The Theory and Politics of Civil-Military Relations* (Cambridge: Belknap Press, 1957), pp. 7-8.
6.  Sir John Hackett, *The Profession of Arms* (London: Times Publishing, 1962), p. 3.
7.  Amos A. Jordan, "Officer Education," in *The Handbook of Military Institutions*, ed. Roger W. Little (Beverly Hills: Sage, 1971), pp. 211-45.
8.  Douglas S. Holmes, "A Report on an Evaluation of Twelve Brigadier General Designees," (unpublished report, Center for Creative Leadership, Greensboro, North Carolina, 1972), pp. 27-39. For a current analysis of findings at the Center for Creative Leadership, based on test profiles of roughly 160 Army brigadier generals, see David Campbell, "The Psychological Test Profiles of Brigadier Generals: Warmongers or Decisive Warriors?" Address before the American Psychological Association Convention, August 30, 1987.

This article appeared in the no. 2, vol. IV, 1974 issue of *Parameters* under the title "The 'Modern Major General' (Vintage 1980)." The article has been updated for the present book.

# About the Editors and Contributors

LIEUTENANT GENERAL WALTER F. ULMER, JR., U.S. Army Retired, received his B.S. degree from the U.S. Military Academy and M.A. from Penn State. He is also a graduate of the Command and General Staff College and Army War College. In addition to serving two tours in Vietnam, he was commandant of cadets at the Military Academy, commanding general of the 3d Armored Division in Germany, and, for 39 months, commanding general of the III Corps at Fort Hood, Texas. General Ulmer is now president of the Center for Creative Leadership in Greensboro, North Carolina.

COLONEL LLOYD J. MATTHEWS, U.S. Army Retired, is editor of *Parameters: U.S. Army War College Quarterly.* He holds a B.S. from the U.S. Military Academy, an M.A. from Harvard University, and a Ph.D. from the University of Virginia. Colonel Matthews served as an infantry officer in the Vietnam War during 1964–65, later commanding a battalion at Fort Ord, California. A graduate of the Army War College, Colonel Matthews has served as a professor and as the associate dean at the Military Academy.

CAPTAIN DALE E. BROWN, U.S. Army, is assistant editor of *Parameters: U.S. Army War College Quarterly.* He earned an M.A. in history from the Ohio State University. Captain Brown is an air defense artillery officer and has served in a variety of air defense assignments in the United States and Europe, including command of a missile maintenance company.

★ ★ ★

COLONEL DONALD F. BLETZ, U.S. Army Retired, received his B.G.E. degree from the University of Omaha, Nebraska, and M.A. and Ph.D. in international studies from American University, Washington, D.C. He held a variety of infantry command and staff assignments during World War II and the Korean and Vietnam wars. In Vietnam, he was deputy commander, 173d Airborne Brigade. Colonel Bletz served on the faculties of the Command and General Staff College, the National War College, and the Army War College. Before joining the Army War College faculty, where he chaired the department of National and International Securities Studies, he was a fellow at the Harvard University Center for International Affairs. Following retirement from the

163

Army in 1975, he joined the faculty of Wilson College in Chambersburg, Pennsylvania, where he served as interim president from 1979 to 1981. He is currently director of the business and economics departments at Wilson.

GENERAL OF THE ARMY OMAR N. BRADLEY was born in Clark, Missouri, on 12 February 1893. Following graduation from the U.S. Military Academy in 1915, he served with the infantry in a variety of assignments and later at the Military Academy as an instructor and tactical officer. Early in World War II, he commanded the 82d and 28th Infantry Divisions. In 1943 he commanded II Corps during the Tunisian and Sicilian campaigns; he was also commanding general of the First U.S. Army during the famed Normandy invasion in June 1944. Later, in 1944–45, he served as commanding general, 12th Army Group, during campaigns in France and Germany that ended the war. General Bradley was named Veterans Affairs administrator in 1946, occupying that position until he was recalled to active duty in 1948 as Chief of Staff, U.S. Army. In 1950, he was promoted to General of the Army while serving as chairman of the Joint Chiefs of Staff. General Bradley died on April 8, 1986.

MAJOR GENERAL CLAY T. BUCKINGHAM, U.S. Army Retired, is a graduate of the U.S. Military Academy (1949) and the U.S. Army War College. During the Korean War, he was a tank platoon leader and company commander in the 3d Infantry Division. In Vietnam, he was a sector advisor in Hau Nghia province. Thereafter, General Buckingham enjoyed a succession of important command and staff assignments in the United States and Germany. During the last six years of his career, General Buckingham occupied all the Army's principal positions in the management-information and computer systems fields. He retired from the Army in 1982 and is currently president of the Association of Military Christian Fellowships.

LIEUTENANT GENERAL ARTHUR S. COLLINS, JR., graduated from the U.S. Military Academy in 1938. In May 1942, he joined the 130th Infantry and remained with the regiment for four years, commanding a battalion in combat on Morotai and Luzon. A U.S. Army War College graduate, he served on the faculty of the War College from 1956 to 1959. General Collins subsequently commanded the 4th Infantry Division, deploying it from Fort Lewis to Vietnam. Later, he returned to Vietnam to command the I Field Force. His final active duty assignment (1971–74) was as deputy commander-in-chief, USAREUR and Seventh Army. General Collins's book, *Common Sense Training: A Working Philosophy for Leaders*, a best-seller, was published by Presidio Press in 1978. General Collins died in 1984.

COLONEL LARRY H. INGRAHAM, U.S. Army, is a Medical Service Corps officer with the department of military psychiatry at the Walter Reed Army Institute of Research in Washington, D.C. Holding a Ph.D. in social psychology from the University of Iowa, he previously commanded the U.S. Army Medical Research Unit (Europe) in Heidelberg, a special overseas activity of the Institute of Research. Colonel Ingraham is the author of *The Boys in the Barracks: Observations on American Military Life* (Institute for the Study of Human Issues, 1984).

DR. KARL KUHNERT is an assistant professor of applied psychology at the University of Georgia. He holds a B.A. from Penn State (1977), where he played football under Coach Joe Paterno. He later received an M.S. and Ph.D. in industrial/organizational psychology from Kansas State University. In the summer of 1987, Dr. Kuhnert was a faculty research fellow at the U.S. Navy installation in San Diego.

DR. PHILIP LEWIS is a professor of psychology at Auburn University, Georgia. He received his A.B. from Hamilton College (New York) and his M.A. and Ph.D. in clinical psychology from Syracuse University, New York. Dr. Lewis was a summer faculty research fellow at Maxwell Air Force Base, Alabama, in 1985.

DR. JAY LUVAAS is professor of military history at the U.S. Army War College, holding the Maxwell Taylor Chair of the Profession of Arms. He is a graduate of Allegheny College, Pennsylvania, where he taught from 1957 to 1982. He has been visiting professor of military history at the U.S. Military Academy and the U.S. Army Military History Institute. Among his works are *The Military Legacy of the Civil War* (1959), *The Education of An Army* (1964), *Frederick the Great on the Art of War* (1966), *Dear Miss Em: General Eichelberger's War in the Pacific* (1972), *The Battle of Gettysburg: The U.S. Army War College Guide* (1986), and *The U.S. Army War College Guide to the Battle of Antietam: The Maryland Campaign of 1862* (1987).

MAJOR ROBERT L. MAGINNIS, U.S. Army, is an operations officer with the 9th Infantry at Fort Wainwright, Alaska. He received a B.S. from the U.S. Military Academy (1973) and a M.S. from the Naval Postgraduate School. He has served with three infantry divisions in a variety of command and staff positions in Korea, Europe, and the United States. Prior to his present posting in Alaska, Major Maginnis was chief of the leadership branch of the Infantry School at Fort Benning, Georgia.

LIEUTENANT COLONEL JOHN T. NELSEN II, U.S. Army, is chief of the War Plans Division, III Corps, Fort Hood, Texas. He is a graduate of Virginia Military Institute and holds an M.A. in European history from the University of Wisconsin and a master of military art and science degree from the School of Advanced Military Studies, Fort Leavenworth, Kansas. He has served in several staff and infantry troop assignments and has taught history at the U.S. Military Academy.

MAJOR JOHN F. SHORTAL, U.S. Army, is a former assistant professor in the department of history, U.S. Military Academy. He is a 1974 graduate of the academy and holds an M.S. from the University of Southern California and M.A. and Ph.D. degrees from Temple University, Pennsylvania. He has served in command and staff assignments in the United States and Korea. Major Shortal is the author of *Forged by Fire: Robert L. Eichelberger and the Pacific War* (1987).

DR. LEWIS SORLEY graduated from the U.S. Military Academy in 1956, later earning an M.A. from the University of Pennsylvania, an M.P.A. from Penn State, and Ph.D. from Johns Hopkins, Maryland. He is also a graduate of the Army War College. He retired from the Army in 1976, joining the CIA, and is now retired from that organization. A prolific author, Dr. Sorley is currently completing a biography of General Creighton W. Abrams, Jr.

GENERAL DONN A. STARRY, U.S. Army Retired, is a graduate of the U.S. Military Academy (1948) and the Army War College and holds an M.S. degree from George Washington University, Washington, D.C. An armor officer who served two tours in Vietnam, he spent many years in high-level command positions, including command of the Armor Center, V Corps, Training and Doctrine Command, and Readiness Command. He is presently a vice president with Ford Aerospace.

COLONEL THOMAS R. STONE, U.S. Army Retired, was director of the Strategic Studies Institute at the U.S. Army War College from 1984 to 1988. A graduate of the U.S. Military Academy (1961), he earned M.A. and Ph.D. degrees in history at Rice University, Texas. His Ph.D. dissertation was a military biography of General Simpson. Colonel Stone taught in the department of history at the Military Academy from 1973 to 1976. His overseas tours have included assignments in Vietnam and Germany and command of a battalion and divison artillery in Korea. Colonel Stone recently joined the management team of Pennsylvania Blue Shield.

LIEUTENANT COLONEL CHARLES G. SUTTEN, JR., U.S. Army, a 1986 graduate of the U.S. Army War College, is a staff officer in the office of the Deputy Chief of Staff for Research, Development, and Acquisition. He is a graduate of the U.S. Military Academy (1967) and holds an M.S. in electrical engineering from Stanford and an M.B.A. from Long Island University, New York. Colonel Sutten served as a signal officer in four different divisions in Vietnam, Germany, and the United States, most recently čommanding an armored division signal battalion in Europe. He has also served in the White House Communications Agency, with duties in command and control and emergency action procedures.

MAJOR JOHN M. VERMILLION, U.S. Army, is G3 Plans Officer in the 24th Infantry Division (Mechanized), Fort Stewart, Georgia. Holder of a B.S. from the U.S. Military Academy (1970) and M.A. degrees from the University of South Carolina and Boston University, he attended the regular course and the School of Advanced Military Studies at Fort Leavenworth before taking up his present assignment. Major Vermillion has had infantry assignments in Vietnam, Korea, and Germany.

LIEUTENANT COLONEL MITCHELL M. ZAIS, U.S. Army, is currently the commander of the 1/506th Infantry in Korea. He is a graduate of the Advanced Military Studies Program at the Command and General Staff College, where he was awarded the master of military arts and science degree. He is also a graduate of the U.S. Military Academy (1969) and holds an M.S.

degree in social psychology from the University of Washington, where he is presently a doctoral candidate. Lieutenant Colonel Zais has taught in the department of behavioral sciences and leadership at West Point. Other positions have included rifle platoon leader in Vietnam; rifle company commander in The Old Guard; mechanized infantry company commander, Fort Riley; and infantry battalion executive officer and S3 in Korea.